Mencius on Becoming Human

SUNY series in Chinese Philosophy and Culture

Roger T. Ames, editor

Mencius on Becoming Human

James Behuniak Jr.

State University of New York Press

Cover art: detail from Shen Zhou, *Three Catalpa Trees* (hanging scroll), about 1481, ink on paper. Used with the kind permission of the Indianapolis Museum of Art. Gift of Mr. and Mrs. Eli Lilly.

Published by
State University of New York Press, Albany

© 2005 State University of New York

All rights reserved

Printed in the United States of America

No part of this book may be used or reproduced in any manner whatsoever without written permission. No part of this book may be stored in a retrieval system or transmitted in any form or by any means including electronic, electrostatic, magnetic tape, mechanical, photocopying, recording, or otherwise without the prior permission in writing of the publisher.

For information, address State University of New York Press,
90 State Street, Suite 700, Albany, NY 12207

Production by Michael Haggett
Marketing by Michael Campochiaro

Library of Congress Cataloging-in-Publication Data

Behuniak, James.
  Mencius on becoming human / James Behuniak Jr.
     p. cm.—(SUNY series in Chinese philosophy and culture)
  Includes bibliographical references and index.
  ISBN 0-7914-6229-3 (alk. paper)
  1. Mencius. Mengzi. I. Title. II. Series.

PL2474.Z7B44 2004
181'.112—dc22
                                                              2003069329

10 9 8 7 6 5 4 3 2 1

For My Family

Shen Zhou, *Three Catalpa Trees* (hanging scroll), about 1481, ink on paper. Used with the kind permission of the Indianapolis Museum of Art. Gift of Mr. and Mrs. Eli Lilly.

Contents

Acknowledgments	ix
Introduction	xi
Sketch of the Argument	xx
Methodology and Key Terms	xxii
Chapter 1 The Cosmological Background	1
Energy and Propensity	1
Shape and Spontaneity	6
Disposition and Spontaneity	10
Zhuangzi and Shape	14
Characteristics of Chinese Cosmology	17
Chapter 2 The Role of Feeling	23
Feeling, Doctrine, and *Dao*	23
Feeling as Transactional	26
Aspiration and Courage	32
Internal/External and the Botanical Model	37
Desire, Coherence, and Integration	41
Chapter 3 Family and Moral Development	47
Spontaneous *vs.* Technical Approaches	47
The Mohist Challenge	50
Recovering the Confucian Measure	53
Family as the Root	59
Family and Extension	64

Chapter 4 The Human Disposition — 73

　　Relationships and the Human Disposition — 73
　　The Human Disposition as Good — 80
　　The Four Sprouts and the Family — 87
　　The Satisfaction of Becoming Human — 90
　　The Value of the Person — 95

Chapter 5 Advancing the Human Way — 101

　　The Constraints on Aspiration — 101
　　The Conditions for Political Legitimacy — 109
　　The Conditions for Human Achievement — 111
　　Human Virtue in the Sacrifices — 114
　　Aspiration and the Human Way — 121

Afterword — 129
Notes — 133
References — 173
Index — 179

Acknowledgments

The present work was completed as a Visiting Research Scholar at Peking University over the academic year 2001/2002. Beijing was an ideal place to work and I am grateful to the following institutions for their support: the Center for Chinese Studies at the University of Hawaii, the Harvard-Yenching Institute at Harvard University, and the Office of International Relations at Peking University.

This work began as a dissertation in the Department of Philosophy at the University of Hawaii. I thank Roger Ames for several years of instruction, endless encouragement, deep generosity, and real friendship while in Hawaii, as well as for many hours of conversation during our year in Beijing. I also thank members of the Ames family, Roger, Bonnie, and Austin, for their hospitality.

I thank Geir Sigurdsson for being a great friend in Beijing and for keeping me relatively sane as I worked on this project. I also owe a lot to Jim Tiles who, from a quarter of the world away, prompted me to think through my argument at every turn. I also thank Eliot Deutsch, Steve Odin, and Edward Davis for their helpful comments on an earlier version of this work. Any weaknesses that carry over into the present draft are my own.

I wish to thank Joseph Grange, who has been a professor, mentor, and friend to me for many years. If I had not wandered into Joe's course in Metaphysics at the University of Southern Maine many years ago, many things including this book would never have materialized. I will never forget that Joe Grange made me a philosopher.

I would like to thank and credit my classmates and instructors from the University of Hawaii, as well as my students and colleagues from Southern Maine, Kalamazoo College, and Sonoma State University, for helping me do philosophy. I thank all of my friends, and I especially thank my wife, Connie, for her patience, encouragement, and love—all under trying conditions. Connie also contributed editorial and research assistance at various stages of this project, which I appreciate.

Finally, I thank each member of my family. If Mencius teaches us anything, he teaches us the profound importance of family affection. I thank them for allowing me to realize this Mencian teaching in my own life. This book is dedicated to them.

Introduction

When peace disintegrates into war, it is not unusual for literary efforts to reflect the breakdown of values and institutions that once distinguished a properly human existence from that of the animal. Mencius thought and wrote during the "Warring States" period in China, a period in which no single authority or common purpose united a belligerent mosaic of states on China's eastern plains. Mencius lived in a time of great anxiety, violence, and appalling carnage. The literature of the period attests to these conditions. From the discourses on warfare circulated in popular military handbooks, to the songs of despair in the *Book of Songs* (*Shijing*), to the pacifist reflections in the *Daodejing*—the writings in this period cope with the realities of war and bloodshed. Among this period's literary efforts, the *Mencius* provides a philosophical vision of what the human experience might become—a vision that asserts itself over and against the reality of what the human experience had become. The Mencian prescription is one among several, advocated in an age that would not allow philosophy the luxury of being a leisurely pursuit.

Mencius is a Confucian. He seeks to reinforce the teachings of Confucius and to some degree "naturalize" these teachings in a manner persuasive and communicable in his own day. His chosen metaphor is botanical. He speaks of the "four sprouts" (*siduan* 四端) of human virtue and likens the cultivation of the person to the growth of a tree. He uses the language of "roots" (*ben* 本), "breaking through the ground" (*da* 達), "disposition" (*xing* 性), "nourishment" (*yang* 養), "life span" (*sheng* 生), and "fruition" (*shi* 實). The botanical metaphor is the vehicle by which Mencius wishes to convey his vision of what it means to "become human."

For one hoping to understand the *Mencius*, it is important to follow the botanical metaphor; but the hermeneutic circle is not tightened until one pauses to think through it. What does the metaphor mean to Mencius? In using botanical imagery, does Mencius mean to suggest that becoming human is an end-driven process: simply a matter of "actualizing" a given, teleological potential? Does he mean to suggest that becoming human is a process like the pre-Darwinian way we as a tradition are given to think about the process of an acorn becoming an oak tree? Does he mean to say that humans possess a predetermined, "natural" end that is antecedently given and unaffected by historical circumstances?

Many of the most qualified interpreters of classical Chinese thought incline towards such an understanding in treating what is commonly understood to be the notion of "human nature" (*renxing* 人性) in the *Mencius*. Benjamin Schwartz understands *xing* 性 to be "an innate tendency toward growth or development in a given, predetermined direction."[1] Robert Eno considers "Heaven" (*tian* 天) itself a "teleological force" that engenders a good "nature" (*xing* 性) in human beings and thereby "indicates what man's purpose, or 'final cause,' is to be."[2] In the same vein, P. J. Ivanhoe submits that for Mencius, to follow one's nature (*xing*) is "the way to both understand and fulfill heaven's plan."[3] A. C. Graham, at one point in his career, considers *xing* to be a notion developed "on lines rather suggestive of Aristotelian teleology."[4] Throughout the secondary literature, the default understanding of *xing* is "nature" with a predetermined end. The botanical metaphor is usually understood as reinforcing the fixity of this end.

In gauging the adequacy of this interpretation, we might begin by paying a visit to Mencius himself. Mencius is interred in a tomb not far from the Mencius Temple in his hometown of Zouxian, in China's Shandong province.[5] The sprawling grounds of the temple host a remarkable grove of trees: a botanical wonder and an apt tribute to the philosopher and his ideas. Today, temple caretakers still supplement with fresh saplings the ancient grove that constitutes the heart of the temple. The layout is designed to highlight the contrast between the fairly uniform, younger trees and the singular, magnificent formations that tower overhead. Mencius maintains that anyone can become a sage, and for those who visit his temple, that doctrine is reinforced by the realization that any one of the undistinguished saplings low in the grove can take on, or even surpass, the majesty of an elder.

One of these gigantic trees, just southwest of the main hall at Zouxian, is particularly impressive. Its lumpy trunk towers straight up some twenty-five meters before splitting into a number of horizontal limbs. Each limb hosts smaller branches, each curling off on a claw-like trajectory. Some of these, in turn, trail off into thickets of tendrils that reach proudly skyward. Most remarkably, at the center top of this tree, a yellowish, bulbous growth of heartwood emerges like a fantastic sculpture—high on a pedestal, never to be touched. It is a breathtaking sight.

At the Mencius Temple, the uniqueness, the form, and the grandeur of each tree are the results of botanical growth. And each tree is absolutely one of a kind. Indeed, everything that grows is one of a kind: a singular expression of the drive of living things to flourish in their habitats by making the most out of their conditions. In the world of singular trees, regardless of species, the result is almost always some aesthetically impressive expression of a living process—a process never, not anywhere, replicated.

In an age shaped by the logic of war, according to which one human casualty might substitute for the next, why not appeal to the aesthetic dimensions of the singular human life? Would it be somehow irresponsible to assume that Mencius' chosen metaphor embraces the notion of becoming a distinct human person? As readers, must we restrict Mencius to the more generic aspects of his metaphor, those with which we might easily identify correlates within our own tradition? Was he merely interested in establishing "humans" as a natural kind, and then designating them uniformly "good" (*shan* 善)? Are we to assume that Mencius was not so interested in the unique qualities of the individual human life? Does the botanical imagery in the text work in any way to foreground the process of becoming distinctly human over the span of a singular life? Does the notion of *xing* 性 allow the metaphor to work in this way?

These are largely hermeneutic questions, so I propose the following exercise: Before we think of the botanical metaphor in terms of an end-driven teleology and equate *xing* 性 with a uniform, predetermined "nature" on that basis, let us briefly attempt to locate this metaphor in its own context. We will ask some odd but important questions: What does it mean to be a tree in classical China? What does it mean to be a "sort" of tree? What does it mean to be a seed? Any answer to these questions that we find in the classical Chinese tradition will more adequately inform our reading of the botanical metaphor in the *Mencius*. This will signal the degree to which that metaphor will tolerate a more particularistic reading.

We can start with Mencius himself. He asks King Xiang directly, "Do you not understand the growth of young seedlings?" Mencius' own account of the botanical process is as follows:

> Should there be drought in June or July, a seedling wilts. Then the sky condenses to produce clouds and it rains in torrents. Then, having been stimulated, the seedling opens out. When it does so, who can hold it back?[6]

When Mencius describes growth, the stress is on the irrepressible process of emergence, a process located within nourishing conditions. The seed is the beginning of an emergent process. Does the seed contain the "final cause" or "end" of that process? In its sole tribute to seeds, the *Book of Songs* relates only that seeds "contain life [*huo* 活] and, abundantly growing, break through the ground [*da* 達]."[7] In the *Zhuangzi*, the "content" of a seed is described only as "the inchoate beginning of a process unfolding" (*ji* 幾).[8] In an episode with Liezi, Zhuangzi traces the career of a seed through various phases: from its life as water plantain to its evolution into a human being.[9] This is a process shaped within environing conditions; it is not teleological in any strict, end-driven sense.

In the Chinese tradition, the seed is not described as containing its own end; rather, the process itself would appear to determine its end, since not all seeds come to fruition. As Confucius laments:

> So it is, there are seedlings that never come to flower. And so it is, there are flowers that never bear fruit.[10]

Generally in this tradition, the mention of botanical growth in a literary context does not evoke generic traits that are simply "actualized" in the process of growth. We can assume that farmers in Warring States China were perfectly capable of distinguishing various seeds according to their generic traits, but this is beside the point. Mencius is not a farmer. Literary treatments foreground the emergent, underdetermined, unique traits of things that grow.

The "Short Preface" (*Xiaoxu*) to the *Book of Songs* relates with more precision how the botanical process is understood in a literary context, and this description lends itself more to a particularistic conceptualization of growth than to a uniform, generic one. This account comes in the form of a commentary on three songs, each of which is missing from the received text. The commentary itself, however, is philosophically interesting. These three songs are said to have represented the following truisms about all things that grow:

1. The ten thousand things attain the emergence (*you* 由) of their ways (*dao* 道).
2. The ten thousand things attain the extremity (*gao* 高) of their magnitudes (*da* 大).
3. The life-span (*sheng* 生) of each one (*ge* 各) of the ten thousand things attains its own fittingness (*yi* 宜).[11]

This is not an account of how a "species" of thing grows. This is an account of how particular things grow: things with their own "ways," "sizes," and "fits." Rather than being an account of generic kinds, this is an account of unique things. As we shall see, the vocabulary used in the *Book of Songs* corresponds to the vocabulary that Mencius himself uses to describe the process of becoming human. It is a process of emerging on a way (*dao* 道) over the span of a life (*sheng* 生), a process that seeks its optimal fit and its most expansive magnitude. The details of this process as they relate to becoming human will be explored in chapters to come.

Mencius clearly does, however, on at least one occasion, intend to classify humans as a "sort" (*lei* 類); this he does most explicitly when he compares humans to rows of barley.[12] But what does this classification mean? What is it to be a "sort" of plant or tree in classical China?

According to Confucius, one goes to the *Book of Songs* if one wishes to learn the names of various plants and trees.[13] The student so inclined is well advised. The *Book of Songs* is classical China's botanical compendium; there are dozens of references to specific kinds of plants and trees. What one finds in the *Book of Songs*, however, is unlike any formal species classification or taxonomy. Instead, there is a recurrent grammatical construction through which one might sort out plants and trees according to the places that "have" (*you* 有) them. The taxonomy is locative.

The south, we learn, "has" (*you* 有) trees with curved drooping branches; the hills of the south "have" mulberry trees, medlar trees, kow trees, and the *ti* plant; the northern hills "have" willow trees, plum trees, *yu* trees, and the *li* plant.[14] The valleys "have" motherwort.[15] Mountains "have" lofty pines, thorny elms, bushy oaks, sparrow plums, mulberry trees, and varnish trees (which are also "had" on hillsides, along with turtle foot and thorn fern).[16] The marshes "have" lotus flowers, rushes, water-polygonum, and valerian.[17] The moor "has" creeping-grass.[18] The wet lowlands "have" white elm, mulberry, chestnut, willow, carambola, and wild pear trees.[19] The central plains "have" pulse.[20] In classical China, everything that grows does so in the environment that will "have" it. Everything that grows is *located*.

In the world that informs the mind of Mencius, to consider the botanical product in abstraction from the location that nourishes it forfeits something of its defining characteristic. If Mencius considers humans to be a "sort" of thing that grows, then we as readers do well to locate *where* this growth is understood to take place. In a reference to becoming human, Mencius speaks of the trees that Ox Mountain ideally "has" (*you* 有).[21] The appropriate question then is "What kind of environment is Ox Mountain?" In other words, what are the unique conditions that nourish humans as a sort?

The argument below is that Mencius means to classify humans by locating them in the family. It will be argued that those features that condition human growth are family-borne features. Like everything else that grows in early China, humans are rooted and nourished *somewhere*. So, if it can be said that the southern mountains "have" mulberry trees, it is suggested here that families "have" humans.

Based on examples of botanical thinking in the Warring States period itself, I am not inclined to take the botanical metaphor in the *Mencius* as suggesting that *xing* 性 is a shared, generic "nature" that can be considered in abstraction from the process and location of its growth. Instead, I understand *xing* as a "disposition" that arises in the process of transaction within a set of localized conditions, and this process results in the formation of something aesthetically distinct. As things stand, however, I am not obliged to base such an interpretation solely on conjecture. Documents recently unearthed from the Warring States period leave little doubt that, in Mencian circles, *xing* was understood as something that took shape in transaction with environing conditions (*ming* 命). The title conferred upon the most important of these documents states as much: *Dispositions Arise from Conditions* (*Xingzimingchu* 性自命出).

This long-lost Confucian document was recovered in October 1993 inside a tomb in Guodian village, part of present day Jingmen city in central China's Hubei province. The tomb dates to the Warring States period, around 300 B.C., and it appears to have belonged to an individual of aristocratic rank. The title "Teacher of the East Palace" was found inscribed on a wine cup discovered at the site, prompting speculation that the tomb's occupant was a "scholar-official" (*shi* 士) who once served as tutor to the Crown Prince of Chu.[22] The tomb had been opened before and had apparently been looted. It was discovered that rising water levels threatened to destroy the tomb's remaining contents. Chinese archeologists managed to recover a cache of bamboo strips from the tomb before these could be claimed by the encroaching elements. Under a veil of secrecy, experts began working on the restoration and reconstruction of the texts preserved on the strips.

What was recovered from Guodian turned out to be a collection of philosophical works of enormous significance: a collection of primarily Confucian-related texts that included the earliest known version of the Daoist classic, the *Daodejing*. The discovery was made public in May 1998, with photographs and preliminary transcriptions made available at that time. In 2002, complete annotated redactions of the Guodian texts were published in China.[23] *Dispositions Arise from Conditions* is arguably the most substantial philosophical document in this collection.[24]

One cannot overstate the importance of these and other recent discoveries to our understanding of Warring States thought. The Guodian documents offer historically unprecedented access to the philosophical foundations of early Confucianism. According to Pang Pu, a leading Chinese scholar researching these finds, the Guodian collection "fills out the one-hundred-year gap between Confucius and Mencius" and "mends the broken theoretical lineage."[25] Such a development stands to revolutionize our understanding of Warring States philosophy. As Tu Wei-ming suggests, "Now that the bamboo strips have been unearthed at Guodian, the entire history of Chinese philosophy and of Chinese academics needs to be rewritten."[26] With yet more documents streaming out of the Shanghai Museum and archeological work in China still ongoing, the world of classical Chinese scholarship has entered a state of remarkable fluidity. Even our most hardened assumptions will be tested by recent discoveries.[27]

Since the release of Guodian materials in 1998, most attention in the English-speaking world has been directed towards the very compelling, early version of the *Daodejing* unearthed at the site.[28] Chinese scholars have meanwhile taken the lead in researching the Confucian-related texts. Ning Chen reports that a 1998 conference in China resulted in consensus that "the Guodian bamboo texts were probably available to Mencius and offer fresh insight into the ideological background of the Mencian discussion of human nature [*xing* 性]."[29] While it is beyond the scope of the present study to survey the most current research in great detail, some general remarks about recent scholarship on the Confucian-related Guodian materials and particularly on the *Dispositions Arise from Conditions* document are in order. It will be stated briefly where the present study stands in relation to some of the positions currently taken by Chinese scholars.

Scholars such as Pang Pu and Li Xueqin have speculated that *Dispositions Arise from Conditions* was once part of an early Confucian collection named after Confucius' grandson, Zisi (子思), a collection similar to a *Zhuangzi*. Ding Sixin, in a dissertation completed at Wuhan University, is representative in maintaining that the text was most likely authored by either Zisi or by his teacher, Zengzi (曾子).[30] Zengzi lends his name to one of the "eight schools" of Confucianism that arose after the death of Confucius. The *Records of the Historian* (*Shiji*) attributes the *Zhongyong* to Zisi and identifies Mencius as a student in this branch of Confucianism.[31] Hence, the school initiated by Zengzi and leading through Zisi to Mencius is referred to as the "Si-Meng lineage" (*Simengpai* 思孟派). While it is difficult to date the *Zhongyong* as a whole with any precision, it is plausible that the *Mencius* lies chronologically between the earlier Si-Meng materials, which include the now recovered *Dispositions Arise from Conditions* document, and the later sections of the received *Zhongyong*—sections that elaborate upon certain themes in the *Mencius*, specifically the notion of "integration" (*cheng* 誠).[32]

There is insufficient evidence to state conclusively what the exact chronology is among texts in the Si-Meng lineage. I concur with the majority, however, in maintaining that the *Mencius* is most adequately treated as a Si-Meng text and that the interpreter of the *Mencius* is obliged to take into account the general themes of this school, which do exhibit some degree of continuity. Generally, the *Zhongyong, Dispositions Arise from Conditions*, and another recently recovered Si-Meng document, the *Five Modes of Conduct* (*Wuxing* 五行),[33] are each concerned with the kind of ethical development that turns virtue into personal character. Each text is interested in cultivating sagacity. Each text foregrounds the emotional dimension of becoming well integrated as a person. To read the *Mencius* as part of the Si-Meng lineage is to put more stress on these dimensions of its thought.

In defining the philosophical relationship among texts in the Si-Meng lineage, there are differing opinions. Pang Pu maintains that the *Dispositions Arise from Conditions* document represents the position that the human "heart-mind" or "feeling" (*xin* 心), and by extension the human "disposition" (*xing* 性), does not have a predetermined direction; it is, in his words, "like a locomotive without the tracks."[34] This position he compares with statements by Gaozi in the *Mencius*, statements to the effect that the human disposition has no fixed direction, "like whirling water it will flow north or south."[35] On the basis of this comparison, Pang Pu distinguishes the philosophy of the Guodian strips from Mencius' own position: that the human disposition indeed has a tendency in a direction that is labeled "good" (*shan* 善).

Other scholars such as Chen Lai, Liao Mingchun, and Ning Chen find more continuity between the *Mencius* and the findings at Guodian. Chen Lai maintains that the Guodian documents reflect an evolving stage between Confucius and Mencius during which the human disposition was not yet considered to have either good or bad tendencies.[36] Liao Mingchun maintains that the philosophy of the Guodian texts represents part of a chain of ideas that stretch between the ideas of Confucius and the *Zhongyong*, neither of which maintains a position on the tendencies of the human disposition, and that this chain of ideas influences both Mencius and Xunzi but is not strictly consonant with either of their positions.[37] Ning Chen argues that the Guodian texts and the *Mencius* have "tangible ideological linkages" that include a similar conception of the human disposition, but that the Guodian texts have a more "ambivalent" position on the tendency of human feeling (*xin* 心) than does the *Mencius*.[38]

I agree with Pang Pu concerning the nature of "disposition" (*xing* 性) in the *Dispositions Arise from Conditions* document. The trajectory of *xing* in this text is not predetermined; it is a process notion and, as such, something like a "locomotive without the tracks." I respectfully part with Pang Pu, however, over the question of how the nonpolemic treatment of *xing* discovered at Guodian fits into the debates that later register in the *Mencius*. *Dispositions Arise from Conditions* is a philosophically sophisticated account of what a disposition is, how it is formed, and how it relates to human feeling (*xin* 心), emotion (*qing* 情), and aspiration (*zhi* 志). This account does not present itself in the style of a doctrine (*yan* 言) that is implicated in any debate over human tendencies. Instead, *Dispositions Arise from Conditions* would appear to be the conceptual background against which the debate over the human disposition is eventually played out. Conclusions at this stage must be tentative, but on my reading, *Dispositions Arise from Conditions* would appear to be a source from which Mencius draws his own ideas about the human disposition. The strong conceptual and linguistic resonance between the Guodian strips and the *Mencius* suggests to me that these are kindred philosophies.

I propose using the teachings of the Guodian documents to better understand Mencian thought, and I attempt to do this in chapters four and five below. While it is true that the Guodian materials do not assert that the human disposition is "good" (*shan* 善), as Mencius must later do in the face of his adversaries, the Guodian finds challenge us to understand exactly what Mencius means by calling the human disposition "good" given the fact that he belongs to a school in which the most philosophically complete statement on "disposition" (*xing* 性) renders it a decidedly process-oriented term.

Sketch of the Argument

To those accustomed to a more generic reading of human development in the *Mencius*, the argument ahead might be anticipated as radical. I feel, however, that what follows is the more conservative reading. To read the notion of human development as end-driven in the *Mencius* is to present Mencius as a truly revolutionary theorist of "human nature" in classical China. I am not prepared or inclined to argue such a radical interpretation. The following assessment is more modest. I maintain that Mencius is working within the parameters of certain commonly held assumptions: assumptions about botanical growth, transformation, development, and about the behavior of "configurative energy" (*qi* 氣).

In chapter one, I attempt to locate the notion of *xing* 性 within the framework of Warring States cosmology, which tacitly assumes the role of "configurative energy" in the kind of processes that interest Mencius.

Rather than entailing the notion of a fixed "nature," I maintain that this cosmology more readily sponsors the notion of dynamic "dispositions" that "take shape" in transaction with formative conditions and issue into unique qualities over the span of their development. If Mencius overrides assumptions such as these and proclaims a fixed, transcendent "nature," he goes against the grain of classical Chinese thinking. I claim that he does not.

In chapter two, I move to the notion of "heart-mind" or "feeling" (*xin* 心) in the *Mencius*. The Mencian understanding of *xin* is consistent with the assumptions of the cosmology explored in chapter one. I argue that "feeling" in the *Mencius* is most adequately understood as the terminal result of transactions conditioned by a "disposition" (*xing* 性) embedded in a world animated by "configurative energies." The role that feelings play in Mencius' rejection of the Mohist doctrine of "impartial concern" (*jianai* 兼愛) will be interpreted on this basis. According to Mencius, the Mohists locate appropriateness (*yi* 義) "outside" (*wai* 外) the circuit of felt experience. Mencius, in turn, situates the standard of appropriateness within the process of growth itself, a process that is nourished by *qi* 氣 energies. One's "feeling" and "disposition" are both enlarged over the process of integrating (*cheng* 誠) "inner" and "outer" in a manner context-dependent and fitting. This is how Mencius understands the growth of character.

In chapter three, I move from "feelings" (*xin* 心) generally to the most important kind of feeling for Mencius: family affection (*qin* 親). For Mencius, human development is rooted in family affection. Becoming human in the *Mencius* is largely a process of preserving and extending family-borne feelings over the course of developing one's personal character. The Mohists have a different approach towards moral development: they employ an external, utilitarian standard that does not entail the integral growth of a person's original, family-borne disposition. The Mencian and Mohist differ most sharply on this point.

In chapter four, the features of a properly "human" (*ren* 人) disposition are considered at greater length. As anticipated in chapter three, I argue that for Mencius the proclivity toward "human" virtues arises from family-borne conditions. This, however, is also associated with the historical work of sages. The "human" designation in the *Mencius*, as I understand it, is in large part a product of history: it consists of a range of "human relationships" (*renlun* 人倫) instituted by cultural heroes in the distant past. These are the "five relationships" that first separated humans from other animals. These relationships, however, are not the end of human development; they are rather a dynamic place to *begin* the process of becoming human within one's own relational context through a Confucian educational program. Thus, as it stands in the *Mencius*, the four human virtues, spoken of as "four sprouts" (*siduan* 四端), are not defined as fixed quantities. In keeping with the botanical model, these sprouts are "extended" in the process of determining what it means to become human. I maintain that, for Mencius, the human experience is still very much in the making.

In chapter five, the notion of becoming human in the *Mencius* is located within the context of the Si-Meng lineage. The *Dispositions Arise from Conditions* document asserts that "making the human way" (*rendao* 人道) is an "art" (*shu* 術). Mencius shares this sensibility with the Si-Meng authorship. He also provides a more developed picture of how social, political, and economic conditions pose constraints upon the project of making the human way. The role of aspiration (*zhi* 志) will be considered in relation to these practical concerns. The notion of aspiration, along with the notions of "forces" (*tian* 天) and "conditions" (*ming* 命) that are explored in this chapter, also suggest the more profound dimensions of Mencian thought. Human beings in this tradition, through the flourishing of associated humanity (*ren* 仁), are responsible for bringing the human experience to fruition in the historical moment. "Becoming human" in the *Mencius* is a work in progress; and the results of that work, as Mencius sees it, can be as great as humans aspire to make them.

Methodology and Key Terms

In our attempt to bring Warring States thought into sharper focus, it is crucial that we reflect upon our methodologies and address how it is that we propose handling certain key terminological issues. The present holds the potential for unprecedented progress in the field, and now is the time to reconsider and restate the assumptions upon which we intend to move forward.

Generally speaking, in a work on Chinese philosophy, there are two criteria for adequacy in translation and interpretation. The first criterion measures the degree to which English renditions of key terms are consistent with the philosophical assumptions of classical Chinese thought in general. Here, chapter one will be devoted to sketching these assumptions as I feel they bear on the *Mencius*. As I have already said, I do not find the English term "nature" to be consistent with the assumptions of mainstream Warring States thought, particularly when the teleological dimension of that term is stressed. Hence, I develop "disposition" as an alternative translation of *xing* 性 on the basis that this term is more consistent with early Chinese assumptions. In translating classical Chinese terms adequately, however, it is rarely as easy as presenting single, isolated argument for each particular translation choice, and this leads to the second criterion.

The second criterion for adequacy in treatment measures the degree of coherence and consistency that can be brought to an object text when it is focused through a particular vocabulary. Rather than a series of isolated arguments for each translation choice, what follows is an extended argument for the viability of the whole cluster of translations used here to render the *Mencius* coherent. The key terms in the text are relatively few, and they are translated below with some consistency. The following terms might be considered at the outset, while the adequacy of these translations will be reinforced over the course of this study:

天 *Tian*: "Forces."

We begin with a term that has no satisfactory correlate in English. In most cases, *tian* will be left untranslated, allowing associations to accumulate around the Chinese term. Some associations, however, are importantly different in the *Mencius*. Mencius disassociates *tian* from the more anthropomorphic "Heaven" of Mozi, which results in a more secular notion of "forces." This does not diminish the awe and respect that Mencius attaches to the term, however. Where I do translate or gloss *tian*, it is usually as "forces" or "the broadest set of interlocking patterns" within which events proceed.

In the *Mencius* and other Si-Meng texts, the cosmological significance of *tian* transmutes into the equally significant notion of "forces" in the realms of culture, politics, tradition, social institutions, and economics, associated with the "age" (*shi* 世) in which one lives.

命 *Ming*: "Conditions."

Ming, like *tian* 天, is a term that commands the awe and respect of Confucians. The notion of *ming* is closely connected to *tian*. If *tian* are the "forces" that shape events in the Chinese world (*tianxia* 天下), *ming* are the "conditions" or "circumstances" under which those events proceed, conditions that "forces" mandate.

It is argued in chapter five that in the Si-Meng school the social and political dimension of "forces" and "conditions" becomes more pronounced. Mencius also represents this shift. He also exhibits a unique understanding of the role that Chinese history, culture, and families play as "conditions" under which the human experience is possible.

性 *Xing*: "Disposition," "to Cultivate as Disposition."

As stated above, my intention is to present *xing* in a manner that is more consistent with classical Chinese thought. Chapter one addresses issues in Warring States cosmology, a cosmology that in my estimation does not exhibit a notion of causality that readily lends itself to the idea of an end-driven "nature." The translation of *xing* as "disposition" is developed instead. In chapter four the historical, cultural, and uniquely human dimensions of the "human disposition" (*renxing* 人性) are explored at greater length.

Xing is also a verb in the *Mencius*; hence, "to cultivate as a disposition" is used on occasion.

心 *Xin*: "Feeling," "Feelings," "Heart-Mind."

This term is absolutely central to the thought of the *Mencius*, one that the text develops into a major Confucian theme. The conventional translation of "heart-mind" is retained here and used on occasion. However, in chapter two, it is argued that in the *Mencius* the term is most adequately understood as a function rather than an organ. *Xin* can be identified with "thoughts" as well as with "feelings," as there is no sharp distinction between the two in classical China. However, it is maintained here that Mencius intends to foreground the function of *xin* as "feeling" in opposition to a more technical mode of moral deliberation and reasoning. Hence, "feeling" is the translation most often employed. Much of chapter two is devoted to explaining what "feeling" means in the present study.

誠 *Cheng*: "Well Integrated," "Integration," "Integrity."

Cheng is relatively underdeveloped in the *Mencius*, but it becomes important in the Si-Meng lineage as the central term in the *Zhongyong*. In the *Mencius* the term exhibits a range of meaning, from the vernacular "genuine" or "true" to the more philosophically significant "integration" or "integrity." On these latter, more philosophical occasions, *cheng* involves feeling the world truly and adjusting one's habits of engagement accordingly. As such, *cheng* can be considered among the normative measures that guide the project of personal growth in the *Mencius*.

The term also reflects the Mencian position in the ongoing debate over whether appropriateness (*yi* 義) is "internal" (*nei* 內) or "external" (*wai* 外). In Mencian thought, the moral sense is best described neither as internal nor as external, but rather as "integral" (*cheng*). This is how the term, and the debate, is understood below.

德 *De*: "Character," "Force of Character," "Quality."

In both the *Mencius* and other Si-Meng materials such as the *Five Modes of Conduct*, *de* is understood as the "character" of a person. "Character" embraces the notion of fortifying moral habits and attitudes in a disposition (*xing* 性) and thereby influencing others by the force of example. That personal character itself has an efficacious "quality" is an extension of this notion of influence. In chapter one, Zhuangzi's understanding of *de* as the unique "character" or "quality" of something is discussed, as it provides a useful point of contrast between the philosophy of the *Zhuangzi* and that of the *Mencius*.

仁 *Ren*: "Associated Humanity."

"Associated humanity" is a human virtue that extends directly from the family. "Humanity" in this instance is not a shared, essential attribute with which all Homosapiens are endowed; it is rather a form of human experience that arises from the dynamics of associated life itself, which begin in the family. Associated humanity, for Mencius, consummates in what is understood as "human" (*ren* 人) and generates qualitatively "human feeling" (*renxin* 人心).[39]

In the *Mencius*, *ren* also refers to a form of government in which associated life is allowed to flourish. In advocating *ren* as a social and political ideal, Mencius exhibits an activism evident elsewhere in the Si-Meng school.

義 *Yi*: "Appropriateness."

Yi is a social sensibility that enables one to behave in a fitting manner. There is some debate in the Warring States period over the "internal" (*nei* 內) and "external" (*wai* 外) features of *yi*, and this debate makes its presence felt in the *Mencius*. Mencius charts his way through the middle of this debate without taking a side. "Appropriateness" is neither internal nor external for Mencius; rather, it is situated within a mode of experience that precedes the distinction. Further along in the Si-Meng line, the Mencian position becomes more explicitly identified with the notion of "integration" (*cheng* 誠). In the *Mencius*, it is evident that the "appropriateness" of an action is measured in relation to the quality of one's "associated humanity" (*ren*), which is relational rather than strictly internal or external.

志 *Zhi*: "Aspiration."

The Guodian finds confirm that "aspiration" plays an important role in the Si-Meng school. In the *Mencius* the term is presented on two levels. On a psychophysical level, "aspiration" is a function of living bodies related to the "configurative energy" (*qi* 氣) that animates them. On a sociopolitical level, "aspiration" is related to the role of the "scholar-official" (*shi* 士) in advancing the "human way" (*rendao* 人道).

In this study, *zhi* is treated on the psychophysical level in chapter two, while in chapter five it is treated on the sociopolitical level. In the latter treatment, the activism of the Si-

Meng Confucians is once again recognized in the *Mencius*, this time in its attitude towards the social and political conditions that the Confucian scholar-official "aspires" to overcome.

As with any set of key translations, this set involves some degree of compromise. One cannot hope to evoke in any translation the entire, seamless range of meaning that attaches itself to an ancient Chinese term. The preliminary terminological discussions above should alert the reader to my general approach. This approach remains to be tested. If what follows is both sensitive to its Warring States context and reasonably coherent, then the adequacy of the preceding vocabulary is recommended.

Of course, the hazard is that the coherence brought to this text will be more the coherence between English words in my head and less the coherence between Chinese words in the *Mencius*. I consider this danger to be unavoidable, no matter how careful one is. The risk of reading oneself into the tradition is significantly lessened, however, if the first criterion for adequacy in treatment is taken seriously. In what follows, I make every effort to read the *Mencius* as a text in context. I have already tried to establish the proper context for reading Mencius by considering the botanical metaphor in the classical Chinese world. I continue to reflect on the broader context of Warring States thought in the pages to come. I reference a range of texts in proximity to the *Mencius*, including those that Mencius himself reads and makes reference to, plus the newly discovered archeological finds.

Despite all individual efforts, however, the interpretation of any classical text is finally a shared effort. We do our best, and then we rely on an active community of readers to determine the strengths and weaknesses of what we have contributed. What follows is an interpretation, and as such it is fallible. But it is nonetheless an argument. Two convictions motivate this argument. The first conviction is that newly unearthed documents from Guodian provide evidence for a more progressive, process-oriented interpretation of Mencian thought. In attempting to inform our reading of Mencius with these documents, I mean to challenge a well-established, default reading that persists in spite of them.

My second conviction is that the *Mencius*, while a difficult and sometimes opaque text, contains a coherent argument that is not indecipherable in our own age. The wisdom of the *Mencius*, as I understand it, speaks quite audibly to the intelligent reader who has an interest in ordinary human occupations such as raising a family, cultivating a character, and improving the conditions under which people live. Above all, I hope that this study succeeds in communicating some part of that wisdom.

Chapter 1

The Cosmological Background

Energy and Propensity

The notion that *qi* 氣 or "configurative energy" animates the world is among the most common assumptions in Warring States literature.[1] The language of *qi* serves as a sort of metaphysical vernacular throughout the period's literature, and the *Mencius* is no exception. By exploring the notion of *qi* one reconstructs the worldview from which Mencius thought and wrote.[2] The *Zuozhuan* teaches that *qi* in its various phases and permutations give rise to a variety of qualities: the "five flavors," the "five colors," the "five modes of music," and when out of balance, the "six illnesses."[3] As the qualities of taste, sight, and sound, *qi* represents the transactions between an organism and its environment. As the measure of health and spirit, *qi* represents the animating energies of the living body: the vitality derived from environing conditions that cause physical growth and sustain life.[4] *Qi* concentrates in living things as a kind of vital fluid, and in the natural world as a kind of vapor; it constitutes both the emotional and the meteorological environment of life as the prevailing "atmosphere" or "weather."[5]

As a metaphysical notion *qi* 氣 presents a challenge: it defies any sharp distinction between form and matter or being and modality. *Qi* is not the inert material of a thing, for it is presented as hylozoistic and dynamic, and it is identified with a variety of qualities. These qualities, however, do not correspond to the essential attributes of any discrete, ontologically primary subject. The qualities of *qi* can be designated as phases of *yin* 陰 and *yang* 陽, but these designations do not belong to any primary being as an essential feature. *Yin* and *yang* do not operate as formal properties. As Nathan Sivin observes:

> *Yin* 陰 is always defined with respect to *yang* 陽, and vice versa. An old man is *yin* with respect to a young man, but *yang* with respect to a woman. The idea that *yin* or *yang* is a property—for instance, that all men are always *yang*, or conversely that *yang* is masculine—is not a Chinese idea. A relationship, if not stated, is always implied.[6]

Yin and *yang* express qualities that arise from relations between things (*wu* 物), and things are always dynamically configured. The way things internally relate to one another gives rise to *yin* and *yang*. As the *Daodejing* says:

> The ten thousand things shoulder *yin* 陰 and embrace *yang* 陽; they are a blending of configurative energy into harmonies [*he* 和].[7]

Achievements of equilibrium or harmony (*he* 和) describe the blending of things into relations that configure *qi* and consummate in qualitative relationships designated *yin* or *yang*. Such relational states entail neither ontologically primary subjects nor the essential attributes thereof. Such states entail only the continuity of transforming *qi*. Zhuangzi also understands the transformation (*hua* 化) of correlative, qualitative states as resolving into the incessant reconfiguration of *qi*. He presents this understanding in the form of a common saying: "Throughout all the world is the continuity [*yi* 一] of configurative energy [*qi*]."[8]

Qi 氣 is understood to express a wide range of qualities at various levels; biological, emotional, meteorological, spiritual, and so on, according to how it is harnessed, blocked, released, or lost in dynamic configurations. In a world animated by *qi*, things spontaneously manifest a particular quality or character by virtue of their relational configurations. The spontaneous nature of qualitative experience in this cosmology is an aspect of the form/function dynamics it entails. There is no primary distinction to be made between form and function in a *qi* cosmology; qualities are discharged and undergone spontaneously by virtue of dispositions that are always both formal and functional. As Judith Farquhar observes:

> *Qi* 氣 is both structural and functional, a unification of material and temporal forms that loses all coherence when reduced to one or the other "aspect."[9]

As things are dynamically configured and reconfigured, material/temporal formations become modally disposed to discharge or undergo qualitative experience immediately. Any standard form/matter or being/modality distinction breaks down.

As we entertain a Warring States cosmology, other familiar notions also begin to dissolve. Without the presence of discrete, primary subjects or formal attributes, standard models of causality become difficult to conceptualize. There is nothing that clearly corresponds to efficient or final causality in the functioning of configurative energy. In the *Zhuangzi*, Ziqi is asked to discuss the "pipes of heaven" and he relates the following:

> The world emits a configurative energy [*qi* 氣] that we'll call a "wind." If only it would not blow, but it does, and the myriad apertures begin to howl. Have you alone not heard their drawn out sounds?

Ziqi then describes the contours of the earth, which like "nostrils," "mouths" and "ears," are configured to give rise to perceptible qualities, the metaphor being various sounds. He continues:

> The myriad sounds produced by the blowing are all distinct, for all the blowing does is elicit from the apertures themselves [*ziji* 自己] their own natural inclinations [*ziqu* 自取]. Who would be the initiator of this?[10]

According to Ziqi, everything derives by virtue of its "shape" a spontaneous propensity towards certain qualities in the incessant blow of *qi*. There is no antecedent force that determines the advent of these qualities in any given configuration, and there is nothing apart from the inclination of the configuration itself that determines the qualities of its own expression. Neither efficient nor final causality is implicated in the "blow" of *qi*.

In place of efficient and final causality, there is an alternative notion of causality suggested in a *qi* 氣 cosmology. However elusive the notion, sensitive scholars consistently detect its presence. It is suggested in what Herbert Fingarette labels "magic" in the *Analects*.[11] Fingarette senses, even in the *Analects*, the presence of a causal reasoning that differs considerably from standard Western models. It is also suggested in what Tu Wei-ming calls the "continuous interaction" of *tian* 天 and *ren* 人 in the early Confucian tradition.[12] *Qi* causality is also suggested whenever the word "organic" is used to distinguish a Chinese mode of thinking from dominant Western modes.[13] The term "organic" calls attention to the interrelatedness of things, highlighting the absence of discrete objects in linear, causal relations in absolute space and time. If causality is not linear in this sense, then what is causality in the Chinese tradition?

The notion of causality operative in classical Chinese thought is difficult to articulate in the familiar terminology of cause and effect. Attempts to describe how Chinese causality differs from linear causality employ the language of "configuration," "resonance," and "propensity." Léon Vandermeersch, writing on the *Book of Changes* (*Yijing*), describes the Chinese notion of causality in the following language:

> From one event to another, the relation revealed by the science of divination [in the *Book of Changes*] is not presented as a chain of intermediate causes and effects, but as a change in a diagrammatic configuration.[14]

Carine Defoort suggests that, for the Chinese,

> Events were not seen as caused by one powerful and preceding event but as woven in a network of inter-dependent nodes, a colossal pattern in which things reacted upon each other by a kind of mysterious resonance rather than mechanical impulsion.[15]

François Jullien has perhaps developed the Chinese notion of causality most fully.[16] He focuses on a single character, *shi* 勢, which in various contexts admits translation as "position," "power," "circumstances," and "propensity." Apart from its use in early militarist texts and its eventual adoption by Legalist thinkers,[17] *shi* never became a highly developed philosophical topic in the tradition. The explanation for this, according to Jullien, is that "the intuition of [*shi*] is common enough in China that it fails to give rise to any abstract reflection," since "to the Chinese, the idea of *shi* seems self-evident."[18] Jullien penetrates an elusive subject matter, one he describes as "difficult to capture in discourse: namely, the kind of potential that originates not in human initiative but instead results from the very disposition of things."[19]

This elusive kind of potential that Jullien locates involves notions of natural efficacy and tendency that rely on neither efficient nor final causality. Instead, *shi* 勢 represents the propensity of a situation or event to ripen into efficacy completely of itself. The notion of propensity is contrary to that of making something happen through any external form of causal force. Mencius himself relates an old adage of the Qi people, illustrating the notion:

> One might be clever, but it's better to make use of propensity [*shi* 勢]. One might have a garden hoe, but it is better to wait for the season to arrive.[20]

Propensity (*shi* 勢) refers to the causal force that circumstances themselves implicate. It is the spontaneous efficacy of a given state or condition of things that relies on no discrete causal agent or principle. Jullien specifically presents the "logic" of *shi* as an alternative to the "extrinsic relatedness" of mechanistic causality and commensurate with the Chinese "indifference to any notion of a *telos*, [or] final end for things."[21] Rather than rely on regressive, causal analysis or the projection of teleological ends, Chinese thinkers interpret reality in terms commensurate with Ziqi's howling apertures: as configurative dispositions that sponsor the spontaneous emergence of events with qualitative character.

The notion of "disposition" involves both configurative arrangement and spontaneous efficacy, notions that are consistent with a *qi* 氣 cosmology. That spontaneous efficacy arises according to the manner in which things are arranged is consistent with the idea that configurative energy disperses in always-qualitative concentrations throughout its field of deployment. In a world charged with configurative energy, every shift of position is a change in disposition and has an immediate, qualitative effect. In the *Mencius* this is reflected even in vernacular contexts.²²

Causality in the Warring States period refers to the dynamic whereby concentrations of *qi* 氣, shored up in fluent configurations, punctuate as qualitative events. A qualitative event, in this respect, can be thought of as a process in which a quality (*de* 德), engendered within the field of becoming (*dao* 道), "takes shape" (*xing* 形) within its environing conditions, and culminates (*cheng* 成) through the force or propensity (*shi* 勢) that these conditions implicate. The formula is presented in the *Daodejing*:

> A process of becoming engenders them, a quality rears them, things shape them, and the propensity of circumstances completes them.²³

Events occur by virtue of the limits implicit in the conditions that sponsor their emergence. Emergence is a process of taking on shape, and shape entails a pervasive quality (*de* 德) that rears a trajectory towards completion (*cheng* 成). Understood discursively, this consummatory instance is itself among the conditions that define the next phase of formation. The process described here is seamless.

Shape and Spontaneity

Admittedly, the cosmological assumptions of the Warring States period are not easy to reconstruct. Extending this discussion to other texts, however, can grant further insight into the assumptions that underwrite the vocabulary of shape and configurative energy in the world of Mencius. The *Book of Changes* is particularly helpful.

The *Book of Changes* is constructed around two hexagrams that symbolize the two salient traits of reality: the "generative" (*qian* 乾) and the "receptive" (*kun* 坤). The "generative" is identified with the incipience and continued novelty of a process as it "takes shape," as well as the seamless continuity among various phases of the process itself:

> Great indeed is the sublimity of the "generative," to which all things owe their beginning [*shi* 始] and which interconnects

tian 天. Clouds move along and the rain spreads, and various things flow in shape [*shunxing* 順形].²⁴

The "receptive" represents the boundless potential for transformation; it cooperates with the "generative" in bringing about the conditions for momentarily definite, yet ever transforming shapes. In the *Words of Wen* (*Wenyan*) commentary on the second hexagram, we read:

> The "receptive" is most pliant, but when considered in agitation [*dong* 動] it becomes firm [*gang* 剛]. It is in equilibrium [*jing* 靜], and owing to unique qualities [*de* 德] it manifests definite trends [*fang* 方].²⁵

"Qualities," as an aspect of the "receptive," delimit events by focusing them within the limitless continuity of the "generative," and reflect that which is determinate about them. Qualities (*de* 德) initiate and direct the trajectories of discursive events and remain, through various phases of development, their defining characteristics. Hall and Ames describe *de* as a "focus" that gathers momentum around itself in a "field."²⁶ Any particular "focus" becomes definite by construing an entire field from the time and location it sustains. Owing to agitation (*dong* 動), also an aspect of the "receptive," the "focusing" that makes things definite is always discursive. The "generative" aspect of reality lends endless potential for novelty and growth. In the *Great Commentary* (*Dazhuan*) of the *Book of Changes*, as in the *Daodejing*,²⁷ this process of growth, exhibiting both agitation and equilibrium, is described as opening and closing a gate:

> [The early sages] called the closing of the gate the receptive, and the opening of the gate the generative.²⁸

The passage continues by defining what it means to "endure through alteration" (tongbian 通變) in those terms:

> The alternation between closing and opening they called "alteration" [bian 變]. The coming-and-going without limit [from one alteration, on to the next] they called "enduring through."

The notion of "alteration" (bian 變) in the *Great Commentary* can be further understood as transformations in shape:

Transforming [hua 化] while cutting a shape [cai 裁] is called "alteration."[29]

"Enduring through" (*tong* 通), in the same passage, refers to the continuity exhibited by shapes-in-process as they move though alteration:

That there is extension [*tui* 推] while traveling along [*xing* 行] is called 'enduring through' [*tong* 通].

The notion of "enduring through alteration" (*tongbian* 通變) in the *Great Commentary* reflects both the boundless novelty of an emergent process as well as the actual "shapes" attained in that process: both the limitless potential for growth and the delimiting constraint of shape are accounted for. The world of the Chinese thinker is one in which "taking shape" and "enduring through alternation" happen endlessly. These processes are simply called "events" (*shi* 事).

We learn more about this cosmology by considering the manner in which Zhuangzi makes sense of his wife's death. At first he says he did not understand his loss. Eventually he peers back into her beginnings (*shi* 始) and uses this insight to make sense of her demise. He finds that there was a time before the configurative energy, shape, and life-span (*sheng* 生) of his wife emerged from an amorphous (*za* 雜) state, prior to her existence.[30] Her existence, he comes to realize, was simply an alteration (*bian* 變) from some state that precluded her into that configurative energy (*qi* 氣), shape (*xing* 形) and life-span (*sheng* 生) that was *her*. Her death is understood as a seamless return to that "formless" state from which she had emerged.[31] Understanding this, Zhuangzi ceases mourning and begins to celebrate her memory. Zhuangzi considers his wife not as a discrete entity now annihilated, but rather as a process that literally "took shape" over the course of a life span (*sheng*), and now consummated, makes for a memorable experience.

Throughout the *Zhuangzi*, life is viewed as alteration (*bian* 變): it is a "taking shape" from some previous phase while death is the perfectly natural transformation into something else. Things do not emerge from sheer nothingness nor disappear into sheer nothingness. There is no substantial generation or corruption. Life and death are simply alterations in functional arrangements of configurative energy, phases in the endless transformation from one shape into another.

Given the fact that no shape is immutable in this cosmology, shape must be considered not as the fixed "nature" of a thing but rather as the momentary consummation of an ongoing process—one that is, in itself, the dynamic starting point for the next phase of transformation. Shape, then, is something that indicates a "disposition" rather than a fixed "nature." By virtue of causal propensity (*shi* 勢), the "disposition" of any configuration issues spontaneously into features that both define and reconfigure the trajectory of its discursive formation.

We must give careful consideration to the notion of "spontaneity" that is being developed here, as it will often be appealed to in the coming discussion of the *Mencius*. "Spontaneity" does not mean "randomness," "haphazardness," or "unpredictability." The "spontaneous" qualities that arise from the propensity of a particular disposition do not emerge randomly; rather, they express the history and continuity of the discursive formation of that disposition.

Taking a step closer to Mencius, let us consider a botanical example. The young oak tree that stands near the baseball field will not "spontaneously" become a giraffe. There are certain "spontaneous" things, however, that we can expect from this oak tree: the turning of its leaves in autumn, the habit of its branches to reach for sunlight, the thickening of its bark, and so on. One might take such "spontaneous" behaviors to illustrate this oak tree's "formal" definition, essential "nature," or "final cause." To do so would be reasonable, but it would be to entirely miss the thrust of Warring States thought. The "spontaneous" behavior of this oak tree, from the perspective of the Warring States thinker, signals the seamless continuity of its emergence, not its "nature" or "final cause." This oak tree is "disposed" to do such things by virtue of its history. In twenty years time, depending on conditions as yet undetermined, this oak tree might be flourishing magnificently in a form all its own, lying on its side providing shelter to a rat snake, or exhausting its fibers providing warmth to someone's living room. In transaction with conditions, it may develop the "disposition" to perform these or any number of functions "spontaneously" so long as these functions retain continuity with its previous form and function. For the Warring States thinker, these potential scenarios are not "actualized" on account of something immutably "fixed." It is instead the continuity of transactional formation within determinate conditions that enable forms to evolve and functions to be discharged "spontaneously" according to situations as they become configured.

This idea will be developed in pages to come. "Spontaneity" will be understood as the unmediated discharge of a function configured in a dynamic disposition. In the next chapter, I will discuss the Mencian notion of "heart-mind" or "feeling" (*xin* 心) along these lines. Dispositions themselves arise from conditions (*ming* 命), such that they "take shape" discursively in transaction with conditions as they are met. This is the theme of the newly discovered *Dispositions Arise from Conditions* document. This idea will be further developed, and in chapters four and five I will treat the Mencian notion of "human disposition" (*renxing* 人性) along these lines. For Mencius, dispositions can be cultivated in such a way that they issue spontaneously into appropriate (*yi* 義) feelings and behaviors. This will be discussed presently.

Disposition and Spontaneity

A. C. Graham was the first to suggest the relevance of a notion of spontaneity to Chinese ethics generally: "Chinese ethical thinking starts from the spontaneity of inclination and the value of wisdom."[32] Graham proceeds to discuss spontaneity in Chinese ethics in terms of a "quasi-syllogism" under which spontaneous approaches might be evaluated in practice. As Graham is well aware, however, spontaneity precludes such discursive reasoning altogether. He writes:

> No thinker in this tradition objectivises the spontaneous in man, as morally neutral inclination to be utilized or checked in the service of ends chosen independently....

He then asks himself frankly:

> Is it a limitation of Chinese thought that it overlooked the approach which seems natural to ourselves? It may be profitable to ask the questions from the opposite direction. How did I as a Westerner get trapped into pretending that I can fully objectivise the spontaneous in myself, shrink myself into a point of rational Ego pursuing ends independent of my spontaneous goals, observing unmoved even my own emotions? What have I gained from following a line of thought which first detached supposedly rational ends from the goals of inclination, then failed to discover any rational grounds for them?[33]

If the young oak tree by the baseball field could speak, it might pose the same questions to those strange onlookers who ascribe its spontaneous behavior to its "species," "nature," or teleological "end."

Graham is keen to point out that spontaneity in ethics is a theme across the spectrum of thinkers and schools in classical China. The notion of spontaneity will be used in chapter three to distinguish the Mencian approach to ethics from the more technical Mohist approach. There is some ground to cover, however, before we are clear about how the Mencian notion of "disposition" works to refute the Mohist by appeal to spontaneity.

From the standpoint of Warring States cosmology, the notion of disposition (*xing* 性) is similar to that of "shape" (*xing* 形) in that each addresses the formal aspects of a *qi* 氣 configuration. Each sponsors a concentration of configurative energy. Each is a dynamic state or condition that facilitates a spontaneous transaction in the world. And each, in turn, expresses the "quality" or "character" (*de* 德) of the things they individuate. Also, given the assumptions of a *qi* cosmology, both are process-oriented notions. Zhuangzi's wife took on shape over the course of a life (*sheng* 生), and as Graham points out, the notion of life span (*sheng* 生) is closely connected to that of disposition (*xing* 性), the two terms being in some cases interchangeable.[34]

However, a disposition is not identical to a course of life. Graham traces the distinction between *xing* 性 and *sheng* 生 and determines that, by the time of the *Spring and Autumn Annals of Master Lü* (*Lüshichunqiu*), the disposition of a thing is considered "its *proper* course of development during its process of *sheng*."[35] *Qi* 氣 is linked to the normative dimension of a disposition at this stage in the tradition. In a manner that has continued to inform Chinese understandings of health and illness, the *Zuozhuan* describes the human disposition (*xing*) as a *qi* configuration, a functional disposition that one loses (*shi* 失) if the harmony it facilitates is upset:

> In excess, [sensory qualities] confuse and disorder, and people lose their dispositions [*xing* 性].[36]

Here, a disposition is presumed to condition the flow of configurative energies that account for vitality. *Xing* 性 is a configuration that sponsors in some desirable way the flow of these energies. As the passage suggests, transactional perturbations can alter a disposition. Any alteration of state or condition is understood to be an immediate alteration of energy. The result is qualitative and spontaneous; in this case, it is the difference between a state of health and a state of illness.

Health is a state that involves the spontaneous discharge of bodily functions that preserve the optimal vitality and integrity of an ongoing process. When the body is healthily disposed, a person feels great and can enjoy any number of things. If one is feeling ill, one cannot restore a healthy disposition by simply behaving as if one feels great—as if such behaviors themselves will somehow restore one's health. Mencius thinks of the moral disposition in a similar manner. Just as a healthy bodily disposition affords one certain vital energies, the cultivation of a healthy moral disposition concentrates what Mencius calls "flood-like configurative energies" (*haoranzhiqi* 浩然之氣). He explains how such experience is had:

> It is born of accumulated appropriateness [*yi* 義]. It cannot be had by anyone through sporadic appropriateness.[37]

The kind of moral disposition that Mencius advocates cultivating can be termed "habitual." Cultivating habit, in this sense, does not mean establishing a set of routines; instead, habit is the developed proclivity to transact with the world on a spontaneous level. Morality is not a series of randomly discharged acts; it is rather the integration of productive habits into one's person. Productive habits are important to cultivate since they condition the manner in which an organism spontaneously acts upon and undergoes experience in the world. Habit conditions impulse, and as a mode of being is indistinguishable from the proclivities that arise from the propensity of a disposition (*xing* 性).

As Mencius suggests, genuine moral impulse has little to do with the sporadic performance of good deeds based on their stipulated goodness. Mencius subordinates any morality based on doctrines (*yan* 言) that stipulate what is appropriate and advocates in their place a morality based on the spontaneous prompts of feeling (*xin* 心). Feeling represents the structural/functional interface of an integrated disposition. The Mencian project is one of preserving the incipient disposition to feel the world in a certain way and of gradually shaping a better-integrated disposition by cultivating that initial disposition into productive habits of feeling. Forging such a disposition is likened to forging a path. As Mencius instructs Gaozi:

If it is used, a trail through the mountains becomes a well-trammeled path in no time. If it is not used, it becomes choked with grass just as quickly. Right now your feelings [*xin* 心] are choked with grass.[38]

To cultivate a moral disposition is to make moral behavior habitual and hence spontaneous. One's disposition then becomes inseparable from one's very identity (*fen* 分) as a person. According to Mencius, the identity of the exemplary person is composed of virtues cultivated into habitudes rooted in feeling. The more deeply integrated identity is with one's integral feeling, the less likely one is to radically alter one's personality when circumstances shift. Mencius explains:

> What exemplary persons make their disposition [*xing* 性] does not increase if their activities become important in the world, nor diminish if they are relegated to live in poverty and obscurity. The reason is that their identity becomes established [*fending* 分定]. What exemplary persons cultivate as their disposition are the associated humanity [*ren* 仁], appropriateness [*yi* 義], ritual propriety [*li* 禮], and wisdom [*zhi* 知] that are rooted in their feeling [*xin* 心].[39]

Mencius continues by describing the physical manifestations of one's disposition, indicating that the creation of identity implicates the whole person:

> This disposition generates a complexion as a matter of course, visible in the face, manifest in posture, and reaching throughout the body.[40]

There is a symbiotic relationship in the *Mencius* between one's bodily shape (*xing* 形) and one's disposition (*xing* 性) as a person. Hence, Mencius implicates the former in the cultivation of the latter:

> One is disposed towards bodily shape and complexion by *tian* 天, but only by becoming a sage is one able to go anywhere [*jian* 踐] with that shape.[41]

A related idea is expressed in the *Zhongyong*:

> What *tian* 天 conditions is a disposition [*xing* 性]. To further [*shuai* 率] one's disposition is called the 'most productive course' [*dao* 道].[42]

These two passages are similar both conceptually and linguistically. In the above translations, the choice of "further" for *shuai* 率 and "going somewhere" for *jian* 踐 is intended to highlight this similarity. *Shuai* means to "follow" but it also means to "lead." It means both here, just as *jian* means both to "follow" as well as to "tread forward."[43] The idea in both passages is that some initial "shape" or "disposition" is given, but one must "move it forward" in some way by doing the most one can with it; this results in the "most productive course" (*dao* 道).[44] These notions will be further considered in pages to come.

Mencius employs the terminology of disposition to distinguish the Confucian attitude towards human development from other competing attitudes. His contemporary, Zhuangzi, is also concerned with the implications of shape and spontaneity in a *qi* 氣 cosmology. Zhuangzi bypasses the notion of disposition (*xing* 性), however. *Xing* 性 appears nowhere in the "Inner Chapters" of *Zhuangzi*; neither is it in *Daodejing*. Rather than focus on developing a moral disposition, these texts focus instead on the inherent uniqueness of the shape (*xing* 形) of things. From the standpoint of a *qi* cosmology, both the notion of shape (*xing* 形) and that of disposition (*xing* 性) can be understood as affective states in a world charged with configurative energy. Reading the *Parity of Things* (*Qiwulun* 齊物論) chapter of the *Zhuangzi* side-by-side with the *Mencius* suggests the functional similarity of these terms.

Zhuangzi and Shape

Zhuangzi responds directly to a Mencian line of thinking in the *Parity of Things*. He agrees that lived configurations issue directly into spontaneous feelings (*xin* 心). He writes, "With the transformation of shape [*xing* 形], feelings transform naturally."[45] Zhuangzi does not, however, as Mencius does, advocate developing one's shape into a putatively moral disposition (*xing* 性) by reinforcing certain habits of feeling; he advocates instead the abandonment of this project. His rationale is this:

If the idea is to follow one's integral feeling [*xin* 心] as a guide, then who is without such a guide? Why must it be only those who understand the on-going development of things and choose for themselves what to feel that have such a guide? Even the dull-witted have one.[46]

Zhuangzi considers the conventionally "wise" no better than the purportedly "dull-witted." These are, Zhuangzi would maintain, not absolute distinctions. He maintains that given the continuity and parity of all things, no lived configuration in the world grants one exclusive access to moral feeling.

According to Zhuangzi, the error of the Confucian sages is that they seek to "rectify the shape [*xing* 形] of everything with their bowing and scraping to ritual forms and music."[47] And this encapsulates the Mencian project: Mencius wishes to "shape" a qualitatively human disposition (*xing* 性) through Confucian practice, Confucian education, and the extension of Confucian moral feeling. For Zhuangzi, however, it is wrongheaded to distinguish such human achievement from human failure when even "human shape" (*renzhixing* 人之形) in the span of "ten-thousand transformations" is not necessarily preferable to other forms of existence.[48] Zhuangzi asks the empty skull if it would like its "shape" restored to a living, human status, and the answer is unequivocal: "Never!"[49] For Zhuangzi, each and every configuration of existence is utterly unique and self-justified. There is no absolute standard by which the worth of various forms can be measured.

This explains why Zhuangzi's dialogues are populated with grotesque creatures, twisted trees, and disfigured criminals. Zhuangzi is keen to assert that these seemingly inferior or undesirable states of existence are all of commensurate importance and capable of contributing unique worth to the totality. Each shape is possessed of an inherent, distinct "quality" (*de* 德) irrespective of any perceived worthlessness. The images Zhuangzi uses to render his point are perfectly suited to frustrate the Mencian project. Mencius sometimes employs woodworking metaphors in speaking of moral development and refuses to surrender the "plumb-line" (*shengmo* 繩墨).[50] Zhuangzi, in turn, exalts a tree so gnarled that it "cannot center a plumb-line [*shengmo*]."[51] The twisted tree is celebrated as useless to the carpenter, useless, that is, to anyone for whom trees represent something to develop.

In rejecting the idea of developing one's shape (*xing* 形) into a thus termed "moral" disposition (*xing* 性), Zhuangzi in effect downplays the importance of shape and elevates the notion of "quality" or "unique character" (*de* 德) in its place. This is most clearly expressed in the *Character Satisfies the Tally* (*Dechongfu* 德充符) chapter.[52] The image that provides the title for this chapter appears in the *Daodejing* as well, where it is related to the impartiality of *dao* 道:

> The sage holds the left half of the tally yet does not exact her due from others. A person of character [*de* 德] is in charge of the tally. A person without character is looking to collect on it. The course of *tian* 天 is impartial; it invariably benefits all people.[53]

Contributing the uniqueness of character is compared to "holding a tally" but not collecting on it. In other words, the contribution of uniqueness involves no debt or restitution. This does not mean, however, that there is nothing of value exchanged. Character "satisfies the tally" by contributing its worth irrespective of the standard implied in any external obligation to do so. Uniqueness is self-justified; the insistent particularity of each thing must be taken at face value. There is no derivative, objectified standard that governs the exchange of such values: uniqueness of character "satisfies the tally."

The implications are clear in the *Character Satisfies the Tally* chapter, wherein a parade of mutilated figures, each of whom would not be expected to have much worth by community standards,[54] win people over by the force of their character and thereby make their unique contributions. Despite the bodily shape he is stuck with, one "lame hunchback without lips" manages to alter Duke Ling's standards of judgment by the force of his unique character. Zhuangzi comments:

> Thus, to the extent that one's unique character [*de* 德] stands out, one's shape [*xing* 形] is disregarded. When people notice what is usually forgotten, and forget what is usually noticed, this is genuine forgetting.[55]

What is "forgotten" here is shape itself: that which invites Confucians to evaluate a properly "human" deportment. Zhuangzi identifies such standards with provincial distinctions, all of which form a seamless continuity (*yi* 一) one to the next.

The projects of Zhuangzi and Mencius differ in priority, but each share cosmological assumptions rooted in notions of "shape" and configurative energy. Zhuangzi encourages one to think beyond the configurative limits of shape (*xing* 形) and ride through existence "with only *qi* 氣 as one's chariot."[56] Mencius advocates shaping a disposition (*xing* 性) that configures the emergence of a morally nourishing "flood-like" *qi*. There are cosmological assumptions that unite these thinkers within the overall context of Warring States thought. Establishing such a context by means of overview is an important preliminary step in understanding the *Mencius*.

CHARACTERISTICS OF CHINESE COSMOLOGY

In his 1935 article "Exposition on the Unique Kind of Basic Spirit in Chinese Culture," Tang Junyi provides an overview of Chinese thinking that both summarizes and corroborates the assumptions here proposed. Tang Junyi identifies seven characteristic views that he feels underlie all Chinese thinking. Each of these views has some bearing on the matters considered in this chapter, and they assist in establishing parameters for our interpretation of the *Mencius*. The seven views are: that there is no substratum (*wudingti* 無定體), that everything is two-way (*wuwangbufu* 無往不復), that having/not having and agitation/equilibrium are each united (*heyouwudongjing* 合有無動靜), that one/many is inseparable (*yiduobufen* 一多不分), that determinism does not apply (*feidingming* 非定命), that process is incessant (*shengshengbuyi* 生生不已), and that dispositions issue directly from the course of *tian* 天 (*xingjitiandao* 性即天道).[57]

If we take seriously the view that there is no substratum (*wudingti* 無定體), a host of substantive concepts are immediately disqualified from interpretive service. We are not entering a world of discrete things with simple location in space and time. The world of configurative energy is not populated with ontologically primary "things" but rather with events, states of becoming that resolve not into static substances, but into transformational processes. Bodies and forms are not fixed entities; they are dynamic *states* that configure an ever transforming energy. Bodies convey the history of a functional transaction with the world, and this transaction is, in turn, formative. Hence, as Tang Junyi confirms, in the Chinese view, "function manifests form and form issues into function."[58]

This leads to the view that everything is two-way (*wuwangbufu* 無往不復), which entails both the reciprocal nature of processional development and the nonlinearity of the Chinese notion of causality. In the absence of discrete substances, form and quality are truly inseparable. Forms take shape within matrices that leave room for the unique, qualitative expression of those forms to present themselves. As qualities emerge in the transaction between an organism and its environment, those qualities are not simply located but rather consequent of the reciprocal shaping of events. The mutual shaping of events precludes the notion of accidental qualities, simply located. Tang Junyi cites the *Daodejing*, which, in stating that "reversal is the movement of the *dao* 道,"[59] suggests that qualities phase into their contrary states on a continuum "shouldered" by the configuration of events.[60] To say that everything entails its opposite is to suggest that events emerge together and shape one another's qualitative dimensions.

This, in turn, leads to the view that having and not having are united (*heyouwu* 合有無). The cooperation of having (*you* 有) and not having (*wu* 無) is an aspect of form/function dynamics. Function (*yong* 用) is an operational limit enabled by what formation affords, yet this is also a consequence of what it lacks. In the *Daodejing*, it is what is not inside the jar (*wu*) that makes the form it has (*you*) potent and functional (*yong*).[61] Zhuangzi echoes this in suggesting that all positions entail function only in relation to space unoccupied:

> One needs only space enough to plant one's feet, but if one were to dig away all the space that those feet did not occupy, to the depths of the Yellow Springs, would the space still have function [*yong* 用] for the person?[62]

Function requires space and time with which to operate. Space and time, however, only describe a potential afforded when forms function in relation to one another. Ever emergent forms interlace in delimiting their regions of functional operation and leave no gaps. Apart from form and function there is no spatial relation, and apart from formation and functioning, no temporal relation. The Newtonian model, wherein space and time are empty and bodies are full, is inverted in the Chinese world: space and time are full, and bodies continually empty into their successors.

This coalesces with the view that agitation and equilibrium are united (*hedongjing* 合動靜). The dynamics of form and function involve adjustment to the emergent conditions under which shape is taken.

Shape is always reshaping, and form is always reforming. The temporal sensitivity of the *Book of Changes* and its prognosticative function validate that, in the Chinese world, experience is regularly viewed as unbalanced and in need of adjustment. The pairing of the generative (*qian* 乾) and receptive (*kun* 坤) underscores the notion that adjusted emergence entails both novelty and continuity. The novel perturbations that challenge equilibrium call for the seamless, novel reconstitution of form. The botanical imagery so ubiquitous in the *Mencius* reflects Mencius' own sensitivity to the lack of absolute discreteness between older and newer forms in the emergence of adjusted development. Growth is the balance of form and function, continually undergoing adjustment. When something grows, the history of the equilibrium (*jing* 靜) maintained over the course of that growth is the same as the agitation (*dong* 動) that occasions those adjustments.

This brings us to the view that the one and the many are inseparable (*yiduobufen* 一多不分). In presenting this idea, Tang Junyi cites two passages in the *Daodejing*, the first stating, "one brings about two, two brings about three, and three brings about ten-thousand things," and the second, "the ten-thousand things attain one and thereby come about."[63] In articulating the view that there is no substratum, Tang Junyi appeals to the process corrective to substance ontology offered by Alfred North Whitehead.[64] In the present context, it is also Whitehead who serves us well. Whitehead expresses the unity of the one and the many in the following formula: "the many become one and are increased by one."[65] This account of creative advance, which for Whitehead is the "category of the ultimate," is consonant with the discursive process of "taking shape" in the Chinese world. Shape is a definite "one." All shapes, however, are temporary. Attaining "one" is a process of synthesis and integration: the "one" emerges from the coffers of the "many" and then returns to increase its bounty. Becoming "one" is an achievement of synthesis that entails some level of integration within the ongoing process (*dao* 道) of the ten thousand things. Mencius displays sensitivity to the dynamics of creative advance in the process of developing one's person (*shen* 身): "The ten-thousand things are here in us," he says, "there is no greater joy than inspecting one's person [*shen*] and finding it well-integrated [*cheng* 誠]."[66] The notion of integration will be further explored in chapters to come.

The stress on creative advance leads to the view that determinism does not apply (*feidingming* 非定命). The classical formulation of determinism entails necessity and requires a linear, causal relationship, and such notions do not factor importantly in the mainstream Chinese tradition.[67] Determinism also entails that emergent events are dictated by conditions. The idea that events are "shaped" by environing conditions is an important component of Warring States cosmology. However, an analysis of the formal constraints upon emergence will never deliver a complete account of any occasion. Another description must take into account the self-creativity that marks that particular occasion as a novel unity of antecedent factors in the present moment. In a *qi* 氣 cosmology, the incessant "blow" of *qi* lends propensity (*shi* 勢) to configurations that ripen so-of-themselves (*ziran* 自然). This moment of self-creation implicates itself in all subsequent moments; hence, creativity in a Chinese world is cocreativity. The two-way relationships that characterize this world ensure that its future is an open prospect. The past does not become the future without the present, and the present is an instance of sheer self-expression. This is what gives the present its aura of unprecedence.

What renders all of these notions coherent is the view that process is incessant (*shengshengbuyi* 生生不已). Tang Junyi identifies this view as one that "Chinese thinkers have unceasingly maintained."[68] Certainly, the case for imputing a process orientation to the *Mencius* is strengthened by the vast preponderance of process commitments evident elsewhere in the tradition. The *Zhuangzi* and the *Book of Changes* provide two dramatic examples of process thinking in Mencius' immediate milieu. The process orientation in classical China is so pronounced, in fact, that the burden of proof most fairly lies with those who would introduce nonprocessional notions as interpretive categories. By my lights, in a world animated by configurative energies, in which "things" are always dynamic and "forms" are ever in formation, the reduction of reality to fixed essences or ends is not a very feasible option. What is determinate in a process-driven world must be accounted for in some other manner.

The notion of "disposition" (*xing* 性) accounts for the determinate structure of experience in a manner that does no violence to a process worldview. The seventh view that Tang Junyi considers, that dispositions issue directly from the course of *tian* 天 (*xingjitiandao* 性即天道), provides an account of structured emergence that is consistent with a process-oriented cosmology. By saying that dispositions issue directly from *tian*, attention is called to the embeddedness of form in a Chinese world. When something "takes shape," it textures the ongoing totality by sculpting out of its background conditions a unique, discursive inscape of concentrated energy (*qi* 氣).[69] This emergent form contributes something irreplaceable to the ongoing totality, while remaining indelibly woven into its environment. There is no slippage between forms, functions, and evolving conditions. As Tang Junyi puts it, "*tian* and dispositions match up."[70]

The notion of disposition (*xing* 性) developed in these pages elides any metaphysical distinction between being and modality. Things are always already disposed; to *be* is to be disposed. Furthermore, a disposition is neither genetic nor teleological. Dispositions are proclivities made determinate by the inherited structures that brace their emergence, yet they are left open by virtue of the dynamics of self-expression, changes in conditions, and creative advance. Disposition, as A. C. Graham suggests, is a "spontaneous development in a certain direction rather than its origin or goal."[71]

Recalling the *Zuozhuan* illustration, a "proper" disposition, normatively speaking, is one that maximizes the integrated functioning of the ongoing process that it represents, in this instance, the human body. The human body grows; its forms and functions develop while its structure adjusts to countless factors in its environment. Its growth is measured by the degree of integration it manages to pattern over the course of its emergence. To realize the optimal degree of integration is to enjoy a heightened state of vitality and energy (*qi* 氣). To lose that optimal disposition is to feel a life deteriorate. As Mencius extends these notions beyond the biological order into the human and moral order, the growth model takes on a whole new dimension.

Chapter 2

The Role of Feeling

Feeling, Doctrine, and *Dao*

In order to understand the growth model and how it relates to human development in the *Mencius*, it is important to understand the function of feeling (*xin* 心) and how it relates to a cluster of important terms in the text. The terms "feeling" (*xin*), "doctrine" (*yan* 言), and *dao* 道 establish the context in which *xin* is a polemic reaction to Mencius' non-Confucian interlocutors. When *xin* is understood in relation to *dao* and *yan*, the argument at the heart of the *Mencius* surfaces.

In Confucian discourse, *dao* 道 most often signifies the optimal course of affairs proceeding in a sociopolitical context.[1] Precisely what this course entails becomes a matter for debate in Mencius' time. Mencius insists that the optimal course is not as difficult to advance as people think: "*dao* is near at hand, yet it is sought after as if it were far."[2] The most productive course, Mencius says, "is like a great road, it is not difficult to realize; the problem with people is that they do not seek it out."[3]

The principal obstacle to *dao* 道, according to Mencius, is the proliferation of philosophies that advocate alternative courses (*dao* 道). In this context, the term *dao* is understood as "teachings" as it refers to the "courses" advocated by these alternative schools. When Mencius speaks of the *dao* of the Mohists, he is referring to the "most productive course" according to the Mohist school of thought. The *dao* of a person or school is their proposed "way" of forging ahead in the world, a path of development reflected in whatever doctrines (*yan* 言) they formulate in its defense.[4] In Mencius' day, *dao* and *yan* signify positions in a newly developed arena of disputation (*bian* 辯).[5]

While Mencius engages in disputation, he does not do so with enthusiasm. Asked by Gongdu whether it is true, as rumor had it, that he actually enjoys disputation, Mencius replies, "I am not fond of it but rather compelled to do it."[6] By Mencius' own account, he enters into argument with reluctance, only to stave off the doctrinal threats mounted against Confucianism by the Yangist and Mohist schools.[7] Not interested in argument for argument's sake, Mencius is critical of those who engage even his own rivals solely for the purpose of defeating them:

> These days, those who argue with the Yangists and Mohists act like they are chasing a stray pig. It is not enough for them to return the pig to the sty; they have to go on to tie its feet up.[8]

Mencius is opposed to the overall argumentative tone of his day. He laments the disastrous impact of staking out and defending inflexible doctrines and advocates a more flexible approach:

> Yang holds to his egoism. If by plucking one hair from his body he could benefit the world he would not do it. Mozi holds to his concern for each. If by shaving his body from head to toe he could benefit the world he would do it. Zimo holds a balance. By doing so he is closer to the mark. Yet to hold that balance without weighing circumstances is no different than holding to one or the other extreme. Holding fast to a single position disgusts me because it cripples the most productive course. One position is taken up and a hundred others go by the wayside.[9]

Mencius, like Confucius before him, prefers not to cling dogmatically to a single position and responds negatively to inflexibility.[10]

Mencius locates himself above the purveyors of doctrine. He stands apart and claims to command an understanding of all the various doctrines of his day and to have the ability to adjudicate between them.[11]

When it comes to his own "doctrine," he appeals to feeling (*xin* 心). When describing the differences between Gaozi's orientation and his own, Mencius says:

> Gaozi claims that what is unobtainable in doctrine [*yan* 言] cannot be expected from feeling [*xin* 心], and what is unobtainable though feeling cannot be expected from configurative energy [*qi* 氣]. The idea that what is unobtainable through feeling cannot be expected from configurative energy is acceptable. The idea that what is unobtainable through doctrine cannot be expected from feeling is unacceptable.[12]

Gaozi does not believe that feeling alone can provide the type of moral guidance that doctrine provides. Mencius disagrees. Feeling, says Mencius, guides us more surely than doctrine in charting the most productive course. This is perhaps why Mencius felt *dao* 道 was always so close at hand.

Mencius agrees with Gaozi, however, that configurative energy does not provide moral guidance. *Qi* 氣 is morally indeterminate if not referenced in a specific configuration.[13] In stating that feeling provides normative insight where *qi* does not, Mencius is saying that feeling represents a certain quality of engagement. In other words, *xin* 心 is the outcome of a specific kind of disposition (*xing* 性) actually embedded in the world. Rule-based doctrines are more abstract and thus at a remove from the feeling (*xin*): they do not entail the quality of engagement that dispositions do. As a result, Mencius feels that doctrines cannot be relied upon to satisfy the vicissitudes of a concrete moral situation. Feeling, however, particularly if fortified in a well-integrated disposition, can be relied upon.

What the "heart-mind" or "feeling" (*xin* 心) is and how it functions in moral guidance are among the topics explored in this chapter. To understand the debate between Mencius and the Mohist school, it is crucial to recognize how feeling-based morality differs from a more doctrinaire form of moral deliberation. When Mencius refers to one's sudden "feeling of distress" (*ceyinzhixin* 惻隱之心) upon seeing a child about to fall into a well, the point is that no abstract, mediate deliberation is involved in the genuine moral impulse. There are no calculations of benefit, no thoughts of personal advantage, and no projection of consequences.[14] Moral feelings are spontaneous in those disposed to feel them. Moral doctrines, according to Mencius, will only obscure the self-evident prompting of such feelings. So while Mencius on occasion calls his position a doctrine (*yan* 言), he simultaneously distances himself from a doctrinaire form of thinking. Feeling is not a doctrine; it represents something else.

Feeling as Transactional

Occurring only six times in the *Analects*,[15] *xin* 心 is a term that the *Mencius*, with one hundred and nineteen occurrences, develops into a major Confucian theme. The character descends from a drawing of the anatomical heart.[16] As early as the *Book of Songs*, however, the term is used in connection with a wide range of emotions and sentiments, usage that blurs any sharp distinction between the location, structure, and function of feeling.[17] Treating *xin* simply as "feeling" rather than "heart-mind" avoids anatomical reification in translation, a reification that often results in awkward and misleading connotations. For instance, in appealing to one's *ceyinzhixin* 惻隱之心 in the "Child at the Well" passage, Mencius is not making reference to a specific, anatomical organ that relays distress; he is rather reporting that such a situation results in a "feeling" of distress.[18] In the *Mencius*, it proves adequate to translate *xin* as "feeling" in most contexts. Dobson, Legge, and Chan each opt for this translation in crucial instances.[19] We stay primarily with this translation.[20]

As argued in chapter one, there is no sharp distinction between form and function in a *qi* 氣 cosmology. This is reason enough to be cautious about reifying *xin* 心. Mencius describes what *xin* is by describing what it does. On one occasion, he speaks of its "function" (*guan* 官).[21] The function of *xin* is "thoughtfulness" (*si* 思). It is the function of thoughtfulness that distinguishes *xin* from the eyes and ears. Mencius explains:

> The functioning of the eyes and ears does not involve thoughtfulness; hence, things mislead them. As things set into relation with one another, one lures the other away; that is all. The functioning of *xin* 心, however, is thoughtful [*si* 思]. When thoughtful, one achieves some engagement [*de* 得] with things. In the absence of thoughtfulness, one does not achieve engage-

ment with things. These functions are what *tian* 天 bequeaths to us.[22]

The identification of *xin* with "thoughtfulness" (*si*) underscores the inseparability of feeling and thinking in this tradition. And "thoughtfulness" is merely a generic label that covers various modes of thoughtful engagement: pondering, directing concern, imagining, reflecting, considering, and so forth. All of these functions are *si* and are not clearly distinguished in classical texts.

As Hall and Ames report, the *Shouwen* lexicon defines "thoughtfulness" (*si* 思) as "a deep river gorge" and the commentary of the Qing dynasty scholar Duan Yucai offers the following explanation: "Deep passageways are generally called deep river gorges; that it is used to define *si* here is because thereby one can pass through things deeply."[23] In the *Mencius*, feeling (*xin* 心) would appear to entail some depth of engagement (*de* 得), such that the function of feeling denotes a greater degree of involvement with the world than do more passive functions like looking or hearing. The idea is that, without such thoughtful, heart-felt engagement, "looking" is not "seeing," and "hearing" is not "listening."

The *Great Learning* (*Daxue*), like the *Mencius*, also identifies the latter, more active forms of engagement with feeling. The opening passage of the *Great Learning* reads, "to cultivate the person, one first effects proper order at the level of feeling [*xin* 心]." The text then clarifies:

> The meaning of "cultivating the person" lies in effecting proper order at the level of feeling. If the lived body is in anger or rage, then the proper order is not obtained. The same applies if the person is in fear or dread, affection or pleasure, melancholy or misery.
>
> When feeling is not present, one looks but does not see, hears but does not listen, and eats but does not taste. What is entailed in cultivating the person lies in effecting proper order at the level of feeling.[24]

Feeling points to a dynamic interface and a depth of involvement that is inseparable from the disposition and activity of the person. As such, it is the terminal result of a transactional engagement with the world.

The idea that "thoughtful" (*si* 思) engagement is transactionally involved rather than passive or disconnected is also suggested in the *Analects*, where the notion of thoughtfulness is understood alongside learning (*xue* 學). "Learning without thoughtfulness leads to perplexity," Confucius teaches, while "thoughtfulness without learning leads to peril."[25] Without an anchor in learning, one's reflections might become irrelevant. Without thoughtfulness, however, learning is merely the passive exposure to curricula and does nothing but confuse. Confucius elsewhere warns against being overly thoughtful, to the detriment of learning, thereby once again rendering thoughtfulness and learning interdependent.[26] Confucius' point is that when genuine education takes place, one's encounter with curricula is thoughtful; it is more than mere exposure.

In the *Mencius*, there is an analogous relationship between the functioning of the heart-mind and the things (*wu* 物) implicated in experience. In the absence of thoughtful, heart-felt engagement, things tend to elude and mislead. In other words, just as passivity in education will only leave one perplexed, becoming emotionally disengaged from one's surroundings will only alienate and misdirect action. The function of "thoughtfulness" denotes involvement; and such thoughtful engagement points to *xin* 心. To focus overmuch on the anatomy of *xin* clouds the attention that Mencius pays to its function in one of his most important treatments of the term.

The world is engaged on many levels, one of the most important of which is the physical. In presenting feeling as a source of moral wisdom, Mencius intends to appeal to the empirical evidence of one's physical reactions, and these consummate in the body. The feelings of distress and concern that emerge upon suddenly spotting a child dangerously close to a well are visceral: increased heart rate, heightened tension, and shortness of breath. The physical dimension of feeling is illustrated throughout the *Mencius* in a manner consistent with the assumptions of a *qi* 氣 cosmology. For the body to fall or run, Mencius tells us, involves a reconfiguration of energy (*qi*) that registers directly as feeling.[27] Tears and perspiration are understood to flow spontaneously from one's feelings through the face and eyes.[28] There is no sharp distinction between feeling and its physical manifestations.

Mencius notes that the Confucian virtues, which are rooted in one's feelings, find direct expression through the shape and complexion of the body itself. This notion was touched upon in chapter one, where the following passage was considered:

> What the exemplary person cultivates as a disposition [*xing* 性][29] is associated humanity, appropriateness, ritual propriety, and wisdom. These are rooted in feeling [*xin* 心]. The complexion that is borne of this is radiance in the face; it manifests itself in posture and extends to the four limbs. The four limbs do not speak words [*yan* 言], yet they are expressive.[30]

Physical comportment is considered to be inseparable from character; for in Mencian circles, "whatever is present on the inside takes shape [*xing* 形] on the outside."[31] Particularly expressive in this regard, we learn, is the pupil of the eye.[32]

In a *qi* 氣 cosmology, the body is understood as a focus of energies that manifest qualities. According to Mencius, *qi* "fills the body" (*ti* 體).[33] The *Guanzi* contains a nearly identical statement, only in the *Guanzi* "body" (*ti*) is replaced by "person" (*shen* 身),[34] underscoring the overlap between body and personal character in this cosmology. For Mencius, the notions of disposition and personal character are closely related. He says that Yao and Shun cultivated a disposition (*xing* 性) and Tang and King Wu later personified (*shen* 身) it.[35] The difference between the two is not great. If dispositions give shape and content to one's feeling, the cultivation of a disposition is inseparably linked to the character of one's person.

Since the human body is understood to be a configuration of *qi* 氣, it is appropriate to revisit that vocabulary in order to understand further the relationship between body and feeling. Not long after Mencius, *qi* becomes implicated in "arousal/response" (*ganying* 感應) thinking, a development that provides some insight into the notions of both causality and emotion in classical China. In a study of the Han text *Huainanzi*, Charles LeBlanc describes *ganying* as "resonance," a notion according to which phenomena are considered to spontaneously "stimulate" and "respond" to one another in the context of an organic field of relations.[36] As John Major points out, such "resonance" is conveyed through *qi*.[37] Resonance is a name for what occurs when two disparate things are correlative under a third category naming a quality that unifies the two. After enumerating various mutual responses that occur between natural and social phenomena, the *Huainanzi* reports:

These are indeed the evidences of the mutual influence of the marvelous *qi* 氣. Hence, mountain clouds are prairie grass. River clouds are fish scales. Drought land clouds are blazing flames. Torrent clouds are billowy waters. Each thing is affected inasmuch as it resembles the shape and sort of other things.[38]

Certain phenomena, while disparate, resemble one another once cast in juxtaposition. Similarity is evoked seemingly out of nowhere, suggesting a mysterious and inexhaustible source out of which affective qualities emerge to unify disparate elements of experience. The resonance between "river clouds" and "fish scales" inaugurates a feeling not felt prior to the comparison being made. An emotional tone arises from the relation itself and pervades that relation as a unifying quality. Cataloging the qualities that emerge through such relations and issue into "arousals of mood" (*xing* 興) becomes an important part of literary theory in the Chinese tradition.[39]

John Henderson suggests that *ganying* 感應 "appears to have been a later scholastic rationalization of resonant effects," tacitly presupposed much earlier in Chinese thinking.[40] If Henderson is accurate in this assessment, *ganying* might be considered a rationalization of the notion of causality spoken of as "propensity" here in chapter one. In a world animated by *qi* 氣, dispositions issue spontaneously into felt qualities by virtue of the propensity they have to configure its flow. This notion of "resonant effects" is broad enough to include the recontextualization of affective words and images.[41] Just as it is when it becomes implicated in *ganying* thinking, *qi* in earlier periods involves the spontaneous manifestation of a felt quality, something that arises directly from the deployment, configuration, or placement of phenomena in a dynamic field of relations.

There is room for misunderstanding, however, if an occurrence of *ganying* 感應 is equated with an occurrence of stimulus and response. Since *ganying* and its related, correlative mode of thinking are not grounded in a notion of causal relations in absolute space and time, it is inappropriate to think of *ganying* in terms of a discrete, passive object being aroused by an external object in a sequence that begins in stimulus and terminates in response. What LeBlanc and Major, who follows Joseph Needham,[42] refer to as the Chinese thinker's "organic" view of nature precludes the possibility of positing stimulus and response as external relations between discrete entities in a mechanistic causal scenario. Stimulus and response in a *qi* 氣 cosmology are not metaphysically separable.

John Dewey offers a corrective to stimulus/response thinking in his landmark article "The Reflex-Arc Concept in Psychology," a critique that illuminates what is at stake in raising this point. Dewey considers how the concept of the reflex arc imposes an analysis in which stimulus and response are separate and how it thereby obscures what is otherwise a coordination of ongoing activities. "The result," says Dewey,

> is that the reflex arc idea leaves us with a disjointed psychology.... [It fails] to see that the arc of which it talks is a virtual circuit, a continual reconstitution, it breaks continuity and leaves us with nothing but a series of jerks, the origin of each jerk to be found outside the process of experience itself, in either an external pressure of "environment," or else in an unaccountable spontaneous variation from within the "soul" or the "organism."[43]

For Dewey, the relationship between organism and environment is such that the functions perceivable in the former amount to the ways in which the latter enter into its respective activities. Stimulus and response for Dewey are merely aspects of what is actually a transaction between an organism and its environment. To isolate and disjoin the two distorts the fact that both "in reality [are] always inside a coordination and have their significance purely from the part played in maintaining or reconstituting the coordination."[44]

The effects that arise from *ganying* 感應 are synchronic "resonances" rather than a sequence of disjointed "jerks." According to *ganying* thinking, when things of a sort (*lei* 類) move or stir (*dong* 動) one another, efficacy between them is considered mutual (*xiang* 相). *Huainanzi* observes that "when meteors fall, the seas immediately swell."[45] The type of causal common sense that sequences such occurrences into prior cause (meteor falling) and subsequent effect (sea swelling) is not that of the *Huainanzi*. Things and events do not *cause* one another; they *correlate* with one another. In this manner, things and events are conceived as embedded in dynamic, relational matrices of mutual shaping and mutual coordination taking place on multiple levels simultaneously. In the configurations that result, the redeployment of any element is enough to "trigger" (*ji* 幾) systemic alteration instantly.[46]

There is no absolute separation of cause and effect; instead, various phenomena index a whole situation as it manifests its unmediated causal propensity.

If one wishes to conceive of "feeling" in the *Mencius* along lines that lead eventually to *ganying* 感應 thinking in the Han, then Dewey's transactional model is one to consider. Feeling points to a degree of involvement. The quality of one's experience, for Dewey, is the terminal result of transactional involvement. As such, it can be understood as the qualitative result of what Mencius calls "engagement" (*de* 得) in the world. The transactional model furnishes an understanding of *xin* 心 adequate to Mencius' description. *Xin* is spontaneous feeling, inseparable from the disposition of the lived body itself. For Mencius, one might say, "experience is emotional," as Dewey writes, "but there are no separate things called emotions in it."[47]

Aspiration and Courage

It is difficult to come away from the *Mencius* with a complete and unambiguous account of its terminology. The *Mencius* presents us with an account of aspiration (*zhi* 志), but the notion is only explained sparingly and left opaque. When aspiration is discussed on the psychophysical level, however, it is though a vocabulary suggestive of a *qi* 氣 cosmology. Mencius says:

> Flowing water is such that it does not proceed unless it has filled all of the hollows. As for the exemplary person's aspiration [*zhi* 志] to proceed along the most productive course [*dao* 道], this does not break forward without a pattern being brought to consummation.[48]

One cognate of *zhang* 章 or "pattern" is *zhang* 障, meaning "dam" or "dyke."[49] Preserving the fluid metaphor in this passage, one might think of "bringing a pattern to consummation" (*chengzhang* 成章) as analogous to what occurs when water breaks over a dam. Something fills up and spills forward; this is aspiration (*zhi*). In this instance, thinking of configurative energy (*qi*) as what "fills the hollows" accords with a discussion we find in the *Zuozhuan* in which configurative energy is said to be what "fills out" (*shi* 實) one's aspiration.[50]

One might visualize the relationship between configurative energy and aspiration in the *Mencius* by picturing a fluid meniscus breaking forward over a containing shape, in this case the body itself. Hence,

> As for aspiration, it is the leader of configurative energy [*qi* 氣]. *Qi* is what fills the body [*ti* 體].[51] Aspiration [*zhi* 志] arises where *qi* stops.[52] Thus it is said: "Manage your aspiration and do not abuse your *qi*."[53]

Aspiration (*zhi*), a cognate of *zhi* 至 "to go forward" written with the heart radical,[54] is like a forward-breaking meniscus of the *qi* 氣 that brims in the physical frame of the living body. *Qi* is something that shores up and spills over into aim, ambition, intention, and efficacy.[55]

That aspiration entails directing and discharging a mounting *qi* 氣 is suggested by the metaphor of "leading armies" that often attends the term.[56] One manages and directs the configurative energy that issues from the body just as a field commander manages and directs his forces in battle. Keeping in mind the contemporaneous militarist tradition, we know that this involves managing the propensity (*shi* 勢) of a disposition situated within a dynamic field of engagement. Aspiration, then, is not an agency wholly separable from the world; it is not a volitional event separate from actions undertaken. It is rather the resultant propensity of one's disposition insofar as that disposition is located within the transactional circuit of engagement itself. Aspiration indicates the propensity to alter conditions through aiming the focus of configurative energies shored up in the body.

Archery is another metaphor associated with *zhi* 志 in the early literature.[57] In the Confucian tradition, images of archery are suggestive of the kind of "propensity" here associated with a *qi* 氣 cosmology. The art of archery involves the unity of placement and execution. To hit the mark requires skill in positioning and power in discharge. Mencius likens skill in archery to wisdom (*zhi* 知) and strength in archery to sagehood (*sheng* 聖). In hitting the mark, wisdom involves skill at the commencement of an undertaking, and sagehood, the power that carries it through.[58]

While Mencius does not use the archery metaphor explicitly in his discussion of human aspiration, the elements of "position" and "discharge" are reflected in his treatment. Asked by Prince Dian what the affairs of the scholar-official (*shi* 士) are, Mencius answers simply, "aspiration" (*zhi* 志).⁵⁹ For the scholar-official, Mencius continues, this entails being "positioned" (*ju* 居) in associated humanity (*ren* 仁) and "proceeding out" (*you* 由) in appropriateness (*yi* 義). The position and discharge motif is reflected in the Mencian treatment of these human virtues. The roles of aspiration on the sociopolitical level and of the scholar-official in charting the "human way" (*rendao* 人道) will be explored in chapter five. At this juncture, we remain focused on the manner in which the notions of position and discharge in the archery metaphor relate to the virtues of associated humanity and appropriateness, and also to human courage.

One is "positioned" (*ju* 居) in associated humanity (*ren* 仁) insofar as *ren* is the foundation upon which interpersonal experiences take shape. According to Mencius, if one fails to effectively communicate one's concern for others (*ai* 愛), one must turn to examine one's own associated humanity.⁶⁰ Similarly, when one is treated inconsiderately, it is also to one's associated humanity that one must return.⁶¹ Associated humanity is also the foundation to which one returns when one feels ashamed or humiliated. And it is in this context that associated humanity is likened by Mencius to archery: "archers make sure their stance is correct before letting the arrow fly; if they fail to hit the target, they do not blame the winner, but rather turn to seek the reason in themselves."⁶²

To think of aspiration in terms of the archery metaphor suggests that the measure by which such aspirations are "discharged" appropriately (*yi* 義) is a measure that resides within associated life. If archers are firm in their stance, their arrows will hit the mark. Likewise, having a solid grounding in associated life sanctions the appropriateness (*yi*) of actions effected by the force of one's aspiration in a social context.⁶³ Engendering hostility, shame, or slight in the world indicates a weakness in associated humanity—either in oneself or in another. In moments that call for judgment as to which, one is first to consider the quality and sincerity of one's own relationships. As Mencius says:

> Exemplary persons differ from others in that they maintain their feelings [*cunxin* 存心]. Exemplary persons maintain their feelings through associated humanity [*ren* 仁] and ritual propriety [*li* 禮]. The person of associated humanity has concern for others. The person who has ritual propriety has respect for others. The person who has concern for others is consistently

shown concern; and the person who respects others is consistently shown respect.

In the event that someone treats her in an unacceptable manner, the exemplary person will turn to herself and say: "I must be lacking in associated humanity and be without ritual propriety; otherwise, how could such things happen to me?" If, upon self-reflection, she finds herself established in human association and not lacking in ritual propriety, and yet the unacceptable behavior continues, she will turn to herself and say, "I must have failed to give this person my best [*zhong* 忠]." If, upon self-reflection, she finds that she has given this person her best, and yet the unacceptable behavior continues, she will conclude, "This is an unrestrained person. As such, how can he be distinguished from an animal? Why should I contend with an animal?"[64]

For Mencius, the warrant to pass moral judgment on others is granted by maintaining moral feeling (*xin* 心), and moral feeling is maintained according to how integrally one is disposed in relationships of concern and deference in a social framework. In appealing to feeling in moral judgment, Mencius is not appealing to some incorrigible, inner standard. He is instead appealing to a standard measured by the degree to which associated living (*ren* 仁) enables one to adopt the feelings and concerns of others (*shu* 恕). For Confucius as well, the warrant to pass moral judgment depends on the quality of one's associated living: "Only the person of associated humanity can be approving or disapproving of others."[65] For Mencius as for Confucius, the moral sense is ultimately a social sense.

While associated humanity (*ren* 仁) is something one "returns" to or is "positioned" in, appropriateness (*yi* 義), conversely, is spoken of as a road (*lu* 路) that one "proceeds out" (*you* 由) upon.[66] The fortitude involved in persevering on this road accounts for the close association between appropriateness and the notion of courage (*yong* 勇).[67] Recall that Mencius says that the dispositions (*xing* 性) of those who have established identities do not shift as fortunes change.[68] Elsewhere in the *Mencius*, the issue of sustaining one's ethical character despite a shift in fortune occasions the discussion of "unagitated feeling" (*budongxin* 不動心) and courage.[69] Mencius is asked whether a powerful political appointment would agitate his heart-mind (*xin* 心). He responds by saying that his heart-mind has not been agitated since the age of forty.[70] A discussion of three types of courage ensues; each one is presented as a way (*dao* 道) of developing unagitated feeling.

The first form of courage is that of Beigong Yu. His courage entails never yielding to others, never accepting insults, and never allowing himself to be outstared. The second form of courage is that of Mengshi She. His courage entails going ahead without fear, not being deterred by circumstances, and accepting defeat as a victory. Mencius is uncertain which is the superior form of courage, but surmises that Mengshi She maintains a sense of what is important (*yue* 約).[71] Mengshi She, Mencius says, retains command of his configurative energy (*qi* 氣). His sense of what is important, however, is deemed inferior to that of Zengzi, who represents the third and greatest form of courage.

This greatest form of courage (*dayong* 大勇) is one that Zengzi learned from Confucius himself. This form of courage entails self-reflection (*zifan* 自反). If upon self-reflection one finds oneself well integrated and attuned, then one can go forward against a multitude; however, if upon self-reflection one finds oneself maladjusted and out-of-touch, then even a single, frail adversary will inspire fear. The form of courage attributed to Confucius maintains the unity of self and circumstance by reflecting on engagement in a social context. The greatest form of courage directs action in a manner appropriate (*yi* 義) given the integration of self and other in associated humanity.[72]

The discussion of courage would appear to be related to a larger debate in the *Mencius* over the notions of internal and external factors in moral motivation and judgment. Beigong Yu represents a form of courage conditioned by external circumstance; his concern is with disgrace in the face of others. Mengshi She represents courage fueled by unbending internal conviction; external circumstances will have no bearing on his conduct. Each form of courage disconnects the transactional circuit of human engagement by introducing either an internal factor, resoluteness, or an external factor, conditioning. The inflexible posture of each form of courage results from the reduction of human conduct into one or the other category. By virtue of this reduction, both Beigong Yu and Mengshi She come across as obstinate rather than courageous. The form of courage that Mencius endorses, however, restores continuity between the internal and the external (*nei/wai* 內外), something that Mencian notions consistently do.[73]

Internal/External and the Botanical Model

In the midst of discussing configurative energy (*qi* 氣) and aspiration (*zhi* 志), Mencius is asked abruptly to explain to his listeners how he surpasses Gaozi.[74] Mencius replies, "I understand doctrines [*yan* 言] and am good at nourishing my 'flood-like' *qi*."[75] No enthusiast of ethical doctrines, when asked what he means by "understanding" them, Mencius proceeds to catalogue their various deficiencies:

> From the biased ones, I understand the blindness. From the extravagant ones, I understand the catch. From the heretical ones, I understand the deviance. From the evasive ones, I understand the poverty.[76]

Of his other quality, his "flood-like" *qi*, he says:

> It is hard to explain. It is a *qi* 氣 that is extremely vast and strong. Nourish it with genuineness and avoid injuring it and it will fill up the space between heaven and earth. It is a *qi* that is the counterpart of appropriateness and the most productive course [*dao* 道], without which it will be starved off. It is given life through a steady accumulation of appropriate behavior. It will not be acquired through a sporadic show of appropriate behavior. If one behaves below the standard of one's feelings, this *qi* will be starved off. This is why I say that Gaozi has never understood appropriateness, since he makes it external [*wai* 外].[77]

Mencius' intention here is to legitimize Confucian ethics by connecting it, however obliquely, to the notion of *qi* and to remind his audience that he does so in contrast to doctrines that rely on external (*wai*) factors. He assures his audience that a habit of appropriateness, if steadily cultivated, finds its sustenance on a cosmological rather than theoretical level.[78] The metaphor of starving employed to illustrate his point is botanical: Mencius is saying that only the securely rooted plant receives the requisite nourishment for growth. Before pursuing the botanical imagery further and locating the notion of "flood-like" *qi* within Mencian thought, we need to reconstruct the polemic context.

One of the most discussed debates in the *Mencius* is that between Gaozi and Mencius over whether appropriateness is internal (*nei* 內) or external (*wai* 外). In the primary exchange on this issue,[79] Gaozi and Gongduzi claim that appropriateness is external, while Mencius and Mengjizi resist the claim. There are a number of interpretations of what is at stake in this debate, and one would find it difficult to improve upon Kwong-loi Shun's analysis of the viability of the most prominent ones.[80] My own interpretation accords with Shun's; that is, the Mencian claim that appropriateness is not external amounts to a claim that one's "recognition of what is *yi* 義 derives from certain features of the heart-mind" (*xin* 心) as opposed to "circumstances that obtain independently" of it.[81] Another way of saying this is that Mencius resists locating the elements of appropriateness in a rule- or principle-based ethic that purports to trump feeling in a concrete context.

The argument goes as follows. Gaozi considers one's respect for elders an example of appropriateness and proceeds to abstract an independent class of things that one deems fit for such respect, namely, those of old age. Gaozi considers this classification an external (*wai* 外) factor; thus, what one considers appropriate is externally determined by whatever goes into the definition of this class. Mencius' response to Gaozi illustrates his preference to avoid such pan-contextual thinking. He chides Gaozi by saying, in effect, "Does your categorical claim mean we have to pay respect to old horses too?" Mencius is not interested in formulating ethical principles based on class distinctions that in turn become standards that determine what is appropriate in every context.[82]

Mencius does not argue here or elsewhere that appropriateness is internal (*nei* 內).[83] His purpose, as D. C. Lau suggests, is only "to show that his opponents failed to establish positively that *yi* 義 is external [*wai* 外]."[84] The analogy that the Mencian side employs to counter the externalist camp—"In winter I drink hot water, in summer I drink cold water"—hardly establishes that anything is strictly internal.[85] Mencius is not interested in tracing out internal/external distinctions. He treats such analysis as absurd:

> Our enjoyment of roast meat prepared by a person of Qin is no different from the enjoyment of that which we prepare for ourselves. So even here, in cases such as these, we are presented with something such as this. Is there, then, to be something external [*wai* 外] in the enjoyment of roast meat?[86]

The point Mencius is making is that an internal/external (*nei/wai*) dichotomy is, as Lau suggests, "too simple for the statement or solution of the problem."[87] Hence, *nei/wai* is never the language Mencius employs in articulating his own philosophy.

The vocabulary Mencius prefers is one of botanical growth and its related imagery: water, roots, shoots, cultivation, nourishment, and the like. The botanical metaphor is the vehicle Mencius chooses to describe the process of cultivating the person:

> As for a *tong* or *zi* tree a few spans thick, anyone caring to keep it alive will know how to nourish it. When it comes to one's person, however, they are at a loss regarding how to nourish it. Is it that one's concern for one's person is less than that for these two trees? This is a case of failing to think.[88]

In order to understand the Mencian position on personal cultivation within the framework of the internal/external debate, we must pursue the botanical imagery.

One element vital to botanical growth is an ample source of water. Mencius discusses the virtues of spring-fed water over standing water in a language that alludes to configurative energy (*qi* 氣):

> Xuzi said, "More than once, Confucius expressed his veneration for water, saying 'Oh, water! Water!' What did he see in water?"
>
> Mencius said, "Water from an ample source flows incessantly day and night, breaks forward only after the hollows are filled,[89] and then drains into the sea. Anything that is rooted to a source [*ben* 本] is like this. What Confucius saw in water is just this and nothing more. If a thing is not rooted to a source, it is like the rainwater that collects after downpours in May and June. It may fill the gutters, but if we stand and wait it will evaporate."[90]

There are a number of points being made here. Keeping in mind previous discussions, let us assume that Mencius is talking about growing a person, a process that entails the development of a disposition (*xing* 性), and that he is recommending that this project be rooted in configurative energy (*qi*).

First, to recommend *qi* 氣 as a source of nourishment is to suggest that one develop one's person with roots in feeling (*xin* 心). Recall that feeling is the qualitative result of a transactional engagement with the world through a disposition (*xing* 性). Disposition is the coincidence of form and function in a world charged with *qi*. Mencius advocates remaining tapped into the vital energies of *qi* by not becoming alienated from the feelings that issue directly from engagement in the world. Maintaining and developing feeling amounts to maintaining and developing a particular disposition.

Next, let us assume that the root (*ben* 本) spoken of here nourishes the growth of a disposition that configures a "flood-like" *qi* 氣, and that in "filling out the hollows" of this disposition this *qi* sustains and propels its growth. This would amount to saying that there is a natural momentum to moral growth based in feeling (*xin* 心). This momentum is what recommends feeling over doctrine as the source in which to root the moral growth of the person. Doctrine is at a remove from the prompts of feeling and as such is external (*wai* 外) to the process of generating habit in the deep sense.[91] In the "Water, Water!" passage above, the image of standing water, stagnant and evaporating, is that of doctrine (*yan* 言) employed as the sole source of moral growth. Meanwhile, feeling (*xin*) is the incessant nourishment issuing from the spring-fed source, configurative energy (*qi*). So when Mencius speaks of "not behaving below the standard of feeling," he is encouraging the cultivation of a constitutive habit of feeling that stabilizes the growth of a disposition rooted in that spring-fed source. Deepening the roots and broadening the span of a moral disposition configures a "flood-like" energy. This energy promotes growth that is "optimally vast" (*zhida* 至大) and "optimally firm" (*zhigang* 至剛) like that of a flourishing tree.

Lastly, let us address the apparent circularity of the Mencian project of "growing" a moral disposition. Mencius advocates drawing on feeling to nourish a disposition that itself *facilitates* feeling. This seeming paradox is resolved in the botanical model. Cultivating the person is likened to growing a tree. It involves an accretion of feeling and behavior that reinforces and enlarges a pattern of growth over the span of a life (*sheng* 生). Just as the extension of limbs and the habit of branches signals the uninterrupted development of a tree, the extension of feelings from their germinal states (*duan* 端) indicate the continuous self-emergence of a disposition (*xing* 性). What appears to be circularity is in fact the continuity of growth. Growth is a continually reconstituted propensity to emerge. When something grows, there is a seamless continuity between its more integrated form and the germinal state from which it arose.

The botanical model of moral development that Mencius employs is fundamentally creative. That Mencius spurns fixed doctrine in personal development indicates that, for him, a moral disposition is precisely *not* the patterning of conduct in accordance with an externally stipulated outline, schema, or design. A moral disposition, like a plant, must develop of itself in its own native environment and at its own speed, or else it perishes. The story of the man from Song who attempts to hasten the growth of his plants by tugging at their stalks makes this point.[92] Upon announcing this undertaking to his family, the man's son rushes out to the fields to find all of his father's plants have shriveled up. The point is clear: no desired standard of development can be reached without a genuine process of maturation. One cannot simply comply with a standard of conduct, "impartial concern" for instance, and call that one's moral disposition. Just as a seedling will not mature into a tree without incorporating into itself the requisite nourishment for growth, a disposition will not develop productive moral habits without the nourishing reinforcement of genuine feeling.

The botanical model reduces the pertinence of external (*wai* 外) standards or rules to the moral development of the person. In this way, the model serves to close the *nei/wai* gap. However, in asserting feeling over rule-based doctrine, Mencius is not in turn positing moral feeling as internal (*nei* 內). The function of feeling is presented here as a coordinated transaction between the organism and its environment. To better understand how feeling works in relation to the *nei/wai* debate, a fresh cluster of terms needs to be considered.

Desire, Coherence, and Integration

In the *Mencius* we encounter psychological reflections of a kind absent in earlier texts such as the *Analects*. In the *Xunzi* these reflections reach a higher degree of articulation.[93] In the *Xunzi*, as in the "Outer Chapters" of the *Zhuangzi*, the appendices of the *Book of Changes*, and the collected chapters of the *Book of Rites* (*Liji*), texts most of which postdate the *Mencius*, such reflections are increasingly presented through a vocabulary of "resonance" (*ganying* 感應). Neither *gan* nor *ying* are employed in any technical sense in the *Mencius*; similar discussions employ the language of internal/external (*nei/wai* 內外) instead.[94] In later texts that employ a *ganying* vocabulary, internal/external distinctions sometimes emerge as the topic turns to "desire" (*yu* 欲). We find this for instance in the *Discourse on Music* (*Yueji*) section of the *Book of Rites*, a passage nearly identical to one that appears in the *Tracing Dao to its Source* (*Yuandao*) chapter of the *Huainanzi*.[95] The following formula, which employs a Mencian vocabulary, apparently enjoyed wide circulation in the Han dynasty:

> One is born in equilibrium [*jing* 靜]; this is one's disposition [*xing* 性] from *tian* 天. There is a response to things and agitation [*dong* 動]; this becomes the desires [*yu* 欲] of one's disposition. Things come along. More and more is experienced. Eventually likes and dislikes are shaped [*xing* 形]. When likes and dislikes are not managed on the inside [*nei* 內] experience is led away by what is outside [*wai* 外]. Being unable to restore oneself, the natural coherence [*tianli* 天理] is destroyed.[96]

According to this passage, one's disposition evolves over the course of experience.[97] Desires and preferences become shaped (*xing* 形) and this in turn forms one's transaction with the world. In the *Discourse on Music*, to adjust oneself on the inside (*nei*) helps narrow an internal/external gap that emerges with an undue level of desire and preference. The goal of such adjustment is to "restore" the coherence and equilibrium of one's initial disposition (*xing* 性).

The concern over desires in this passage echoes Mencius' own concern over the accumulation of desires. The best way to nurture (*yang* 養) one's feeling, Mencius says, is to make one's desires few; one thereby "maintains" (*cun* 存) that which is most important within the process of development.[98] Maintaining one's feeling is a consistent theme in the *Mencius*.[99] It is the maintenance of feeling that distinguishes the exemplary person (*junzi* 君子) from all others.[100] The *Discourse on Music* speaks not of maintaining (*cun* 存) but of restoring (*fan* 反). The main idea, however, is the same: there is a correlation between undue desire and a rift in one's activities, purposes, and relations in the world. This rift is treated in the *Discourse on Music* as an emergent inner/outer (*nei/wai* 內外) distinction, one that is distinguished from an abated coherence.

It is difficult to establish precisely what "coherence" (*li* 理) means in this context or in the *Mencius*. The *Shouwen* lexicon associates *li* with "dressing or polishing jade" and "the veins or striations within the jade." The former activity is recognized as the art of bringing out the latter. In the *Book of Songs*, *li* is associated with dividing fields into smaller plots by paths and ditches;[101] again, this is a process of bringing out patterns inchoate and not fully realized. The idea that dispositions commence development in a state of coherence that is upset by agitation (*dong* 動) and restored by equilibrium (*jing* 靜) is consistent with the process-oriented cosmology of "taking shape" (*xing* 形) in the *Great Commentary* of the *Book of Changes*, discussed here in chapter one. That undue "desire" for objects also disturbs the coherence of a developing disposition suggests the presence of an inchoate quality at the incipience of the process that can be productively augmented so long as nothing "external" to its native proclivity is introduced. In the *Discourse on Music*, this quality is something that one "restores" (*fan* 反) when cohesion is lost; in the *Mencius*, it is perhaps best understood as something that one ideally "maintains" (*cun* 存) within the process of growth.

The translation of *li* 理 as "coherence" is meant to capture a range of notions that seem to be at work here: notions such as pattern, unity, order, cohesion, integration, and formation. The notion of coherence is important to Mencius. He teaches that the feelings of humans are similar (*tong* 同) in that they find satisfaction in two things: coherence (*li*) and appropriateness (*yi* 義).[102] But what does he mean by the former?[103] There is sufficient overlap in terminology between the *Mencius* and the *Discourse on Music* to justify using the latter as a template for approaching the question.

The course of forming a disposition begins, presumably at birth, in a state of "coherence" between the disposed and its environment. The development of certain desires, over time, corresponds to a compromise of this original quality. The result is a derivative bifurcation of experience into "internal" *nei* 內 and "external" *wai* 外 factors that become implicated in the project of "restoring" the lost coherence.

In the Mencian botanical framework, moral growth rooted in feeling maintains over the course of development a state of "coherence" between the self and its surroundings. In the process of personal growth, to lose the feelings (*xin* 心) that emerge in the transaction between self and surroundings by entertaining "external" standards of appropriateness is to disconnect from the world and its nourishing energy (*qi* 氣). Once disconnected, what was once growing begins to disintegrate and will ultimately perish.

In the search for a standard of appropriateness, to disregard felt experience is to ignore the terminal qualities of engagement (*de* 得) that arise from the very fact that one's activities are always located in concrete circumstances. Mencius stresses that the standard of appropriate conduct is not located elsewhere, waiting to be discovered; it resides within the transactional circuit of experience itself. As always, in presenting his position, Mencius avoids the term "internal" (*nei* 內):

> "By seeking it, it is obtained, and through neglecting it, it is lost."[104] When this is so, seeking leads to obtaining and we are seeking something that resides with us [*zaiwo* 在我]. "Seeking it entails a method [*dao* 道], and to obtain it is a matter of conditions [*ming* 命]." When this is so, seeking does not lead to obtaining, and we are seeking something that resides outside [*zaiwai* 在外].[105]

For Mencius, the standard of appropriateness is located within experience, in the feeling that arises directly with it. There is no method (*dao*) or doctrine (*yan* 言) that can direct one towards appropriate behavior in so broad a variety of circumstances as can feeling. As long as one maintains coherence between self and surroundings, one has a moral compass in one's feelings. For Mencius, as for Confucius, the apex of personal development is to flourish by maintaining a state wherein one may "give one's feelings free rein without overstepping the mark."[106]

The question that now arises is this: if feeling is the standard of appropriateness, what is the standard of feeling? What measure resides *within* experience that indicates the grade of one's moral feeling? As noted earlier, Mencius advocates self-reflection (*fanzi* 反自) in the face of social transgression. This is likened to the archer turning back to inspect her stance in the event of misfiring.[107] As the base of one's social sensibilities, associated humanity (*ren* 仁) is the target of moral self-reflection. It is from here that interpersonal experiences take shape. If upon self-reflection one finds oneself sincere in one's associated living, then one can trust one's moral feelings and judgments. Establishing a strong sense of associated humanity involves achieving a self that is transparently integrated (*cheng* 誠) with things and sensitive to the feelings and concerns of others (*shu* 恕). Mencius explains:

> Everything is here in us. There is no greater joy than inspecting one's own person and finding it integrated [*cheng* 誠]. To conduct oneself in a way that shows persistent consideration of the standpoint of others [*shu* 恕]: this is the shortest route to associated humanity [*ren* 仁].[108]

Moral standards, for Mencius, arise from associated living: "everything is here in us." It is the integration of self, other, and world that facilitates the moral wisdom to do what is appropriate (*yi* 義). The more deeply integrated one becomes, the more attuned one is to the standpoint of others, the only real factor in morality. So long as one remains socially robust and committed, one cannot go far wrong morally in Mencius' estimation. As Confucius says, "Indeed, if one's aspiration is set on associated humanity [*ren* 仁], one can do no wrong."[109]

The *Zhongyong* develops the notion of integration (*cheng* 誠) in a way that accomplishes more explicitly Mencius' objective, that is, to overcome *nei/wai* 內外 by locating the standard of appropriateness (*yi* 義) within a framework that precedes the distinction. Integration is neither strictly internal nor strictly external; it is instead a continually reconstituted synthesis. In the *Zhongyong*, this synthesis is the final cosmological fact:

> Integration [*cheng* 誠] is self-consummating. Its course is self-directing. Integration is the beginning and end of things. Without integration there would be nothing. This is why exemplary persons consider integration important. It does not just terminate with one's own self-consummation; it is the means by which everything finds its consummation. Consummating oneself, this is associated humanity. Consummating things, this is wisdom [*zhi* 智]. This is the character [*de* 德] of a disposition, the course [*dao* 道] integrating the internal [*nei* 內] and the external [*wai* 外]. Thus whenever one applies it, it is fitting.[110]

As presented in the *Zhongyong*, the notion of integration (*cheng*) restores coherence by closing the *nei/wai* gap, and in providing the measure for what is "fitting" (*yi* 宜), it leads one directly to appropriateness (*yi* 義).[111] This is the direction in which Mencius wishes to go. The above passage also maintains the assumptions of a *qi* 氣 cosmology: culmination (*cheng* 成) is identified with the immediate, qualitative character (*de* 德) of a disposition. This disposition is fully embedded in the world; thus, it is reducible neither to internal nor external factors. The passage summarizes the more important philosophical assumptions tacit throughout the *Mencius*.[112]

On the basis of the previous discussion, we can conclude by locating the notion of "flood-like" *qi* 氣 in Mencius' thinking. Keeping in mind the transactional model of feeling and disposition, this energy, "extremely vast and firm, and filling the space between heaven and earth,"[113] configures itself in any disposition that is well integrated in the world. This energy is the "counterpart" to feelings that attune one to appropriateness (*yi* 義) and to the most productive course (*dao* 道), "without which," Mencius says, "this energy will be starved off."[114] Sustained through the steady accumulation of appropriate behavior, this energy will only fortify the genuine, habitual disposition (*xing* 性). Such a disposition maintains the "coherence" of experience in the uninterrupted circuit of self and world. "External" factors like doctrines (*yan* 言) and undue desires (*yu* 欲) will only interrupt that circuit and retard the growth of a moral disposition; hence, the "flood-like" *qi* is associated with feeling (*xin* 心) and disassociated from what is external (*wai* 外).

The growth of a genuine, moral disposition is the kind of personal growth that remains situated, heart-felt, and involved. What remains to be explored are the kinds of feelings Mencius recommends developing into dispositions, how this process is understood to take place, and for what reason it is undertaken. Addressing these issues will involve taking a closer look at the Mohist challenge and at the profound commitment Mencius makes to the institution of family.

Chapter 3

Family and Moral Development

Spontaneous vs. Technical Approaches

We saw in chapter two that Mencius prioritizes feeling (*xin* 心) over doctrine (*yan* 言) in his debates with the Mohists. The Mencian position on the role of feeling in moral development is formulated in the presence of an ongoing debate over the internal/external (*nei/wai* 內外) dimensions of appropriateness (*yi* 義). Mencius claims that Gaozi does not understand appropriateness because Gaozi renders it "external."[1] In response to this position, Mencius does not render appropriateness "internal," but rather, by appealing to the heart-mind, situates appropriateness within the transactional circuit of felt engagement (*de* 得). Mencius thus begins to formulate the notion of "integration" (*cheng* 誠), a notion that reaches its philosophical maturity in the *Zhongyong*.[2]

In this chapter, we examine the Mohist challenge in greater depth and develop the Mencian counterposition more fully. We will see that, for Mencius, it is morality rooted in family affection (*qin* 親) and filial piety (*xiao* 孝) that provides the alternative to the principle-based, doctrinaire morality proposed by the Mohist school. Mencius' emphasis on family is consistent with his emphasis on felt engagement. Mencius identifies spontaneous, family-borne feeling as the source of moral feeling in general and, in keeping with the botanical model, considers family experience the "root" (*ben* 本) of all subsequently well-integrated moral growth.

It is helpful at this juncture to once again consider Mencian thinking within the broader context of Warring States thought. There is a pervasive fault line that defines points of contention between various schools in this period. This fault line separates the more "spontaneous" from the more "technical" approaches to morality and political practice. Mention was already made in chapter one of the role of spontaneity in Chinese ethics generally, as developed in A. C. Graham's work and as it relates to the notion of disposition (*xing* 性) developed here. "Spontaneity" can be distinguished from a more "technical" approach that concerns itself with the establishment and application of pan-contextual laws or principles. Both Daoist and Confucian thinkers tend to define themselves against such technical thinking and thereby station themselves on the more "spontaneous" side of the philosophical divide.[3]

For instance, the author of the received *Daodejing* associates the Confucian virtues of wisdom, associated humanity, and appropriateness with a remedial, technical morality that surfaces only when a more spontaneous way is eclipsed.[4] In a similar, more satirical vein, the *Zhuangzi* routinely presents Confucian practice as programmatic and officious. The error of the Confucians is that they seek to "rectify the shape [*xing* 形] of things with their bowing and scraping to ritual and music," thus Zhuangzi regards ritual form as something stipulated and forced upon more spontaneous forms of expression.[5] Thinkers conventionally labeled "Daoist" see themselves as garrisoned on the "spontaneity" side of the fault line against the more "technical" Confucians.

Many Confucians, however, are equally critical of technical approaches to morality and politics and see themselves as defenders of spontaneity against Legalist tendencies. This friction dates back to the *Analects*. Confucius is keen to distinguish ritual (*li* 禮) from punishment (*xing* 刑) as a method of maintaining social order.[6] Hence, Confucians regard penal laws (*fa* 法) as tools that impose order at the expense of more participatory, self-determinative forms of order. Ideally, according to the Confucian, ritual enables more spontaneous moral and political orders to emerge by creating avenues for productive self-expression. Whereas in a law-based society socially undesirable elements are simply punished or eliminated, in an ideal ritual-based society ritual shapes behavioral dispositions that preclude the emergence of socially undesirable elements from the outset, resulting in spontaneously moral behavior. Hence,

> The instructive, transforming influence of ritual is subtle. It stops depravity before it has even "taken shape" [*xing* 形]. It allows people to advance productively on a daily basis and remain far from blame without them even realizing it.[7]

Rather than resort to the technical apparatus of law and punishment, Confucians entrust moral and political order to the kind of social intelligence that emerges without coercion within associated life (*ren* 仁).[8] Most Confucians see themselves on the more creative, "spontaneous" side of the fault line when it comes to the ritual/law distinction.[9]

In prioritizing feeling (*xin* 心) over doctrine (*yan* 言), Mencius is positioning himself on the "spontaneity" side of the pervasive divide. In defending the promptings of the heart-mind, Mencius is taking a stand against technical morality in general. He associates doctrines (*yan* 言) about the human disposition (*xing* 性) with attempts to "bring something about" (*gu* 故) through forced reasoning, while he sees himself as "not imposing anything" (*wushi* 無事) on spontaneous tendencies.[10] The "spontaneity" of Mencius is reflected in his understanding of the emergent human disposition (*renxing* 人性) and further in the botanical model he employs in his treatment of moral growth. These aspects of Mencian thought will be the focus of this chapter and the next.

It is important to recognize the difference between the spontaneous and technical orientations in Chinese thought. Thinkers often use a similar vocabulary to make different points, and without a general idea about how thinkers differ, one risks equating ideas that are, in some instances, quite distinct. For example, Confucians, Mohists, and Legalists each use the term *fa* 法 to speak of "laws," "standards," or "models." For the Legalist, *fa* is a "law" that regulates human behavior under threat of punishment.[11] For the Mohist, *fa* is used as a term that designates a normative "standard" endorsed by an anthropomorphic "Heaven" (*tian* 天); this standard is instantiated in a particular instance or applied in practical reasoning.[12] In virtually every case, however, when Mencius uses the term *fa*, it is understood as a "model" embodied in a particular person like Shun or King Wen without reference to rule, law, or deity.[13] "Models" (*fa*) in the *Mencius* evoke participation in a norm inspired by the achievements of particular persons. Models are neither applied, like the laws of the Legalists, nor instantiated, like Mozi's universal standards; rather, models for Mencius arouse (*xing* 興) others to embody a norm (*jing* 經) in their own contexts under the influence of another person's force of character (*de* 德).[14]

Those who employ "laws" and "standards" are the more technical thinkers; they lean more heavily toward abstract conceptions of what is good.[15] Those who use "models" rely more heavily on the spontaneous response elicited by human exemplars in a concrete instance; they are not given to generate abstract conceptions of the good later to be "applied" by either fiat or practical reason. The manner in which *fa* 法 is used signals important differences in normative thinking among competing schools.

As we will see, family affection and filial piety play a central role in giving Mencian philosophy its "spontaneous" alignment. Family, for Mencius as for other Confucians, is the model of an unforced, harmonious order. The importance of family in Mencian moral thought cannot be overstated. Family-borne feelings are the kind of feelings Mencius has in mind when he speaks of spontaneous, moral feelings. Hence, as Mencius surveys his adversaries and finds that the technical morality of the Mohists poses the greatest threat to the family, he vigorously attacks the school. Any threat to family is a threat to Mencian thought as a whole.

The Mohist Challenge

Mozi is notably the first historical figure in China to self-consciously establish standards of evidence and argument in philosophical discourse.[16] In evaluating the rival doctrines of his day, however, practical utility is the criterion that Mozi deems most important. Mozi says:

> Doctrines that allow for translation into conduct should be advocated. Doctrines that do not should not be advocated. To advocate doctrines that do not allow translation into conduct is to wear out one's mouth.[17]

Mozi's own doctrines are guided by a version of the utilitarian principle. He claims that those doctrines and practices that "benefit" (*li* 利)

the world ought to be affirmed and those that harm the world, avoided. What Mozi does with his standard of benefit is probably more important than its precise formulation.[18] He puts his standard to work in criticizing the institutions and practices of his day. He condemns offensive warfare and improvident government expenditure.[19] He denounces the funding of royal extravagance through taxation and argues that public emoluments be awarded solely by merit.[20] His interest in social welfare aligns him squarely with the poor; he repeatedly calls attention to the conditions under which the less fortunate majority is condemned to live.

Mozi's most vigorous assaults are against the Confucians. He rails against the allocation of state funds for extravagant Confucian rituals, specifically, elaborate funerals and expensive musical performances.[21] He laments the growing secular attitude towards the world of ghosts and spirits that he relates with the Confucian movement.[22] He also denounces what he considers to be the fatalistic, Confucian understanding of "circumstance" (*ming* 命).[23]

His most potent critique, and the one that reverberates most strongly in the *Mencius*, is against the "partiality" (*bie* 別) of Confucian thinking. Mozi is particularly opposed to the "partiality" of the Confucian notion of family affection (*qin* 親).[24] The target of this critique, however, is larger than the special devotion one shows to one's family. While such devotion is indeed suspect, so too are the ritual forms (*li* 禮) to which family affection ultimately gives rise.[25] Mozi considers ritual propriety, like the family-centric reflex, to be unintelligent practice, the desirability of which goes unexamined.[26] Mozi's formulation of the doctrine of "impartial concern" (*jianai* 兼愛) is a response, then, to Confucian practice as embodied both in the institution of family and in ritual form.

Mozi's argument in favor of a more "impartial" set of practices stems from his utilitarian standard of benefit. Mozi surveys the calamities of his day, among them, warfare, deception, robbery, and oppression, and asks from what kind of disposition they arise. They arise, he says, from a disposition to injure. If one were to ask whether those who injure are partial (*bie* 別) or impartial (*jian* 兼) in their concern for others, the answer is clearly the former. Thus, argues Mozi, being partial in one's concern is not ultimately beneficial (*li* 利). Hence, partiality of concern should be abandoned and impartiality adopted.[27]

Mozi appeals to the impartiality of *tian* 天 to bolster support for the standard of benefit, but *tian* does not underwrite the doctrine of impartial concern. Mozi does not conflate standard (*fa* 法) and doctrine (*yan* 言); he considers the doctrine of impartial concern preferable *based* on the utilitarian standard of benefit endorsed by *tian*. He acknowledges that impartial concern is not the accustomed disposition of a person; it is instead a doctrine that must be self-consciously accepted and put into practice (*xing* 行). He has already argued that to do so is beneficial. All that remains then is for Mozi to persuade his audience that impartial concern is indeed a serviceable doctrine, that is, one that satisfies his own criterion of practicality.

The practicality of a doctrine hinges on its ability to translate into practice. Mozi begins his defense of the practicality of impartial concern by arguing that people readily affirm that it is in fact preferable. Mozi considers this an empirical question. He fashions a hypothetical scenario in which one is forced to entrust the well-being of one's family members either to one who exhibits an impartial (*jian* 兼) disposition or one who does not (*feijian* 非兼). All but the fool, says Mozi, would choose the latter, regardless of what his or her stated position is.[28]

Given that people readily affirm that impartiality is preferable, and assuming that people should wish to adopt what is preferable, Mozi next considers whether or not impartial concern is within the capacity of people to adopt. This is addressed by historical example. Mozi argues that six former sage-kings exhibited impartial concern, and hence it is possible for any person to do so. If impartial concern is both preferable and achievable, then it is certainly something that can translate into practice.

Mozi acknowledges one's reluctance to move beyond one's accustomed family preference and put the doctrine of impartial concern into practice. He ultimately appeals to the standard of benefit and admonishes willingness. He knows that one has partial feelings towards one's own family to begin with. Why else would one hesitate to entrust one's family members to the partial caretaker? Mozi cleverly appeals to the fact of partiality in arguing for the adoption of impartial concern. He assures his audience that impartiality will in fact reinforce the well-being of one's family by securing it under the stanchions of a more general social practice. Concern for one's family naturally entails the desire to have others treat them well. And the best way to secure this,

Mozi argues, is to show impartial concern for the family members of others, who will then in turn show concern (*ai* 愛) for one's own. Impartial concern benefits all involved.[29]

Mozi's argument for impartial concern is subtle and logically sophisticated, merits not overlooked by Mozi himself. He writes:

> My doctrine is sufficient. To cast aside my doctrine and go on thinking is like casting aside the bounty while continuing to harvest the grain. To take one's own doctrine and refute mine is like throwing an egg against a rock. All the eggs in the world will be used up and the rock will go unscathed.[30]

Recovering the Confucian Measure

Like Mozi, Mencius trusts the merit of his own thought. Mencius' attitude, however, is different from that of Mozi. Mencius is confident that his way (*dao* 道) will naturally attract those of kindred feeling (*xin* 心). He does not intend to pursue adherents with the tools of logical persuasion. Mencius explains:

> In forwarding my course of study, I do not go after those who leave, and I do not refuse those who come. As long as people come aboard with optimal feeling [*xin* 心], I simply accept them.[31]

The stress on feeling (*xin* 心) is what distinguishes the Mencian program from that of the Mohist. For Mencius, if a moral teaching is not rooted in feeling, then it stands little chance of developing genuine moral habits and attitudes. Mozi's project is admittedly not oriented towards the habitual feelings of the average person. His course must be argued for, accepted, and put into practice. This is supposed to result in moral people. Mencius defines himself against such "technical" projects. For Mencius, one cannot change what people do without changing their heart-felt dispositions. The goal for Mencius is to cultivate people who are "spontaneously" moral by virtue of the habits and attitudes that define their characters.

As presented in chapter two, the Mencian resolution to the *nei/wai* 內外 debate is reflected in the notion of integration (*cheng* 誠). To develop one's moral sensibilities requires maintaining the root of feeling that locates one integrally in the world and in associated life (*ren* 仁). For Mencius, when one gives favor to standards "external" to such everyday experience, one is uprooted from one's ground in feeling and one's moral growth is retarded. Conversely, associated humanity and appropriateness ally themselves with the project of becoming integrated and developing a disposition (*xing* 性) that issues spontaneously into moral sensibility and behavior. In doing so, associated humanity and appropriateness present an alternative to Mozi's standard of benefit, or so it is suggested in the opening passage of the *Mencius*, where Mencius visits King Hui of Liang:

> "Sir," said the King, "you have come all this way, thinking nothing of the distance; surely you have some way to benefit [*li* 利] my state."
>
> Mencius answered: "Why must you mention benefit? All I bring you is associated humanity and appropriateness [*renyi* 仁義]. If a King asks, 'How can I benefit my state?' and a counselor asks, 'How can I benefit my family?' and officials and commoners asks, 'How can I benefit my person?' those of all ranks will be trying to benefit at the expense of others and the state will be in peril. . . .
>
> "No one of associated humanity ever abandoned family affection [*qin* 親], and no one of appropriate conduct ever puts the interests of his prince last. Now you see what I mean, "associated humanity and appropriateness account for everything; why must you mention benefit?"[32]

To Confucius, "benefit" (*li* 利) is usually understood as narrow self-interest: "the exemplary person understands what is appropriate [*yi* 義], whereas the petty person understands only what is of 'personal advantage' [*li* 利]".[33] Mencius retains this pejorative association of *li* with self-interest.[34] Mencius likens the person whose actions are consistently driven by benefit to the most selfish person of all: Robber Chi. In contrast to Robber Chi, Mencius distinguishes Shun, whose actions were consistently driven not by benefit but by what was productive or good (*shan* 善).[35] As A. C. Graham suggests, Mencius comes to associate the term *li* so closely with self-interest that "one can hardly translate him coherently without switching the English equivalent to 'profit'."[36]

Confucians have no inherent problem with the idea of benefit (*li* 利). On occasion, both Confucius and Mencius use the term in a positive sense in connection with benefiting the people.[37] The problem that Mencius has with the idea lies in the tension between benefit (*li*) and the dual virtue of associated humanity and appropriateness (*renyi* 仁義) as sources by which to generate norms of behavior. Mencius feels that there is a significant difference between being motivated (*yue* 悅) by calculations of benefit and harm, which he apparently feels can be nothing but self-interested, and being motivated by associated humanity and appropriateness.[38] The former approach is "technical" and does not lend itself to the cultivation of a disposition, whereas actions that proceed from the latter arise from one's feelings for what is appropriate (*yi* 義) in concrete instances of associated life (*ren* 仁): inclinations solidified in a disposition. In other words, the normative measure that obviates benefit is one resident in associated life itself.

The Confucian normative measure suggests itself in this cluster of terms: associated humanity, appropriateness, and the productive or good. We understand *shan* 善 as "good" with due qualification. *Shan* is fundamentally relational; it is first and foremost a "good at," "good for" or "good in."[39] Only derivatively does one consider *shan* as an abstract concept. As A. C. Graham maintains, however, *shan* in particular lends support to the claim that in the classical Chinese language, "the absence of terminations to mark abstract nouns interferes with forming an abstract concept."[40] According to Graham, moral terms such as *shan* are not designated constants (*chang* 常) in the Chinese tradition; they are instead located through directive concepts such as *dao* 道. Chinese moral terms are primarily relational. The *Book of Documents* (*Shujing*) corroborates Graham's claim:

> Virtue [*de* 德] has no constant [*chang* 常] model; it is oriented towards what is good [*shan* 善]. What is good has no constant orientation; it accords with what is adequate in a single instance [*xieyukeyi* 協於克一].[41]

Given the relational character of *shan*, Graham understands it "not as a quality but as a way of behaving."[42] This way of behaving is one that contributes productively in a real, concrete situation; it is not to be understood or formulated pan-contextually.

Asked to explain *shan* 善, Mencius replies, "It is what is desirable."[43] The *Shouwen* lexicon, stressing the aesthetic dimension of *shan*, glosses it as "synonymous with what is appropriate/fitting [*yi* 宜] and aesthetically best [*mei* 美]."[44] Mencius further relates that Shun adopted from others anything that was *shan*, concluding that

> To adopt from others that which can be rendered productive [*shan* 善] is to help them be productive, and there is nothing more important to an exemplary person than helping others to be productive.[45]

Something that is *shan* contributes itself productively to a greater whole—and this is good. Such a whole can be considered an aesthetic achievement: an integration of disparate elements in a manner both beautiful and "fitting" in a specific context. In this respect, *shan* dovetails with the notion of harmony (*he* 和), the normative measure that I now suggest renders the entire Confucian program coherent.

Confucius teaches that "Exemplary persons seek harmony [*he* 和] over sameness [*tong* 同]; whereas petty persons seek the opposite."[46] Harmony is the stated aim of the Confucian. This aim entails the achievement of an optimally functioning, optimally rich order within a concrete situation, one that most fully expresses the worth of its particular constituents. Harmony can be measured according to how well it promotes that which is most particular about what is harmonized.[47] In the Warring States period, harmony is best and most often illustrated through its association with cooking soup. The *Book of Songs* and the *Book of Documents* both illustrate this association,[48] but the *Zuozhuan* does so most vividly:

> Harmony [*he* 和] is similar to cooking soup. Soup is made by adding various kinds of seasoning to water and then cooking fish and meat in it. One mixes them all together and adjusts the flavor by adding whatever is deficient and reducing whatever is in excess. It is only by mixing together ingredients of different flavors that one is able to create a balanced, harmonized taste.[49]

The harmony of flavorful soup is constituted by its ratio of ingredients: not too much salt, not too much cabbage—just right. The result is a good pot of soup. The harmony of the soup is measured by the degree to which it succeeds in incorporating its particular ingredients in a productive way. Peppercorns are wonderful in soup, but one does not therefore add all the peppercorns at one's disposal. That would disrupt the contributions of the other ingredients and result in disharmony. The more harmonious a soup, the better its ingredients express their particular worth through the order it embodies.

Confucius says that when a state is in harmony (*he* 和), "population is not an issue."[50] For if people can find meaningful, productive "identities" (*fen* 分) in a particular state, underpopulation will not be a concern. Likewise, if that state successfully incorporates the contribution of each of its various members, overpopulation will not be a problem either. A harmonious political order is one that incorporates its constituents such that each one's particular qualities appreciate by virtue of the order, just as the quality of a peppercorn is accentuated in a spoonful of good soup.

For Confucians, harmony is a good; there is no gainsaying this. Harmony itself has worth. It is value added in the achievement of increased togetherness.[51] Of significance to the rejection of Mozi's quest for impartiality (*jian* 兼) is the fact that, according to the Confucians, the goal of forging productive togetherness is not furthered by reducing what is different to what is the same (*tong* 同). The challenge instead is to achieve an order that preserves and accentuates the distinct characteristics of each and every novel constituent. In the *Sayings of the States* (*Guoyu*), the preference for harmony over sameness is presented in terms of novelty explicitly: "harmony produces something new, sameness does not produce anything new."[52] Confucians are disgusted by sameness and uniformity, which they find perverse. The goal is to create soup, not gruel. The Confucian attitude towards the preference for sameness (*tong*) over harmony (*he*) is reflected in a cognate term, "stupidity" (*tong* 侗), a trait that Confucius claims "not to understand."[53]

Harmony (*he* 和) entails both the achievement of a good (*shan* 善) order and the satisfaction of meaningful participation in that order. Soup is one illustration of this notion, and family and music-making are two others. The song "Dried Leaves" in the *Book of Songs* depicts both music and family in terms of harmony:

> Dried Leaves. Dried leaves. How the wind blows.
> Oh uncles, oh uncles. Lead in the singing.
> Young men join in the harmony [*he* 和].

> Dried Leaves. Dried leaves. How the wind blows.
> Oh uncles, oh uncles. Lead in the singing.
> Young men bring it to a close.[54]

The harmony of a family, like that of a song, is an aesthetic achievement that emerges discursively over the process of blending unique voices into a coherent whole. Mencius recognizes aesthetic coherence (*li* 理) as one of the qualities of Confucius himself.[55] It is said of Confucius that before singing in a group he would always ask to hear the song again before joining in. In this instance, Confucius measures the satisfaction of productively contributing himself to a harmony against the shame of disrupting something that was otherwise going well (*shan* 善).[56] Participation in a harmony entails distinguishing oneself in a productive, unique, and meaningful way. This is important in a family just as in a musical ensemble.

In the *Analects*, Master You identifies the achievement of harmony (*he* 和) as the most valuable function of ritual form (*li* 禮); however, he goes on to warn that in troubled times achieving an effete harmony for its own sake is not going to work.[57] Confucius well understood that the danger of a ritual-based society was the imbalance of form over function.[58] The point of ritual is not merely in its form: "In talking time and again about ritual propriety, how can I just be talking about gifts of jade and silk?"[59] The point of ritual is to facilitate a harmonious social order that delineates, supports, and ennobles the human experience by preserving the uniqueness of roles and relationships.[60] Harmony is achievable when there are ample opportunities to be distinctly human and to be appreciated as such.

John Dewey surmises that it is "the deepest urge of every human being to feel that he does count for something with other human beings and receives recognition from them as counting for something."[61] This deep, human urge is what recommends the Confucian program. Humans want to fit in, to cohere, and to be appreciated; in other words, humans want to be like the peppercorn in the good pot of soup. Recall that Mencius considers the taste for fitting in appropriately (*yi* 義) and integrating coherently (*li* 理) to be qualitatively human tastes.[62] What Confucians have to offer is the satisfaction of having a distinct, meaningful identity or share (*fen* 分) in a social environment patterned through ritual form, expressed in associated humanity, and generative of appropriate conduct.[63] In substituting Confucian virtues for the

Mohist standard of benefit (*li* 利), Mencius is recommending the recovery of harmony (*he* 和) as a normative measure.

The popularity of the Mohist School in the Warring States period is not surprising. The Confucians had failed to achieve the level of moral and social harmony to which followers of Confucius aspire. The Mohist course attempts to effect moral and social order by appeal to a doctrine based on a normative standard of benefit (*li* 利). Mozi's remedy for the social ills of his day is well intentioned and carefully presented. Mencius' counterresponse to the Mohist remedy, however, is also considered. The Mencian project is consistent with the alternative normative measure that guides the Confucian program. In seeking to effect moral and social order, Mencius does what the measure of harmony (*he* 和) entails; he returns to the primary ingredients. He begins with the family, the context within which one most readily contributes oneself, and seeks to reestablish moral and social order from there.[64]

Family as the Root

As argued in chapter two, Mencius maintains that personal growth is genuine only when one's feelings are well rooted (*ben* 本). Mencius understands *ben* in the same manner as the author of the *Great Learning*.[65] Both are expressly concerned with the roots of well-ordered empires, states, families, and persons.[66] In both the *Mencius* and the *Great Learning*, the root of social, political, and familial order is always the well-ordered person (*shen* 身) from whom that order emerges and in whom it ultimately remains grounded. In locating the root of the moral and social order in feeling, Mencius is recommending the establishment of order without recourse to stipulated "doctrines" (*yan* 言) of the good. Good (*shan* 善) moral and social order emerges instead from the concretely felt transactions among particular, constituent elements making a moral and social world.[67]

For the Confucian, ordering a world is not an exercise in putting a doctrine or theory into practice. Instead, a world is established through the patterns of deference that emerge through associated living (*ren* 仁) itself. Hence, the locus and root metaphor of social order is the family (*jia* 家), for it is in the family that the feeling of deference within associated life initially emerges.[68] The instructions that Eyin gives the new king Tang in the *Book of Documents* illustrates how social order is initiated in the Confucian world:

> To establish concern [*ai* 愛], have affection for your intimates [*qin* 親]. To establish deference, have respect for your elders. The process commences with the family and state, and consummates with the entire empire.[69]

The appeal to family feeling in effecting order on a broader, sociopolitical scale (*zheng* 政) also finds expression in the *Analects*:

> Someone asked Confucius, "Why are you not employed in effecting sociopolitical order [*zheng* 政]?" The Master replied, "The *Book of Documents* says: 'Merely in being filial [*xiao* 孝] with your parents and being amicable with your brothers is to carry out the work of effecting sociopolitical order.' In doing this I am effecting sociopolitical order. Why must I be 'employed' in effecting sociopolitical order?"[70]

Mencius, like other Confucians, regards family as the native soil from which a productive social, political, and moral order grows. As a corollary, the Mencian notion of personal cultivation entails that one's attitudes and habits of feeling remain rooted in that soil; accordingly, family affection becomes particularly important to one's moral development in the Mencian framework.

The spontaneity that attends family affection (*qin* 親) in a normally socialized human renders this reflex the most sunken root of moral development. Family affection, or the love of a child for his or her parent, is something Mencius considers unlearned (*buxue* 不學). It is from here that all moral order extends (*da* 達). Mencius explains:

> What people are able to do without learning is what they can truly do; what they can realize without having to think about it is what they truly come to realize. There are no young children who do not realize a love for their parents, and when they grow up, none will fail to realize a respect for their elder brothers. Loving one's parent is associated humanity [*ren* 仁], and loving one's elders is appropriateness [*yi* 義]. All that remains is to extend [*da* 達] this to the whole world.[71]

The Mencian position on the root of moral development is echoed in the *Book of Filial Piety* (*Xiaojing*). In this text, the unqualified fact of physical inheritance is held to engender the incipient affection that a child has for his or her parents. This initial affection grows into a sense of social responsibility and culminates in the full-fledged person. Explaining to Zengzi what enabled the ancients to bring about social harmony (*he* 和), Confucius submits:

> It was filial piety, the root [*ben* 本] of character [*de* 德] and the source from which instruction [*jiao* 教] emerges. Sit down, and I will explain for you. Of a person's body, every speck of hair and molecule of skin is received from the parents. One would never presume to cause them harm; this is the commencement of filial piety. To establish one's person by proceeding on the most productive course and to have one's reputation celebrated by future generations, bringing honor to one's parents: this is the conclusion of filial piety. It commences with service to family members, proceeds through service to the ruler, and concludes in the establishment of one's person.[72]

The establishment of one's person (*shen* 身) commences with filial piety, and this begins with unadulterated affection of child for parent. The root of moral development, for Mencius as well as for the author of the *Book of Filial Piety*, is a form of spontaneous feeling indicative of the earliest stages of a human life. Mencius maintains that the person of magnitude (*da* 大) never loses this childlike quality of feeling (*xin* 心).[73] In the well-developed moral person, the root of family affection and the spontaneous form of feeling such affection represents are maintained (*cun* 存).

The Mencian position on moral cultivation is reinforced in the "Two Roots or One" exchange with Yizhi.[74] Yizhi is a proponent of the Mohist doctrine of impartial concern; hence, he endorses the notion that one's concern (*ai* 愛) for other people be impartial. Yizhi wishes to allow, however, that the principle of impartial concern emerges initially from affection for one's family (*shiyouqinshi* 施由親始).[75] Mencius, in turn, accuses Yizhi of positing "two roots" (*erben* 二本), whereas, according to Mencius, "*tian* 天 produces things with only one root" (*yiben* 一本).

That *tian* 天 produces things with only one root simply means that the emergence and maturation of any order takes place in a *specific* location or context. This context is the place from which its nourishment comes forth. To uproot an emergent event from its context is to immediately devitalize it. What is deemed fundamental to any maturing process is the root that initiates and sustains its development. Just as sociopolitical order (*zheng* 政) is an achievement rooted in concrete relationships, moral order is an achievement rooted in the context-specific feeling of family affection (*qin* 親). Moral development, like any emergent growth, must remain grounded where its initial nourishment is elicited. As long as the family context remains secure and nourishing, and adverse circumstances do not intervene, what grows there from will reach its optimal trajectory. The botanical metaphor serves as a reminder that such development is always site-specific. Just as it is difficult to replant a thriving tree, it is difficult to abstract and relocate the moral qualities of a developing person since these qualities emerge through the particular affection of actual families—and nowhere else.

In the episode with Yizhi, Mencius is saying that moral sensibilities cannot be rooted twice, once in one's family and once again in the principle of impartial concern. Human moral sensibilities can have only one "root" or context. The fact that one loves one's own nephew more than a neighbor's child is presented as empirical evidence that human concern is fundamentally rooted in the family and not elsewhere. Affection (*ai* 愛) comes out from (*you* 由) one's family not only initially (*shi* 始), as Yizhi allows, but fundamentally (*ben* 本). Hence, while one's interests and affections expand over the course of a lifetime, one will not lose special concern for one's family if one remains well grounded. Accordingly, Mencius twice lauds Shun for having been fifty years old and still devoted to his parents.[76]

Being rooted in affection for one's family and in deference to one's elders both initially and over the course of a lifetime is absolutely central to Mencius' moral thinking.[77] When Mencius says that each person is able to become a sage like Shun, he is saying that the sage's "most productive course" (*dao* 道) is one that can be cultivated in one's native context through filiality (*xiao* 孝) and fraternity (*di* 弟) alone.[78] In other words, there are no abstract principles or doctrines that inform one's moral development outside of the context from which its incipient nourishment came forth. It is filiality and fraternity at home, and nothing else, that bring human virtues to fruition (*shi* 實).[79] As Mencius says:

> Serving one's parent's is bringing associated humanity to fruition. Respecting one's elder brothers is bringing appropriateness to fruition. Understanding the two and not leaving them is bringing wisdom to fruition. Ordering and embellishing the two is bringing ritual propriety to fruition. Finding joy in and delighting in the two is bringing enjoyment of music to fruition.[80]

Mencius considers all Confucian virtues to be the "fruit" of one's concrete, always singular family relationships. Hence, no stipulated order is introduced to define the emergence of these virtues "outside" (*wai* 外) the context in which one is most intimately involved.

Confucius states explicitly that one's associated humanity is rooted in one's family relationships:

> Exemplary persons concentrate on the root; the root having been established, the most productive course will grow therefrom. As for one's filial and fraternal responsibility, this is surely the root of one's associated humanity.[81]

Characteristically, Mencius employs botanical imagery to emphasize that one's associated humanity is something grown, not given:

> The five grains are the most beautiful of plants. Yet, if they are not allowed to ripen they are worse than the wild varieties. As for associated humanity, the point is also to see that it ripens.[82]

The manner in which one's immediate family relationships ripen into a broader sense of associated humanity is unique in every case. While Shun is the model (*fa* 法), one is bound to remain rooted in one's own circumstances and not in those of Shun.[83] Shun's moral growth came not by leapfrogging over his family to embrace some pan-contextual doctrine, nor were his affections attributable to the operations of some abstract principle in his heart. Instead, he preserved and extended the feelings that located him in his family and thereby became a Shun. Mencius stresses that there is nothing special about Shun.[84] Anyone can become an exemplary person (*junzi* 君子) in his or her own context and chart the most productive course (*dao* 道) in a process that Mencius describes as "self-consummating" (*zide* 自得).[85] So rather than consult the pedagogues of doctrine (*yan* 言), Mencius instructs one to return home and "one will have many teachers."[86]

Family and Extension

While teachers are found at home, the type of moral education one receives from the family differs considerably from what might normally be understood as moral instruction. In fact, Mencius suggests that the home is no venue for instruction (*jiao* 教) at all:

> Gongsun Chou asked, "Why does an exemplary person not instruct [*jiao* 教] his own children?" Mencius replied, "That arrangement will not work. An instructor must resort to correction; and when that does not work, one ends up losing one's temper. When this happens, father and son will hurt one another: 'You instruct me by correction, but you yourself are not correct.' In this way father and son hurt one another. For father and son to hurt one another is unproductive. In ancient times, people instructed one another's sons. Father and son should not demand goodness [*shan* 善] from one another. To do so only estranges them. There is nothing worse than estrangement between father and son."[87]

In the Confucian world, the demand made upon instructors that they "live up to their word" (*xin* 信) is properly reserved for friends (*you* 友) rather than family members. Confucius establishes the relationship between living up to one's word and friendship on numerous occasions.[88] The friends one keeps become one's moral instructors by default; accordingly, Confucius advises one to retain as friends only those who reinforce the level of one's own conduct.[89] As for family members, it is the preservation of loving affection that is paramount. While one may gently remonstrate (*jian* 諫) with one's parents, the point is to maintain the integrity of the intimate relationship:

In serving your parents, remonstrate with them gently. Upon seeing that they do not follow your suggestions, remain respectful and do not behave otherwise. However unbearable, have no resentment.[90]

Moral disapprobation does not belong in the family. As Mencius cautions, "it is the way [*dao* 道] of friends to demand goodness [*shan* 善] from each other; for a father and son to do so will seriously compromise the love between them."[91]

Mencius' concern with shielding family relationships from moral remonstrance reflects an important dimension of his philosophy. Just as moral sensibilities are rooted in the "spring-fed" sources of feeling and family affection rather than in hard-and-fast doctrine, the vicissitudes of integral relationships will trump social rules or mores if the latter are too stringent to accommodate the emergent demands of associated living. One aspect of the botanical model that has yet to be fully exploited is the considerable suppleness it entails. Stipulated patterns of development or conduct devitalize the life process (*sheng* 生).[92] The flexibility that is required for sustained growth entails being rooted in a fluid source and adapting to demands in an ever changing environment. To surrender either root or pliancy jeopardizes the extendibility (*da* 達) of growth. Since moral sensibilities are both rooted in and extended from the family, these relationships in particular must be protected from the suffocation of external rules and standards. Hence, when Confucius is told of a "true" (*zhen* 真) person from a neighboring village who turned his father over to the authorities for stealing a sheep, he replies that in his village a "true" son would cover for his father.[93] Again, nothing should be done to compromise the family relationship.[94]

The care with which Mencius precludes moral remonstrance and "instruction" from family life reflects his interest in the evolving phraseology of education. He explains that "learning" (*xue* 學) in the Xia dynasty fell under the rubric of "instruction" (*jiao* 教); in the Yin, it was "archery" (*xu* 序); and in the Zhou, "nourishment" (*yang* 養). Each of these, he explains, serves to "elucidate human relationships" (*mingrenlun* 明人倫).[95] Mencius appears, however, to understand "instruction" to mean a more disciplined program of moral reproach and correction. His reluctance to relegate it to the home might be explained in part by his conviction that such instruction is the state's responsibility through the village school system.⁹⁶ Mencius considers vigorous state support of public instruction the way for government to win over the hearts (*xin* 心) of the people.⁹⁷ Mencius certainly does not consider formal instruction to be among his own vocations, as he says:

> There are many methods of instruction [*jiao* 教]. My disdain with offering instruction is itself one way of offering instruction.⁹⁸

Turning to what takes place within the home, Mencius does not use the language of instruction, but rather the language of nourishment (*yang* 養):

> Those who are on the mark nourish those who are not. Those who are capable nourish those who are not. This is why people are glad to have good fathers and brothers.⁹⁹

Employing the language of nourishment in this context is consistent with the position that moral education is a process of botanical-like growth located in the family.¹⁰⁰

As the family nourishes the growth of one's person (*shen* 身), one must not only maintain the root of affection for one's parents, but also monitor one's personal character as it extends beyond that affection. Character can be lost (*shi* 失) along the way. As Mencius says:

> What is the most important thing to take care of? It is family affection [*qin* 親]. What is the most important thing to monitor? It is character [*shen* 身]. I have heard of people not losing their character and taking care of family affection, but I have not heard of people who have lost their character being able to do so. There are many things to take care of, but family affection is the most fundamental [*ben* 本]. There are many things to monitor, but character is the most fundamental.¹⁰¹

As one's personal character takes shape beyond the unlearned affection of early childhood, it is possible to lose the very root of its moral growth. This root must be maintained as one extends one's natural affections beyond the family realm.

The notion of "extension" is an important one in the *Mencius*, and this is reflected in a number of ways. Among the terms Mencius employs in his presentation is the term *tui* 推, which means "to push" or "to extend." The extension of one's sensibilities entails the growth of a disposition that registers concern within various realms of felt transaction, including both the human and the nonhuman worlds. While tutoring King Xuan on becoming kingly, Mencius notes that he was once disposed to grudge or show concern (*ai* 愛) for an ox being led to sacrificial slaughter.[102] In aspiring to true kingship, all that remains is for Xuan to extend this kindness (*tuien* 推恩) by making his feeling "reach" (*ji* 及) beyond those parameters.[103] The notion that concern has "reach" underscores the fact that concern is distributed concentrically and to an evolving extent. Mencius says that it is persons of associated humanity who extend the "reach" (*ji*) of their concern from those they care for to those they do not.[104]

Mencius appeals to the fact that King Xuan could not bear (*ren* 忍) to see the suffering of the ox. Mencius contends that every person has that which he or she cannot bear.[105] The development of moral character involves "drawing out" or "extending" (*da* 達) the feelings that attend the spontaneous revulsion toward that which one cannot bear. Mencius explains:

> Everyone has things they cannot bear. To extend [*da* 達] this revulsion into the realm of what they can bear is associated humanity. Everyone has things they are unwilling to do. To extend this aversion into the realm of what they are willing to do is appropriateness. If a person is able to bring to full expression [*chong* 充] the feeling [*xin* 心] of aversion towards injuring others, there will be an overabundance of associated humanity. If a person can bring to full expression the feeling of contempt for boring holes and scaling walls,[106] there will be an overabundance of appropriateness.[107]

To understand Mencius' point here it is important to retain the botanical model. The term *da* 達 suggests "breaking through" as when grains sprout from the earth.[108] Mencius is not talking about "applying" one's feeling pan-contextually as one might apply a rule or principle. In the Mencian framework, the "extension" of feeling is an integral expression of the *growth* of one's disposition (*xing* 性). This growth is registered not as the mental affirmation and application of a moral rule, but rather as the emergence of autogenerative, psychosomatic reactions within a widening realm of felt experience.

Mencius suggests that such spontaneous reactions historically gave rise to customs and behaviors later formalized into articles of ritual propriety. He offers the burial of parents as an example:

> One would presume that in past generations there were instances of people not burying their parents. When parents died, they were tossed in the gullies. One day their children passed by their bodies, eaten away by wild animals and devoured by insects. The children broke into a sweat and turned away, unable to bear the sight. This sweat was not merely sweat for others to see; instead it broke through from their feelings [*zhongxinda* 中心達], and it manifested itself in their faces and eyes. They immediately went home for baskets and spades and covered their parents over. It was genuinely [*cheng* 誠] right for them to cover the bodies of their parents over; hence, for filial children and those of associated humanity to do likewise must be the most productive course.[109]

In the Mencian account, there was no moral deliberation involved in the initial impulse to bury one's parents; it was instead initiated by feeling (*xin* 心). At some point in history, children encountered the decaying bodies of their parents and found that this was something they could not bear to see. Compelled by this, they became disposed to behave in ways commensurate with the enlargement of their sensibilities. This advanced the most productive course (*dao* 道). For Mencius, this episode represents the most "genuinely integrated" (*cheng* 誠) form of moral behavior and growth.[110] In chapter five, the emergence of formal burial rites for parents will be used to illustrate what it means to advance the human way (*rendao* 人道) more generally.

Before proceeding to the final two chapters, let us summarize once again the main difference between Mohist and Mencian thought. Burton Watson suggests that Mohist thought "held little attraction for the men of an urbane and aesthetic-minded society."[111] Watson's appraisal might be better formulated by considering what it means to be aesthetically minded in a Chinese world. Being so minded involves eschewing external principles in the construal of order in favor of focusing on the particularity of an order as it emerges from its own set of factors or constituents. In keeping with the normative measure of harmony (*he* 和), the aestheticism operative here is one sensitive to the emergence of orders that are intrinsically fitting (*yi* 宜) rather than coercively imposed. The growth of a moral order, like that of an empire, state, family, person, or tree, must proceed from the root soil. The courses of such emergent orders are born spontaneously from what is so-of-itself (*ziran* 自然).[112] Moral and social order is not forced when spontaneous feeling is its root. As the *Book of Filial Piety* says, to govern the emergence of social order by maintaining its root in spontaneous, family-borne feeling is to be "effective without being strict."[113]

Feeling is the root of all human virtue for Mencius, and it is the engine that advances the human way. Human virtue emerges (*you* 由) as the fruit of concrete, felt experiences. It does not emerge from anything outside of such experience. As Mencius says:

> Associated humanity, appropriateness, ritual propriety, and wisdom do not come from the outside [*wai* 外] to refine us. They belong to us all along. It is only that we fail to give it thought.[114]

Accordingly, Mencius disapproves of the kind of technical reasoning suggested in the Mohist ethic. In an allusion to the uniquely Mohist distinction between theory and practice, Mencius states that sagely morality is not evaluated in such terms:

> Shun was clear on the basics and he understood human relationships [*renlun* 人倫]. His associated humanity and appropriateness emerged [*you* 由] in due course; he did not put associated humanity and appropriateness into practice [*xing* 行].[115]

Appropriateness and ritual propriety are likened to the road (*lu* 路) and the door (*men* 門), respectively, wherefrom the virtues of the exemplary person emerge (*you* 由) and come out (*chu* 出).[116] There is no outside (*wai* 外) source that serves as a universal "standard" (*fa* 法) of human virtue in the *Mencius*; instead, there are only exemplary human "models" (*fa* 法) that inspire one forward from where one is. Human virtue comes from particular humans. Mencius puts it succinctly: "Ritual propriety and appropriateness emerge by coming out of persons of quality" (*liyiyouxianzhechu* 禮義由賢者出).[117]

In lauding the achievements of Shun, Mencius alludes to the *Book of Songs*: "Ever filial, his filial piety made him a pattern to imitate" (*ze* 則).[118] In the case of Shun, it was the preservation of family affection and filial piety that facilitated the emergence of his moral person. Sages emerge to inspire others to cultivate their own persons within their own family contexts. According to Mencius, the sage serving as model for the moral development of others does far more to inspire that development than do doctrines (*yan* 言). As Mencius reflects:

> When Confucius ascended the Eastern Mountain, he felt that his state of Lu was small. When he ascended Mount Tai, he felt that the empire itself was small. Likewise, for one who has seen the ocean, it is difficult to appreciate mere water; and for someone who has been around a sage, it is difficult to appreciate doctrines.[119]

This passage illustrates once again the difference in normative thinking between the Mencian and Mohist schools. Mencius appeals to the sages as "models" (*fa* 法) of moral cultivation based on the filial piety they exhibit in their persons. Mozi also appeals to the sages as exemplars of conduct, but their morality (*yi* 義) is ultimately the expression of a "standard" (*fa* 法) far removed from the sages' own concrete circumstances. As Mozi says:

> If the kings, ministers, and exemplary persons of the world really wish to pursue the most productive course [*dao* 道] in benefiting the people, ascertaining the root of associated humanity and appropriateness is fundamental. The intent of "Heaven" [*tian* 天] must be accorded with. To accord with the intent of *tian* is the standard of morality [*yi* 義].[120]

Such top-down moral thinking is anathema to the aesthetic sensibilities of Confucians and the antithesis of their normative measure of harmony (*he* 和).

In the final analysis, Mohism lends itself toward theorizing the proper level of concern (*ai* 愛) one ought to feel based on an abstract standard, rationally affirmed. By eschewing such technical thinking and locating the model of moral development in the filial piety and associated humanity of the sage, Mencius advocates extending and developing one's own spontaneous, family-borne feelings into habits and attitudes that he maintains are qualitatively human. The Mencian notion of "human disposition" (*renxing* 人性) will be reconstructed under this assumption.

Chapter 4

The Human Disposition

Relationships and the Human Disposition

As suggested in chapter three, preserving the kind and quality of feeling generated in the family and expressed through filial affection is profoundly important in the Confucian world. Confucius considers filial piety (*xiao* 孝) to be the root from which the Confucian way (*dao* 道) emerges.[1] Similarly, the *Book of Filial Piety*, which asserts that the way of parent and child is the "natural disposition" (*tianxing* 天性) of the human experience,[2] considers filial piety to be the root of excellence in character and the source of all Confucian teaching.[3] In the *Zhongyong*, tributes to great Confucian exemplars commence in recognition of their filial piety.[4] And with the ascendancy of Confucianism in the Han, the epitaph *xiao* is added to the posthumous title of every emperor.[5] The importance of family feeling in this tradition cannot be overstated. In the Confucian world, all qualitatively human relationships are derivations of family relationships.[6] In the absence of family, one has little claim on the designation "human" (*ren* 人).

Mencius is both heir and progenitor to this profoundly family-centric way of thinking. For Mencius, as we have seen, the cultivation of character is a process rooted in feelings of family affection. It is also family affection that serves as a necessary condition for qualifying one as human. On this point, Mencius is unequivocal: "if one is not engaged [*de* 得] in family affection [*qin* 親], one cannot be called human [*ren*

人]."[7] The newly recovered *Six Positions* (*Liuwei* 六位) document from Guodian concurs and is even more explicit, suggesting that family affection is itself a sufficient condition:

> Having affection [*qin* 親] towards one's close and distant relatives: being "human" lies solely in this [*weiqirensuozai* 唯其人所在]. Engage [*de* 得] in this affection and the "human" begins to be present [*ju* 舉]; disengage from this affection and the "human" ceases to be [*zhi* 止].[8]

The Mencian notion of the human disposition (*renxing* 人性) is here understood as a corollary to this Confucian assertion. For Mencius, the giving and receiving of family affection is an essential component of the human experience: it is from associated living in the family that all qualitatively "human" sensibilities stem. Being born into a caring family "disposes" one towards feelings of family affection, and it is the proclivity of this initial, "human" disposition to extend one's family-borne sensibilities into the world and become increasingly "human" along Confucian lines.

This interpretation of the human disposition raises a much debated question in Mencian studies: Is the Mencian notion of *renxing* 人性 genetic or is it cultural?[9] Mencius describes family affection as something "unlearned" (*buxue* 不學),[10] and maintains that the "capacity" (*cai* 才) to become human is something "conferred by *tian* 天."[11] Interpreted genetically, these statements are considered as evidence of Mencius' belief in innate, human characteristics biologically given prior to any social conditioning or contact. If family affection (*qin* 親) is understood to be such a characteristic, then *renxing* for Mencius would be something akin to a biologically given "human nature."

Such a one-sided reading, however, is in tension with the assumptions of a *qi* 氣 cosmology. In a *qi* cosmology, formation and function are inseparable within the process of structured emergence, such that, as Tang Junyi puts it, dispositions (*xing* 性) "match up" with the ongoing process of *tian* (*tiandao* 天道).[12] If we preserve the kind of transactional model that is more consistent with this cosmology, then social and cultural circumstances become factors in the shaping of "unlearned" responses "conferred" by *tian*. If structural emergence is understood as the process of "taking shape" within the layered patterns and processes that are *tian*, then the conditions that sponsor emergence factor into emergent formations and their concomitant functions.¹³ Such an understanding would give more weight to the social, cultural, and historical aspects of the human disposition, and in addition to being more loyal to Warring States cosmology, it would better fit the account of human emergence that Mencius presents in his telling of the Chanxiang episode.¹⁴

This episode involves Xuxing, an uncouth southerner from Chu and follower of the egalitarian, agrarian-based Shenneng ideal.¹⁵ Xuxing settled in Tang and began to attract local followers. One of these adherents was Chanxiang. Chanxiang had formerly been educated under Chenliang, originally a southerner like Xuxing, although one who had come north to be educated in the most productive course (*dao* 道) established by the Confucians. Chanxiang, in transferring his allegiance from the refined, northern-educated Chenliang to the southerner, Xuxing, was abandoning the Confucian course and returning to an agrarian ideology associated with southerners.

While arguing with Chanxiang over the merit of Shenneng ideology, Mencius volunteers a lesson in cultural history. He relates how, before Xie was appointed minister of education under Yao and Shun, the Chinese people existed only at the level of material subsistence. This, Mencius says, was "the most productive course [*dao* 道] that they had." He continues to relate how, "being well-fed and warmly-clothed but dwelling idle without education, they were 'close' [*jin* 近] to birds and beasts." Mencius explains that once Xie was appointed minister, he proceeded to teach the people "human relationships" (*renlun* 人倫): affection between father and son, appropriateness between ruler and subject, distinction between husband and wife, respect of the old by the young, and faithfulness between friends.¹⁶ In the account given in the *Book of Documents*, we learn that Xie's establishment of human relationships was initiated because, without them, people were "not affectionate" (*buqin* 不親).¹⁷ In Mencius' telling, it was Xie's establishment of the human relationships that enabled the Chinese people to "consummate themselves" (*zide* 自得).¹⁸

After recalling the historical establishment of human relationships, Mencius echoes Confucius' praise of Yao, adding that Yao patterned himself after (*ze* 則) *tian* 天 in his accomplishments. In the *Analects*, Confucius' praise reads in part: "How great was Yao as ruler! How majestic his accomplishments, and how brilliant his cultural achievements!"¹⁹ Mencius is matter-of-fact about the superior achievements of

Confucian-based Chinese civilization: "I've heard of Chinese civilization converting barbarians," he says, "but I've never heard of converting back to barbarian!" Mencius cannot accept the fact that Chanxiang would abandon Confucianism and follow the likes of Xuxing, a "twittering-tongued barbarian from the south, whose most productive course is not that of the ancient kings." Mencius lodges his disapproval with a striking image: "I have heard of emerging from a dark ravine to settle in a lofty tree, but I have never heard of descending from a lofty tree to settle in a dark ravine."

Mencius' treatment of Chanxiang is telling. If a human disposition is something that Mencius considers "good" (*shan* 善), then in labeling Chanxiang's conversion back to barbarian ways "not good" (*bushan* 不善), he is suggesting that, in abandoning the human relationships established by Xie, Chanxiang becomes less than human. That non-Confucian practice fails to distinguish "human" experience from barbarism and leaves people closer to animals is always Mencius' position. His main objection to the teachings of the Yangist and Mohist schools is that each undermines one of the human relationships that distinguish the Chinese from animals. He objects to Mohism on the basis that it fails to acknowledge fathers and to Yangism on the basis that it fails to acknowledge rulers, and "without rulers and fathers, we are animals."[20] Mencius' point throughout is that those who are not proceeding on the course established by Xie have lost their human dispositions. They are closer to animals.

The distinction between humans and animals is one that Mencius describes as "slight" (*xi* 希); he explains that the common person loses this distinguishing feature while the exemplary person like Shun, who "has insight into human relationships," preserves it.[21] The five human relationships, which include the putatively "unlearned" feeling of family affection (*qin* 親), are the features that distinguish humans from birds and beasts. These distinguishing features do not appear to be strictly genetic for Mencius; instead, he traces them back to Xie's reforms, which under the wisdom of Yao are patterned like *tian* 天. The Chanxiang episode would suggest that the human disposition, if understood in terms of germinal, moral sensibilities rooted in one's family upbringing, is understood by Mencius more as a historical, genealogical inheritance than as a genetic or biological one.[22]

As Mencius sees it, people are born into a world in which institutions like family have a history. If the human disposition emerges with moral sensibilities and habits shaped by such institutions, then the human disposition also has a history. And history is something always being made. If the sages, who are of the same sort (*lei* 類) as any other person,[23] can pattern themselves after *tian* 天 and contribute to the extension of the human disposition, then any other person can as well. One is not only shaped *by* the institutions that one is born into; one can also contribute to the process of reshaping *them*. As Mencius says: "in building high, one takes advantage of existing hills."[24] The person is both beneficiary and contributor to the structures established by one's predecessors. Just as one's disposition "extends" over the span of one's life (*sheng* 生), the collective, human experience, over time, can be "extended" by the work of sages. The work of the sage is not at an end. Mencius eagerly awaits the emergence of new sages and considers their arrival "overdue."[25]

We can assume that, prior to the achievements of Yao and Xie, Mencius considered people "close" to animals in disposition (*xing* 性), since the word that Mencius uses in this context, "close" (*jin* 近), is the word Confucius uses in reference to *xing*. Confucius says, "In disposition we are close [*jin*], and by habit and experience [*xi* 習] we are distanced."[26] Confucius employs the language of proximity and distance in a manner reminiscent of an episode in the *Book of Documents* involving Taijia, son and successor of Tang, the founder of the Shang dynasty. Here, too, disposition is how people are initially "close" and habit and experience are what introduce "distance."

The *Book of Documents* relates that Yiyin, a minister to Taijia, decided to strategically relocate the palace of his wayward king in order to rehabilitate his ethical disposition (*xing* 性) which had been completely altered by poor ethical habits (*xi* 習). Yiyin declares:

> Now this is inappropriate behavior, and by habit has become established as his disposition [*xing* 性]. I cannot remain close by what I do not accord with.[27] I will build a palace in Tong, where Taijia will be intimately connected to the former Kings.[28] This instruction will prevent him from wandering astray in life.[29]

Tiajia's bad habits lead him so far astray that he develops a completely new disposition, one out of accord with the disposition of those to whom he was once in "close" proximity. Yiyin's solution is to locate him even "closer" to the cultural and historical source of the disposition he left behind. Tiajia's moral disposition is treated exclusively as a cultural product—not as anything even remotely genetic. Mencius is clearly fond of the Tiajia story. In recollecting it, he relates how Tiajia was successfully rehabilitated by the relocation initiated by Yiyin,[30] and how the minister acted out of noble intent in banishing the king.[31] Mencius himself prescribes a similar program for King Yen of Sung.[32]

Read against the story of Taijia, Confucius and Mencius are saying that disposition (*xing* 性) is how "we" are close, an observation of the fact that groups, having achieved some level of common practice and like-mindedness, share certain tendencies and attitudes. Mencius suggests the same in his telling of the Chanxiang episode. While Confucius does not present a position on the "goodness" (*shan* 善) of a disposition,[33] from what he does offer, we can surmise that like Mencius he is not presenting a biological or genetic account of the human disposition. Confucius realizes that dispositions are culturally malleable: those who begin "close" in their culturally disposed tendencies may, like Taijia, become distanced from one another through the undergoing of experience and the formation of habit.

In the *Mozi*, we see just how far groups of people diverge by virtue of their cultural habits. Mozi presents a series of ethnographies intended to illustrate the degree to and frequency with which habit (*xi* 習) replaces appropriate behavior (*yi* 義) and becomes customary (*su* 俗). Mozi's examples are intended to shock. East of Yue, people once chopped up and ate their first-born sons in order to benefit their next born. South of Chu, there are a people who scrape the flesh off the bones of their dead parents and, once they have buried the bones, feel they have "completed the actions of filial offspring." Mozi calls into question the associated humanity of such people:

> Leaders regard these customs as the affairs of governing state, and the people regard them as acceptable procedure; they are performed without cessation and adopted without discrimination or choice. Yet how could it be that they actually represent the most productive course with regards to associated humanity and appropriateness? What we have here are people instituting habitual practices and deeming appropriate their vulgar customs.[34]

Mozi would have custom established on the basis of his utilitarian principle. While he never explicitly links the notion of custom (*su* 俗) to Confucian ritual (*li* 禮), he likely means to suggest that Confucian ritual is equally indiscriminate and established without utilitarian evaluation.[35]

Mencius, however, is equally critical of people's tendency to behave indiscriminately and form habits (*xi* 習) without reflection. As he says:

> The multitudes do not understand what they practice and form habits without their noticing it. Their entire persons emerge without any realization of the course [*dao* 道] they are on.[36]

The Mencian prescription for this malady differs from that of the Mohist. Rather than guide social practice according to the normative standard of benefit (*li* 利), Mencius proceeds in deference to appropriateness (*yi* 義), the "fittingness" that calls to mind the normative measure of harmony (*he* 和). He stresses family affection and filial piety with the aim of eliciting moral, social, and political practices that correlate with the harmony of the family institution established by Xie. The identification of family affection with a qualitatively "human" existence is an endorsement of the Confucian way. The ancient sages, in establishing the five human relationships, began with family affection, and for Mencius, this has been the foundation of "human" experience ever since.

From Mencius' Confucian perspective, the family-borne disposition is morally and socially good. Family affection conditions an initial disposition the proclivity of which is to develop more robust human relationships (*ren* 仁) and more refined moral sensibilities (*yi* 義). That such a human disposition does not reduce to biological functions, "eating and reproduction" (*shise* 食色), for instance,[37] is a point that Mencius wishes to make clear:

> Gaozi said: "Disposition is the life process [*sheng* 生]."
> Mencius said: "To say that disposition is the life process: is this like saying white is white?"
> "Yes."
> "And the whiteness of white feathers is like the whiteness of white snow, and the whiteness of white snow is like the whiteness of white jade."

"Yes."

"Then is the disposition of a dog like the disposition of an ox, and the disposition of an ox like the disposition of a human?"[38]

Kwong-loi Shun's meticulous philosophical and linguistic analysis of this passage yields the following submission, with which I concur:

> [Mencius] wanted to redirect attention to a way of viewing *xing* 性 that does not emphasize the biological. Instead, as seen from his query that ended the debate, he viewed the *xing* of human beings as something that distinguishes them from other animals, rather than as biological tendencies common to all.[39]

This distinguishing feature is cultural. It is "human relationships" that make "human" dispositions possible, not anything strictly biological.[40] Before the advent of human relationships, all beings were more or less animals. Thanks to the family-related institutions established by Xie, becoming "human" is now a "capacity" that people have from birth. If one neglects the cultivation and extension of this capacity over the course of one's life, then one reverts back to being an animal. Confucians, remaining family-centric, identify themselves with the "human" side of this distinction and thus strive to maintain it. As Confucius says, "I cannot go congregating with birds and beasts; for if I am not a member in the human world, then who am I?"[41]

The Human Disposition as Good

Mencius is widely recognized for his optimistic assertion that the human disposition is "productive" or "good" (*shan* 善). Confronted with alternative notions, he explains his position as follows:

> As far as one's emotion [*qing* 情] is concerned, one is capable of becoming good [*shan* 善]. This is what I mean by "good." As for those who are not good [*bushan* 不善], this is not the fault of their capacity [*cai* 才].[42]

In coming to understand the Mencian position, we now benefit from the recently unearthed *Dispositions Arise from Conditions* document that deals extensively with the notions of "emotion" (*qing* 情) and disposition.

The first thing to note about *Dispositions Arise from Conditions* is that it locates emotion (*qing* 情) within a disposition (*xing* 性) not as a fixed attribute, but as the discursively emergent product of experience. The text begins:

> Generally, while people have a disposition [*xing* 性], their heart-minds [*xin* 心] have no fixed aspirations [*zhi* 志]. These wait upon things and events, and only then arise. They wait upon an inclination, and only then enter into action. They wait upon the formation of habit, and only then become fixed. The energies [*qi* 氣] of pleasure, anger, grief, and sadness are a matter of disposition. When they come to be externally manifest, things and events have activated them. Dispositions arise from conditions. Conditions are conferred by *tian* 天. The proper course [*dao* 道] has its beginning in emotion [*qing* 情]. Emotion arises from a disposition. In the beginning stage, the proper course is close to emotion; and in the concluding stage, it is close to appropriateness. Those who understand emotion are able to discharge it; those who understand appropriateness are able to incorporate it. Predilection itself is disposition. Likes and dislikes are a matter of things and events. Goodness [*shan* 善] itself is disposition. Being good or not good is a matter of the propensity of circumstances [*shi* 勢].[43]

In *Dispositions Arise from Conditions*, dispositions (*xing* 性) name the predilections, aspirations, and proclivities developed in transaction with things and in relation to the propensity of circumstances. Apart from the experience of doing and undergoing in the world, disposition (*xing*) and feeling (*xin* 心) are notions void of content. They are "mute." The text explains:

> When dispositions are under consideration, things and events are activating them. Metal and stone have a sound, but if they are not struck they will not ring out. So, although people have

dispositions and feelings, in the absence of things and events to activate them, they would not arise.[44]

Dispositions can only be considered as embedded in the world. Feelings can only be considered as engaged. In other words, dispositions have no transcendent "nature" that is formed prior to engagement in the world. Once a process is commenced, an initial disposition obtains. This disposition is then "grown" over the course of its emergence. The text explains:

> Dispositions have things that agitate them, things that challenge them, things that cooperate with them, things that discipline them, things that produce them, things that nourish them, and things that grow them.

> Things and events agitate dispositions, inclinations challenge them, things already brought about cooperate with them, appropriateness disciplines them, the propensity of circumstance produces them, habits nourish them, and the process itself [*dao* 道] grows them.[45]

With *Dispositions Arise from Conditions* now in hand, little doubt should remain that disposition (*xing* 性) can be understood as a process-oriented notion in the Warring States period and that it is so understood in the Si-Meng lineage of Confucianism.

But what is "emotion" (*qing* 情) and how does it assist us in understanding the Mencian notion of a "good" human disposition? As *Dispositions Arise from Conditions* suggests, "emotion arises from a disposition." The presentation of pleasure, anger, grief, and sadness as *qi* 氣 energy configured in a disposition is consistent with our previous discussion of the transactional nature of feeling (*xin* 心) in chapter two. *Qing* as a neutral term appears to be the most inclusive manner by which to refer to the terminal result of the transactions that issue into various emotional states. These transactions are conditioned by a disposition; hence, emotional content itself "arises" from a disposition. The question to be asked of Mencius can be framed as follows: what is the distinguishing emotion (*qing*) that arises from a qualitatively "human" disposition?

In *Dispositions Arise from Conditions*, dispositions are presented in terms that resonate with the *Mencius* and other writings in the Si-Meng school: they arise from "conditions" (*ming* 命) that are "conferred by *tian* 天." This is to say that dispositions take shape within ongoing processes and are "grown" over the course of adjustment to those processes. Just to be disposed is to have predilection, but the things and events that are experienced must be factored in before predilection becomes actual likes and dislikes. Similarly, just to be disposed is to have some degree of goodness (*shan* 善), but only when the propensity (*shi* 勢) of a set of circumstances is factored in can a disposition become productive or unproductive. Mencius explains that as far as one's emotional content is concerned one is capable of becoming good (*shan*). This, he says, is what he means by "good." With *Dispositions Arise from Conditions* as our guide, we know better what to look for in filling out his position.

First, if Mencius is talking about an emotion, he is also talking about a disposition that facilitates it. Second, if Mencius is talking about a disposition, he is also talking about a set of conditions that sponsor its emergence. Third, if Mencius is talking about a "good" disposition, he is also talking about the propensity of circumstances under which it is so. In keeping with the causal framework of a *qi* 氣 cosmology, all four elements—conditions (*ming* 命), disposition (*xing* 性), propensity (*shi* 勢), and emotion (*qing* 情)—operate in tandem, so we are not looking for disparate explanations. As the family-borne, "human" disposition commences with family affection (*qin* 親), this would be the most likely candidate for the emotion that Mencius has in mind. Family affection is emotion arising from the propensity of a disposition configured within a family. Mencius clearly considers the family to be the most productive (*shan* 善) set of conditions from which to emerge both morally and socially.

Mencius does not use the term *qing* 情 very often. The term "feeling" (*xin* 心) does most of its work. One important occurrence of *qing* is in the "Ox Mountain" passage. The passage can be understood within the framework of the botanical model, and it helps establish the link between *qing*, understood as family-borne feeling, and the "capacity" (*cai* 才) that Mencius refers to in his description of the human disposition as good (*shan* 善). Mencius says:

The trees on Ox Mountain are no longer beautiful. The mountain lies on the outskirts of a large state: its trees are chopped down with axes, so how can they become beautiful? Given a regular hiatus, and the nourishment of the rain and dew, there is no lack of new shoots emerging; but then the cattle and sheep come to graze upon the mountain. This is why the mountain looks so bald. Seeing only its baldness, people think Ox Mountain never had any "wood stuff" [*cai* 材]. But how can this be the disposition [*xing* 性] of the mountain?

And so with humans: how can they be without the feeling of associated humanity and appropriateness? The case of losing this good, fertile feeling is like that of denuding trees with an axe.[46] When these are chopped day after day, how can they become beautiful? Even given a regular hiatus and the energies [*qi* 氣] of a calm morning, the predilections that resemble closely [*jin* 近] those of humans become very few. What is done over the course of the day has a constricting effect and they perish.[47] If this constriction takes place repeatedly, then even the energies of the night will not be enough to preserve these predilections. If the energies of the night are not enough to preserve them, then one is not far from an animal. When humans see such an animal, they will think that it never had the capacity [*cai* 才]. But how can this represent the emotion [*qing* 情] of a human? Hence, anything that receives nourishment will grow; and anything deprived of nourishment will wither away. Confucius said, "Hold it and it is preserved, let it go and it perishes. It comes and goes at irregular periods and no one knows its direction." It is perhaps to the heart-mind that he refers?"[48]

As the "Ox Mountain" passage suggests, the "capacity" to become human can be understood in botanical terms. The term "capacity" (*cai* 才) overlaps phonetically with the notion of "wood stuff" (*cai* 材), which is also understood as the "quality" or "disposition" of an organic material.[49] Kwong-loi Shun argues that the "capacity" to become human in the *Mencius* refers ultimately to the "four sprouts" (*siduan* 四端) of human virtue.[50] It has already been suggested, and will be further argued below, that these capacities are "rooted" in family affection.

Hence, just as the "wood stuff" of Ox Mountain is rooted in mountain soil, the disposition of which is to produce beautiful trees, the "capacity" to remain "close" to humans is rooted in family affection and its related states of feeling (*xin* 心), the disposition of which is to produce beautiful persons. We see once again, in the "Ox Mountain" passage, that it is daily "habit" that gradually overwhelms one's family-borne disposition and results in behavioral tendencies that are no longer "close" to those that are considered distinctly human.

That developing one's human capacity along Confucian lines inflicts no violence upon the initial disposition of the human "wood stuff" is a point Mencius is keen to make in his debates with Gaozi:

> Gaozi said: "Disposition is like the willow tree. Appropriateness is like a cup or bowl. To take a human disposition and make associated humanity and appropriateness is like making a cup or bowl from the willow tree."
>
> Mencius responded: "Can you make cups and bowls in accord with the disposition of the willow tree, or must you mutilate the willow tree in order to make cups and bowls? If you must mutilate the willow tree in order to make cups and bowls, then must you mutilate people in order to make them persons of associated humanity and appropriateness? In bringing disaster upon associated humanity and appropriateness, it will certainly be this doctrine [*yan* 言] of your's that the world will be following.[51]

The family-borne "human" disposition has a tendency toward Confucian development just as water tends to flow downward.[52] One born in family affection need not be forced to create oneself in a Confucian direction.

There is another level of significance to the "Willow Tree" passage. In likening Confucian virtues to objects "made" from a resistant, raw material, Gaozi substitutes a production model for the process-oriented botanical model. According to Mencius, such "technical" separation of ends from means is a property of doctrine (*yan* 言), and he does not allow Gaozi's "willow tree" example to pass without the derogatory classification of his approach to human realization as doctrinaire. The Yangists and Mohists are associated with doctrines that attempt to force upon human development some end-driven result "for the sake of" (*wei* 為) some standard of benefit (*li* 利).[53] Mencius rejects the imposition of fixed ends upon the creative process of human development along with any doctrine formulated to endorse them. Recall that Mencius is "spontaneous" rather than "technical" in his orientation. He recommends not imposing anything on human development and seeks instead to "bring about" only that which will emerge out of the human disposition's own proclivities. He explains his position as follows:

> The world's doctrines [*yan* 言] about disposition [*xing* 性] are simply designed to bring something about [*gu* 故]. Those who would bring something about consider benefit [*li* 利] to be fundamental. What is objectionable in such clever people is their forced reasoning. If the clever were only to act as Yu did in guiding the floodwater, then there would be nothing objectionable in their cleverness. Yu guided the floodwater by not imposing anything on it [*wushi* 無事]. When clever people also proceed without imposing anything, this is great cleverness indeed. While the heavens are high and the stars are distant; if only one seeks what comes about [*gu* 故] in this way, one can calculate the solstices of a thousand years without leaving one's seat.[54]

The movement of celestial objects is conditioned in such a manner that their trajectories are open to forecast by the astute, empirically-minded observer. Mencius maintains that the conditions of human emergence can also be a matter of forecast to the empirical observer. For Mencius, human emergence is initially conditioned by family experience. Accordingly, Mencius forecasts a Confucian direction of development that he alleges will proceed unforced from these initial conditions.

Below, we consider the process of "bringing to fruition" (*shi* 實) the human virtues. We shall see that, while Mencius forecasts the direction of human development in the form of the "four sprouts," he is not establishing their end results. In keeping with the botanical model, the end products of these virtues emerge over the course of their well-integrated (*cheng* 誠) growth and unforced maturation. Mencius is a process-oriented thinker. He does not establish fixed ends antecedent to the process of development. This feature distinguishes Mencius from his principal adversaries, the Mohists and Yangists.

The Four Sprouts and the Family

That humans have certain "shared" traits is an important theme in the *Mencius*. We find the most substantive discussion of this theme in two passages: the "Child at the Well" passage, in which Mencius outlines the four sprouts of human virtue, and the "Barley" passage, in which Mencius likens the process of becoming human to that of growing rows of barley. In order to understand these passages in context, we must bear in mind the principal themes discussed thus far. In what follows, we revisit the internal/external (*nei/wai* 內外) debate, harmony (*he* 和), configurative energy (*qi* 氣), and the botanical model. It will be argued that the common traits that Mencius attributes to humans as a "sort" (*lei* 類) in fact serve to reinforce a creative, particularistic notion of human development, one that he traces back to the family institution.

In the "Child at the Well" passage, Mencius presents the cultivation of one's human disposition as contingent upon the proper extension of feelings from what he refers to as their "sprouts" (*duan* 端). The "Child at the Well" passage is best considered in its entirety. Mencius says:

> Each and every human [*ren* 人] has feelings [*xin* 心] sensitive to the suffering of others. The former kings had such feelings, and these were manifested in their compassionate governing. Putting such feelings to work in governing, they ordered the world as easily as turning it in their palms.
>
> As for each human having feelings sensitive to the suffering of others, suppose a person suddenly sees a child about to fall into a well. Each would feel empathy for the child—not in order to gain the favor of the child's parents, nor to win the praise of villagers and friends, nor out of concern for a potentially blemished reputation.
>
> From this we observe the following: without such a feeling of commiseration one is not human, without a feeling of shame one is not human, without a feeling of deference one is not human, and without a feeling of discrimination one is not human. A feeling of empathy is associated humanity [*ren* 仁] in its germinal state. A feeling of shame is appropriateness [*yi* 義] in its germinal state. A feeling of deference is ritual pro-

priety [*li* 禮] in its germinal state. A feeling of discrimination is wisdom [*zhi* 知] in its germinal state.

People [*ren* 人] have these four sprouts just as they have four limbs. For one to possess these four sprouts yet consider oneself incapable of developing them is self-mutilation; for one to consider the ruler incapable of doing so is to mutilate the ruler.[55]

For anyone having these four sprouts in him or herself, to realize their enlargement and bring them to "fullness" [*chong* 充] is like having a fire catch or a spring break through. If these germinal beginnings are brought to fullness, one might safeguard the whole empire; if they are not, one might not even tend to one's own parents.[56]

In fitting this passage into the Mencian botanical framework, it is necessary to establish the "soil" from which the sprouts that distinguish humans from other sorts of creatures emerge. In the "Child at the Well" passage, "not tending to one's parents" is presented as just as much of a threshold for calling someone "human" as empathy for the child in danger. We have already seen that, according to Mencius, if one fails in maintaining one's family affection (*qin* 親) one can no longer be called "human."[57] Mencius, however, does not identify family affection as a "sprout." It is more likely that family affection is the "soil" from which the "four sprouts" emerge. Hence, if one becomes unhuman to such a degree that one cannot even care for one's own parents, then one's "four sprouts" wilt in the process. All human virtues emerge from and remain rooted in family feeling. Without family feeling one cannot even begin to become human.

To assume that "human" sensibilities are rooted in some source outside (*wai* 外) the family would violate the core of Mencius' position. This is a position reinforced in the "Two Roots or One" episode with Yizhi.[58] Mencius there maintains that moral growth is rooted not in doctrine but in family affection. Again, Mencius is not alone in maintaining his family-centric position; the *Book of Filial Piety* concurs. In the *Book of Filial Piety*, the "human" disposition traces back to the earliest stages of childhood:

In the efficacious virtue of the sage, what was there besides filial piety? Family affection originates at the parent's knee; thereby veneration for one's parents is nourished on a daily basis. The sage proceeds from veneration to the instruction of respect; and proceeds from family affection to the instruction of concern. Sagely instruction is comprehensive without being severe, and sagely government is effective without being strict. They proceed from the root.

The way [dao 道] of a father and his son is a natural disposition [tianxing 天性]; and this is also appropriateness (yi 義) between ruler and subject. This originates from one's parents. There is no greater gift.[59]

Moral development in this tradition traces back to the affections that one is disposed to share with one's parents in the earliest stages of life. Moral sensibilities then "extend" in the form of a disposition to feel and act in a qualitatively "human" way as one's person takes shape. In keeping with the major premise of this tradition, the four sprouts that grant one the capacity to become increasingly human are most adequately understood as extensions of the "unlearned" sensibilities rooted in one's family upbringing. Initially, to be human is to "take shape" in an environment of family affection. It would be difficult to imagine Mencius appealing to the "four sprouts" of the child who did not.

Mencius' description of the human virtues provides further evidence that the four sprouts are rooted in family experience. Recall that the "fruit" (shi 實) of each sprout is developed entirely in terms of family relationships and their embellishments:

> Serving one's parents is bringing associated humanity to fruition. Respecting one's elder brothers is bringing appropriateness to fruition. Understanding the two and not leaving them is bringing wisdom to fruition. Ordering and embellishing the two is bringing ritual propriety to fruition.[60]

Given that the "fruit" of each human virtue matures in a family context, the "fullness" of the four sprouts spoken of in the "Child at the Well" passage can be understood as the unique achievements of persons, like Shun, who have remained consistently rooted therein. Giving "fullness" (chong 充) to something is to be understood as "bringing it to fruition" (shi 實). Together, chong and shi take on the verb/compliment form in the *Mencius*.⁶¹ Hence, the cultivation of what is human, from its germinal state to its achieved form, is a process located in the family context—beginning to end. Humans are creatures who initially emerge from families and sustain that root in cultivating their distinct persons. Shun was such a person, and the sage and we are of the same sort.⁶²

The Satisfaction of Becoming Human

Locating the project of becoming human in the family highlights the personalized, nonprogrammatic nature of this process. Recall the polemic context: Mencius' rejection of the Mohist doctrine of concern for each (*jianai* 兼愛) is based on the contention that no order is to be imposed on human virtues outside (*wai* 外) the process of "bringing these to fruition" (*shi* 實) in one's own concrete relationships. The image of the four sprouts, in keeping with the botanical imagery throughout the *Mencius*, is designed to foreground the creative dimension of growth. As the man from Song learned, things that grow do so in their native environments, at their own speeds, or else they perish.⁶³ The point here is that one cannot force a strict pattern upon growth. Pattern must emerge within the process of maturation; it must "take shape" in transaction with its immediate environment.

Hence, in emerging from particular families and "extending" their sensibilities into the world, individual persons "bring to fruition" what it means to become human. The "human" itself takes shape. There is no strict blueprint by which to govern this process; it is governed instead by allowing the novel development of social patterns that emerge from an extended form of interpersonal feeling that originates with family affection. The *Book of Filial Piety* maintains that the ancient sages "governed" society in such a noncoercive manner and in so doing were "effective without being strict."⁶⁴ The *Mencius* can also be understood as an endorsement of such noncoercive governing. Institutions such as burial rites, relationships such as those between ruler and subject, customs such as dietary habits, even ethical standards such as those governing the proper treatment of animals, will arise and transform of themselves with the "extension" of human sensibilities and the emergent demands of associated living.⁶⁵

The importance of associated humanity (*ren* 仁) in Mencius' thinking thus becomes understandable. Associated humanity grows initially from the family.⁶⁶ To lose family feeling, and by extension one's associated humanity, amounts to forfeiting participation in the novel construction of an emergent human world. Outside the circle of associated humanity lies the perverse world of the animal; within the circle of associated humanity reside the emergent standards of human morality and feeling. As Mencius puts it, "associated humanity *is* human feeling [*renxin* 人心]."⁶⁷ There is no sharp distinction between the process of associated living and the "human" sensibilities that emerge over its course. Hence, for Mencius, the Confucian way (*dao* 道) amounts to "associated humanity coming together [*he* 合] in what is human [*ren* 人]."⁶⁸ The substance of what it means to be "human" emerges in the process (*dao* 道) of associated living. It is this *process* orientation that must be restored to the Mencian position. While one remains nominally "human" when a distressed child elicits a certain response, this "capacity" or "ability" (*cai* 才) to respond to that child becomes by default the *responsibility* to do something and to participate in the process of determining what being "human" in that instance will mean.

While becoming human is a process in the *Mencius*, it is not a haphazard or random development. Becoming human and "giving fruit" to the human virtues is fueled by a spontaneous, creative energy and generative of deep satisfaction. Mencius makes reference to this on two occasions. First, in the "Child at the Well" passage, he speaks of an unstoppable momentum that attends the process of "bringing to fullness" (*chong* 充) one's capacity to become human. He likens this to "a fire catching or a spring breaking through."⁶⁹ Later, when discussing the complimentary notion of "bringing to fruition" (*shi* 實) one's inchoate human qualities, Mencius describes the unstoppable creative energy this generates:

> When joy arises how can it be stopped? Being unstoppable, one dances it with one's feet and waves it with one's arms without being aware.⁷⁰

The spontaneous energy and felt satisfaction that Mencius presents as part of cultivating one's human capacities traces back to his resolution to the *nei/wai* 內外 debate, to his grounding in a *qi* 氣 cosmology, and ultimately to the normative measure of harmony (*he* 和).

The feelings that make one human are rooted in the love one shares with one's family; the "four sprouts" are, by association, also forms of immediate feeling that indicate a disposition that is humanly configured, well integrated (*cheng* 誠), and coherent (*li* 理). Recall that if a disposition remains well integrated as it grows in its broader constitutive habits, it configures a "flood-like" *qi* 氣 that Mencius equates with development that is "optimally vast" (*zhida* 至大) and "optimally firm" (*zhigang* 至剛).[71] By integrating well and preserving coherence over the course of developing as a person, one maximizes in breadth and depth the circuit of one's experience.[72] Mencius resolves the *nei/wai* debate by appeal to the transactional nature of well-integrated growth. The "flood-like" *qi* is the qualitative result of a life configured so as to optimize the felt satisfaction of integrating well into the patterns that constitute one's environment. Maintaining such integrity over the course of personal development maximizes one's life force (*qi* 氣).

As argued in chapter three, the quality associated with integrating things productively (*shan* 善) into patterned wholes—be it adding ingredients to a soup or adding voices to an ensemble—is assessed, in the Confucian tradition, according to the measure of harmony (*he* 和). Mencius uses the same kinds of illustrations, culinary and musical, in describing the pleasure that humans feel in sustaining coherence (*li* 理) and fitting in appropriately (*yi* 義) as they cultivate their incipient human capacities, suggesting that becoming human is also an achievement evaluated in terms of harmony. The pleasure of becoming human, like that of a good culinary or musical experience, is fundamentally an aesthetic pleasure. Such pleasure speaks to the manner in which humans are similar as a sort. We turn now to the "Barley" passage:

> In good years, the young are largely reliable. In bad years, the young are largely impetuous. It is not that the capacity [*cai* 才] conferred by *tian* 天 is radically different. The difference comes about as a result of their feelings [*xin* 心] being blocked.
>
> Consider barley. Allow that we sow barley seeds and cover them with soil. The earth is the same, and the season they are sowed likewise the same. The plants shoot forth, and by summer solstice, each and every one is ripe. While there are dissimilarities, this is due to the various richness of the soil, the nourishment of the rains and moisture, and the disparity of personal attention.
>
> Hence, generally, things of the same sort [*lei* 類] each resemble one another. Why should humans alone be an excep-

tion to this? The sage and we are of the same sort. Thus Longzi said, "In making a shoe for a foot one hasn't known, we know one will not produce a basket." Shoes resemble one another since feet throughout the world are similar.

So it is with taste in food. Palates are similar in their preferences. Yiya was the first to apprehend the preferences of our palates. Were it the case that the disposition [*xing* 性] of palatal preferences differed in humans in the manner that dogs and horses are of different sorts than we, then how could it be that each and every palate in the world pursues the preferences of Yiya? When it comes to taste in food, the fact that the world looks to Yiya shows that all the palates in the world resemble one another.

So it is also with listening to music. The whole world looks to Shikuang, and this shows that all ears in the world are similar. The same goes for what the eye sees. The whole world appreciates the beauty of Zidu; whoever does not is blind. Hence it is said: all palates have the same standard in taste; all ears have the same standard in sound; and all eyes have the same standard in beauty.

When it comes to feeling, is it this alone in which nothing is commonly so? What is it to feeling that is commonly so? It is coherence [*li* 理] and appropriateness [*yi* 義]. The sage was the first to apprehend what in our feelings is commonly so. Hence, coherence and appropriateness bring pleasure to our feeling just as meats bring pleasure to our palates.[73]

This passage suggests that becoming human is a felt pleasure that all humans share. And read within the family-centric framework of the *Mencius*, it also states that despite differences in "nourishment" and disparities in "personal attention," the young, like so many barley seeds, emerge "largely reliable" from the "soils" of their respective families. The conclusion to be drawn from the "Barley" passage, however, is ultimately this: The pleasure of becoming human in a family has as its foundation, like any good musical, culinary, or aesthetic experience, the normative measure of harmony (*he* 和).

Considering the polemic context of the *Mencius*, it is no surprise that the pleasure Mencius appeals to in designating the "human" as a sort (*lei* 類) is the same as that which comes from being a Confucian.

Recall that Confucianism provides the satisfaction of cultivating associated humanity (*ren* 仁) and appropriate conduct (*yi* 義) while meaningfully participating in a world beyond oneself. By preserving integrity (*cheng* 誠), which is something that does not reduce to either "internal" of "external" factors, one is "intensively" involved and "giving one's all" (*zhong* 忠) and simultaneously "extensively" involved and "putting oneself in another's place" (*shu* 恕). The exemplary person is at once integrally present in the world and sensitive to its other participants; this is the "single thread" that Confucius equates with his entire philosophy.[74] Confucians had long considered this pleasure to be found in family experience. Mencius is now isolating that satisfaction and designating it qualitatively "human." He is aware, however, that avenues for this satisfaction are not ahistorical; as he says, "The sage was the first to apprehend what in our feelings is commonly so."[75] It was the historical sage who inaugurated properly "human" institutions (*renlun* 人倫) based on his experience with these feelings.

We can now summarize what Mencius considers humans to share. First, Mencius considers people to have the "capacity" to become increasingly human. This capacity we identify as the four sprouts of human virtue that trace back to being born and nourished in family affection (*qin* 親). This capacity is "conferred by *tian* 天." *Tian* in this context is understood as the history, experience, culture, institutions, and general processes that have shaped human emergence since Xie was minister to Yao and Shun. This disposition (*xing* 性), formed through family affection, is one that over the course of person's life (*sheng* 生) has the proclivity to extend in ways that correspond with traditional Confucian virtues. This disposition is deemed "human," it is productive or "good" (*shan* 善), and it is something that "humans" initially share.

Second, people share an inherent pleasure in sustaining coherence (*li* 理) while fitting themselves appropriately (*yi* 義) into the world over the course of developing their initial, human dispositions. Recall that the coherence of one's disposition is linked to its integration (*cheng* 誠), its propensity to feel and act with spontaneous appropriateness (*yi*). Integrity is upset by desire (*yu* 欲) and doctrine (*yan* 言), each of which mediate experience and compromise the continuity of growth. To preserve and extend one's integral feelings over the course of growing as a person is something that, according to Mencius, each and every human will find pleasure in.[76]

The Value of the Person

That becoming human for Mencius represents something more than just a biological process is also reflected in the "Fish or Bear's Paw" passage. The human life is not one merely "lived"—it is one "lived with self-respect." Mencius explains:

> Fish I want. Bear's paw I also want. If I cannot have both, I would rather take the bear's paw. Life I want. Appropriateness I also want. If I cannot have both, I would rather take appropriateness. While life is what I want, there is something I want more than life. Hence, I will not cling to life at all costs. . . .
>
> There are things one wants more than life, and things one loathes more than death. It is not the person of quality [*xian* 賢] alone that has this feeling [*xin* 心]; each and every human has it. It is just that the person of quality never forfeits it.[77]

The self-respect of a person can be understood in terms of that person's "value" (*gui* 貴), but just as not all humans maintain their self-respect, not all humans realize their own value. Mencius explains:

> The desire for value [*gui* 貴] is a feeling similar [*tong* 同] in humans. In fact, every human has value in him or herself; it is just that this has never been reflected on. What people value is not truly valuable. What Zhaomeng finds value in, Zhaomeng can also depreciate.[78]
>
> The *Songs* say: "Having intoxicated us with wine, having filled us with character [*de* 德] . . ."
>
> This illustrates that, having been satisfied with associated humanity [*ren* 仁] and appropriateness [*yi* 義], one does not long after the exquisite foods that others enjoy. Being worthy of esteem and widely appreciated exhibits itself in one's person [*shen* 身], such that one does not long after the exquisite trappings of others.[79]

When it comes to locating the "value" of a person, Mencius does not appeal to common traits; he is more interested in the end products of those who develop a personal character (*shen* 身) of unique quality and integrity.

In the "Barley" passage, as in the "Child at the Well" passage, Mencius gives a nod in the direction of shared human traits. His main objective in doing so is to defend Confucianism against its adversaries. He is interested in "grounding" Confucian practice in felt experience and in the historical era of the sages: the era that gave rise to the human experience itself. According to Mencius, the sages established human experience and they understood what was pleasurable in that experience. Mencius would like to make it appear that Mohists and Yangists, so far removed from such experience, are neither Chinese nor human. The presentation of "shared" human traits is largely a polemic device that serves this purpose.[80] One wonders if Mencius would ever formulate such notions without the prompting of adversaries. Polemic exigency aside, Mencius has a *genuine* philosophical interest in the novel contributions that individual persons make to human experience over the course of its emergence. He is most interested, and without provocation, in individual particularity and worth.

Mencius understands that shared traits are not enough to secure the worth of human individuals. He relates the following:

> "Since Zengxi was fond of jujubes, Zengzi, his son, could not bear to eat them."
>
> Gong Sunchou asked, "Which is more delicious, roasted meat or jujubes?"
>
> Mencius replied, "Roasted meat, of course."
>
> "So, why was it that Zengzi ate roasted meat but did not eat jujubes?"
>
> "Roasted meat is a common [*tong* 同] taste, but jujubes are a particular [*du* 獨] taste. We avoid the use of another's given name, but we do not avoid the use of one's family name. The family name is what is common; the given name is what is particular."[81]

The significance of this passage becomes clear once we consider the role of names in the Chinese world. Names speak both to the continuity and the particularity that characterizes persons. One's given name (*ming* 名) does not merely signify one's existence; a given name confers distinction in the form of one's "reputation." Given names, we learn in the *Zuozhuan*, "cannot be loaned to others" since "they are used to generate one's credibility."[82] Zengzi cannot adopt the particular characteristics that distinguish his father just as he cannot adopt his father's given name, which itself serves as his father's "claim" to an achieved distinction.[83] Zengzi must distinguish his own "name" and establish his own reputation, a prospect that Confucius holds to be of the highest importance.[84]

Mencius does maintain that humans are similar in that they come from families and find satisfaction in the development of their self-worth. The "value" of humans, however, is based more on the particularistic, achievement end of human development than on the "shared" nature of these base characteristics. In the "Jujube" passage, the sorts of things that humans share, like pleasure in roasted meat or a surname (*xing* 姓), provide insufficient content to distinguish one person from another.[85] Similarly, the virtues that distinguish humans from nonhumans are content-poor without being "filled out" (*shi* 實) in the creative emergence of the particular person. Mencius is more interested in the process of human cultivation than he is in base characteristics. He does designate humans as a sort (*lei* 類), but when he remarks, "the glorious phoenix is the same sort of thing as any bird, and the mighty ocean the same sort of thing that runs in the gutter,"[86] he is not exalting common traits at all but rather celebrating the achievement of distinction.

For Mencius, the achievement of distinct character over the course of a life is what really generates worth and brings each and every human satisfaction. If this satisfaction is as common to us as the pleasures of the palate, then this only means that the creative possibilities of becoming "human" are as varied as those of becoming "delicious." What is important to Mencius is not the common, empty capacity to become human, but rather that some people are "twice, five times, or countless times" better at developing their human capacity than are others.[87] This qualitative disparity among humans is due to the relative inability of some to be productive in "getting the most" (*jin* 盡) out of the capacities furnished through their initial, family-borne dispositions.

Mencius insists that to become sage-like one must "go somewhere" (*jian* 踐) with one's initial disposition.[88] This is done by "pursuing" (*cong* 從)[89] either its lesser or greater components (*ti* 體), and with qualitatively different results. While those who succeed in maintaining a human status do so equally in some general sense, this is not as important to Mencius as how some humans distinguish themselves in a more concrete sense. As Gong Duzi inquires:

> "While equally human, some become greater humans than others, how is this?"
>
> Mencius replied, "Those who pursue the greater component become the greater humans, those who pursue the lesser components become the lesser humans."[90]

The greater (*da* 大) component is the function of feeling (*xin* 心), the root of one's emergence as a "home-grown" human person with distinct moral character. The lesser (*xiao* 小) components include the sensory functions and members of the physical body that have a different "value" and ought not to rank higher than feeling in priority for nourishment and cultivation. The function of feeling rather than the biological body, strictly speaking, is the locus of the capacities (*cai* 才) that enable one to cultivate oneself as human.[91]

As argued above, these sprouts originate and find expression in family experience. Becoming human is the process of getting the most out these sprouts. In so doing, one is bringing something inchoate to "fullness" and thereby "bringing to fruition" one's human virtues.[92] To "get the most" (*jin* 盡) out of one's initial disposition and feelings is to draw out from these everything that they make available. The notion of "getting the most" out of something is reflected in a cognate term, *jin* 燼, which refers to the remnant ashes of something fully combusted. In a Confucian context, this does not mean developing an inherent *telos* toward a predetermined end.[93] In keeping with the normative measure of harmony (*he* 和) that guides the Confucian program, "getting the most" out of a thing means integrating its qualities by facilitating its optimal expression within the aesthetic limits of balance and proportion. That *jin* 盡 involves a balanced, proper measure is suggested in the image of striking a bell from the *Book of Rites*:

> Struck with something small, a bell gives a small sound. Struck with something large, it gives a large sound. But let it be struck leisurely and properly and one "gets the most" [*jin*] out of its sound.[94]

Jin refers to the optimal expression of something. Here, optimal expression involves not just volume but proper proportion, for only then does something productively contribute the full range of its unique qualities.

In the context of bringing about social harmony, to allow people to "optimally express" themselves and to contribute their experiences to that of a collective humanity is considered crucial to securing political legitimacy. In the *Book of Documents* we read:

> If rural men and women are not given the confidence to "get the most out of themselves" [*zijin* 自盡], the people's lord will fail to complete his own achievement of merit.[95]

These passages in the *Book of Rites* and the *Book of Documents* contribute towards a more adequate understanding of *jin* 盡 in a Confucian context. The term involves optimal expression and balanced integration. It also suggests the creation of an environment that facilitates the contribution of each person to an ongoing humanity, and is thereby related to social conditions generally and tied to political legitimacy.

As we see in the next chapter, Mencius and other Si-Meng Confucians understand people's "getting the most" out of themselves in their own circumstances—historical, social, economic, biological, spiritual and so on—in relation to the overall advancement of the "human way" (*rendao* 人道).

Chapter 5

Advancing the Human Way

The Constraints on Aspiration

The notion of a "human disposition" (*renxing* 人性) has been identified with family-borne feelings and tied to the historical work of the ancient sages. Thus understood, *renxing* facilitates personal development along family-centric, Confucian lines; as a result, Mencius regards this disposition as productive or "good" (*shan* 善). Mencius' optimism with regard to the human disposition is tempered, however, by the recognition that there is a propensity of circumstances within which the human experience must make its way. Social, political, and economic circumstances conspire to limit the achievements that might be brought to fruition in the course of human development. While these circumstances will change with time, Mencius strives to optimize human experience and to forge the most productive course (*dao* 道) within the limits of the historical moment. Ideally, he aspires to transform that historical moment. Mencius is very sensitive to circumstances that obtain by virtue of the "age" in which he lives, and his notion of *tian* 天 reflects this sensitivity.

The meaning of *tian* 天 in classical China ranges from anthropomorphic to naturalistic. Mencius exercises the full range of the term's meaning: from the increasingly eulogistic "heaven" that grants good fortune or calamity, to the meteorological "sky" above.[1] Robert Eno finds that, in the *Mencius*, the term *tian* "varies with particular fluidity according to the instrumental context in which [it is] discussed."[2] There is no univocal sense in which the term is used. One aspect of *tian* that Mencius wishes to be clear about, however, is that it "does not speak" (*buyan* 不言);[3] he thus distinguishes himself from the more anthropomorphic Mozi, who contends that *tian* does speak and is clear (*ming* 明) in its pronouncements.[4]

Mencius employs a different vocabulary when he discusses the role of *tian* in human affairs, a vocabulary that suggests a sociological rather than an anthropomorphic understanding. Instead of expressing an aspiration (*zhi* 志), as Mozi contends,[5] *tian* for Mencius is manifested through "occurrences and events" (*xingyushi* 行與事) in the world.[6] Rather than ascribe an anthropomorphic "purpose" to *tian*, Mencius locates *tian* beyond any purposive agency: "What is done without a doer is *tian*."[7] For Mencius, what *tian* "allows" to occur (*shou* 受) is identical to what people themselves allow to occur.[8] Quoting the *Book of Documents*, he explains that "what the people see and hear are the eyes and ears of *tian*."[9] In the *Mencius*, *tian* denotes in part an intangible yet manifest aspect of societal experience and sentiment, something like the "age" in which one lives or the "general conditions of the times." Thus understood, *tian* has the "propensity" (*shi* 勢) to condition the possibilities of experience. In keeping with a mainstream Warring States cosmology, however, such propensity does not reduce to the kind of causal agency that Mozi ascribes to it.

The Guodian strips assist us in reconstructing this aspect of *tian* 天 in the *Mencius*. One document in particular, *Failure and Success According to the Times* (*Qiongdayishi* 窮達以世), expresses a parallel interest and resonates linguistically with the *Mencius*. The document opens with the following observation:

> There is *tian* and there are people. Between them there is a difference. By examining the difference one understands how to proceed. If you have the people but not the right "age" [*shi* 世], even those of quality will not proceed effectively. Yet if the age is right, what difficulties could there be?[10]

The theme of *Failure and Success According to the Times* is echoed in the *Mencius* in an exchange between Mencius and Song Goujian, a fellow scholar-official (*shi* 士) who is traveling from state to state in the hope of influencing the rulers of the day. Mencius advises:

> Hold character in high regard and take pleasure in appropriateness, then you will be content. Scholar-officials do not abandon appropriateness in times of failure [*qiong* 窮], nor depart from the most productive course in times of success [*da* 達]. By not abandoning appropriateness in times of failure, scholar-officials consummate themselves. By not departing from the most productive course in times of success, the people are not deprived of a focus for their hopes. When the ancients realized their aspirations [*zhi* 志], the people were further enriched. When they did not realize their aspirations, they cultivated their persons and presented these to the age [*shi* 世]. In times of failure, they improved their character in solitude. In times of success, they improved the world together with others.[11]

In both of these texts, failure and success (*qiongda* 窮達) depend on circumstances beyond the aspirations (*zhi* 志) of particular persons. If an "age" is not ripe for the realization of certain aspirations, the holders of those aspirations bring them to fruition in their personal characters and present themselves as models to their wayward times.

There is further resonance between the *Mencius* and *Failure and Success According to the Times*. Mencius, reflecting on the failure of Duke Ping of Lu to call upon his own services, relates:

> When a person proceeds effectively [*xing* 行] something facilitates it. When a person is hindered, something interrupts it. Proceeding effectively and being hindered are not within a person's control [*neng* 能]. That it did not come to pass [*yu* 遇] that I would meet the Marquis of Lu is a matter of *tian* 天.[12]

Mencius' language in this context echoes that of *Failure and Success According to the Times*, which states that "What comes to pass [*yu* 遇] and what does not is a matter of *tian* 天."[13] Given the content of *Failure and Success According to the Times*, we can understand Mencius to be referring to the "age" (*shi* 世) when he speaks of *tian* as hindering or facilitating what "comes to pass."

Pang Pu, reading the Guodian strips, asks what it means to consider the "age" in discussing *tian* and draws the following conclusion:

> [*Tian* 天 in these strips] is a force beyond the human being that the human being can neither anticipate nor control—yet must accept. It is an opportunity that comes and goes or appears in cycles, and it is the conditions under which we prosper if we grasp it and decline if we lose it, but we cannot command it. It is an environment people yield to fearfully and rely on to survive. Hence, what was then called "*tian*" took on a special meaning. Using modern concepts, it is actually the social context, social conditions, social opportunities, or simply put, social forces.[14]

Broadly speaking, *tian* denotes the forces and conditions under which all things proceed, forces and conditions either favorable or unfavorable to human aspirations. In the *Mencius*, these "forces" include the social, political, and economic conditions of the "age." Such conditions are established through the policies of rulers; thus, those who would aspire to change these conditions counsel to those in power. In the *Mencius*, it is the function of the scholar-official (*shi* 士) to aspire for such change. Asked what the business of the scholar-official is, Mencius responds with only one word: aspiration (*zhi* 志).[15] Below we consider how Confucians of the Si-Meng lineage understand the role of aspiration in the advancement of the human way (*rendao* 人道). Here the focus will remain on how the scholar-official serves in the *Mencius* to influence the "age" by encouraging rulers to adopt associated humanity (*ren* 仁) in their persons and thereby bring about the conditions for the possibility of that advancement.

Scholar-officials in the *Mencius* encourage rulers to transform the predominant conditions through the rulers' own "force of character" (*de* 德) as persons of authoritative humanity. Rulers are to become what Mencius calls "parents of the people" and thereby evoke spontaneous popular sentiment and unforced order among their constituents—much as parents evoke spontaneous affection and deference in their children.[16] Mencius recommends associated humanity for achieving political legitimacy and characterizes anything short of this as untenable. He quotes Confucius and alludes to the *Book of Songs*:

> Confucius said, "Associated humanity [*ren* 仁] undermines the formation of a social mass. If the ruler of a state favors associated humanity, there will be no opposition in the world." These days, the desire to have no opposition in the world through means other than associated humanity is like taking hold of something hot without having cooled it in water. The *Book of Songs* asks: "Who can take hold of something hot without first cooling it in water?"[17]

Mencius insists that there is no genuine political legitimacy short of that arising from a ruler's own associated humanity. This is consistent with what Mencius identifies as a "common saying," one that captures the Confucian way of bringing about a harmonious social order: "Empire, State, Family: the empire is rooted in the state, the state is rooted in the family, and the family is rooted in the person."[18] On the authority of Confucius, Mencius maintains that in the sociopolitical realm "there are only these two ways: associated humanity and coercion [*buren* 不仁]."[19] In the *Mencius*, the coercive way of exercising power is set in opposition to associated humanity on numerous occasions, and the former is presented as bound to fail.[20]

Mencius claims that associated humanity is an honor bestowed by *tian* 天, whereas political office is an honor bestowed by people.[21] Becoming "parent to the people" and fostering associated humanity, however, have less to do with divine providence and more to do with the implementation of sound social and economic policies. In order for rulers to find themselves "without opposition in the world," Mencius proposes the elimination of duties at border stations, the remittance of property tax on local merchants and on those working public lands into production, and other measures. These economic policies, Mencius explains, will attract commerce and inspire confidence, such that "neighboring states will look up to you as a parent." And since "no one has ever succeeded in inciting children against a parent," the ruler's legitimacy is secure. That ruler is "doing the work of *tian*" (*tianshi* 天史).[22]

The establishment of favorable economic conditions is of great significance to Mencius, for this will ensure that people have "dependable feelings" (*hengxin* 恆心), which he equates with having "dependable means of support" (*hengchan* 恆產). Under such conditions, people can regulate themselves and there is no need to resort to punitive measures (*xing* 刑).[23] The fact that economic policy does the work of *tian* 天 and results in dependable feelings extends the Mencian notion that human feeling is "conferred by *tian*."[24] For Mencius economic conditions are also *tian*, and only once material needs are met will common people be in the position to develop a feeling of associated humanity. He therefore prescribes strategies to increase food production, proposing that "when food is as plentiful as fire and water, then who among the people will exhibit anything but associated humanity?"[25] Economic security is a prerequisite for the widespread transmission of this feeling: only scholar-officials, says Mencius, maintain a sense of associated humanity when economic conditions do not sponsor it.[26] Additional economic proposals aim to ensure the execution of filial piety. The ruler who is "parent to the people" does not force the people to incur debt in carrying out their filial duties.[27] Mencius therefore endorses a family-based economy proposed by King Wen, one that ensures that the material needs of elderly family members are easily provided for.[28]

So while the propensities of *tian* 天 in a given "age" are something that people must accept, this does not mean that people capitulate to conditions and abandon their aspirations for a better world—one that better facilitates productive forms of human feeling. Yet harboring such aspirations can be dangerous. In Warring States China, overt political resistance might easily result in an early death; this fact prompts the Yangists to withdraw from political life altogether and focus their efforts on self-preservation. Mencius has a different attitude toward effecting change in the face of predominant forces (*tian*). As noted above, he recommends that scholar-officials focus on the cultivation of their persons and bide their time. He recommends a similar program to the rulers of oppressed states. He explains:

> When the world is on the most productive course, those of little character submit to those of great character, and those of little quality submit to those of great quality. When the world departs from the most productive course, then the small submit to the big, and the weak submit to the strong. Both of these are instances of "prevalent social, economic, and political forces" [*tian* 天].[29] Those who accord with *tian* are preserved, while those who resist it are annihilated.

Duke Jing of Qi said, "Since we are not in the position to command [*ling* 令], and cannot endure what is commanded of us [*ming* 命], we are cut off from events." In tears he gave his daughter in marriage to Wu.

Currently, small states emulate large states, and yet are humiliated having to endure what is commanded of them. This is like young people feeling humiliated in emulating their predecessors. If one is humiliated in this manner, it is best to emulate King Wen. Emulating King Wen, a large state given five years and a small state given seven will surely bring about order in the world.[30]

Mencius identifies King Wen with the establishment of social, economic, and political conditions that commence an "age" in which human experience flourishes without coercion through the dynamics of associated humanity. The rulers of oppressed states are encouraged to begin the process of bringing this about by initiating certain economic reforms in their own principalities and by providing models of filial piety and personal cultivation in their own persons. Together, these will be the "conditions" under and the "root" from which this sociopolitical order will emerge. Having established these, rulers are to exercise patience and allow time for the influence of their characters (*de* 德) to take effect on the "age."

Mencius considers this a long-term project.[31] Rulers must work within conditions as they are, and even their best efforts may not yield results in their present generations. Mencius relates this process to Duke Wen, who feels threatened by the rising state of Qi:

> If you do your best [*shan* 善], then among your descendents in a future generation there is sure to be a king. All the exemplary person can do in commencing an enterprise is to pass on an inheritance. When it comes to bringing that enterprise to successful completion, this is a matter of *tian* 天. What can you do about Qi? You can only do your best.[32]

Tian as "forces" beyond the ruler's individual efforts must cooperate in bringing about a better world; in order for something to come to pass, the "age" (*shi* 世) must be right.

Mencius feels that his time is one in which things ought to come to pass with greater ease (*yiran* 易然) by virtue of the "propensity" (*shi* 勢) of prevailing circumstances.³³ Mencius sees his world as one that is tired of coercive forms of government and ripe for the advent of a more dynamic form of government through associated humanity (*ren* 仁):

> In the present time [*jinzhishi* 今之時], if a state of ten thousand chariots were to bring about order through associated humanity, the people would rejoice as if being freed from hanging by their heels. With half the effort of the ancients, twice as much can be achieved: such is what is possible in these times.³⁴

Mencius sees promise in his age, but while his efforts as counselor fail, his frustration grows. After failing to influence the course of affairs at Qi, he confides to Chongyu:

> It must be that *tian* 天 does not yet want to bring about peaceful order in the world. If there was a desire for peaceful order in this present age [*jinzhishi* 今之世], then who is there apart from us to bring it about? Of course I am frustrated.³⁵

As James Legge notes, Mencius perseveres in public council for fifteen years beyond this episode before finally retiring to compose his written works.³⁶

Mencius understands the history of human achievement as cyclical. He calculates that the world gives birth to a king in intervals of roughly five hundred years, and he says that "ages" take their names from these kings.³⁷ The more prolific sage (*shengren* 聖人) influences a hundred generations.³⁸ The influence of both the exemplary person and the petty person wane after five generations.³⁹ Mencius employs the "proximity" motif in discussing the influence of the sage. That Confucius is so proximate yet Mencius' age so troubled is a fact that Mencius registers with incredulity, displeasure, and palpable frustration:

> From the time of Confucius to the present is just over one hundred years. We are not yet far from the age of the sage. And we are so near [*jin* 近] to the place that he lived. And yet there is no one. Very well then, there is no one.⁴⁰

However optimistic Mencius is about the capacity of the human disposition, he realizes that *tian* poses a formidable constraint upon the aspirations of humans to advance their way.

The Conditions for Political Legitimacy

Regardless of the constraints posed by *tian* 天, the most productive course (*dao* 道) is one that can always be advanced. On all levels of experience—social, economic, political, biological, spiritual, and so on—there are conditions that provide the baseline against which human progress itself is measured. The Guodian strips suggest that, like *tian*, the notion of "conditions" (*ming* 命) in the Si-Meng school has a rather pronounced social dimension. This is evident in the *Honoring Virtue and Appropriateness* (*Zundeyi* 尊德義) document, wherein the notion of *ren* 人 itself is plausibly understood as "society." The text reports:

> One understands oneself by understanding "society" [*ren* 人]. By understanding society, one understands "conditions" [*ming* 命]. By understanding conditions, one understands the most productive course [*dao* 道]. By understanding the most productive course, one understands how to proceed effectively [*xing* 行]. There are those who understand themselves but do not understand conditions. There are none, however, who understand conditions but fail to understand themselves.[41]

One understands oneself in relation to the possibilities of one's "age" by understanding the "forces" that shape one's historical moment. Once these are recognized, one understands the "conditions" under which humans must make their way. With such an understanding, one can proceed effectively within the given circumstances.

Bringing the social dimension of *tian* 天 and *ming* 命 into the foreground is helpful as we establish the broader significance of these terms, particularly as they are used to express the notion of a socially conferred political mandate. Tang Junyi describes the notion of "*tian*'s charge" (*tianming* 天命) as a negotiation between *tian* and the human being in "their mutual influence and response, their mutual giving and receiving."[42] In the *Mencius*, the potential effect of virtuous character (*de*

德) on society speaks to the "mutual influence" that Tang Junyi calls our attention to. "Forces" (*tian* 天) may begin as constraints, but within these constraints is an opportunity to establish an efficacious character with the power to sway political sentiment and alter "conditions" (*ming* 命) in a favorable manner. If this is accomplished, then conditions come to sponsor the person in the form of *tian*'s charge. The political "mandate" is a negotiation between the propensity of "forces" and the efficacious character of the ruler, a result of their "mutual giving and receiving." This is in keeping with the cosmological assumptions proposed here in chapter one.

Thus understood, *tian*'s charge bears little resemblance to a divinely conferred "mandate" to rule, a point that Tang Junyi wishes to make clear. He explains that the ruler's cultivation of personal character (*de* 德) precedes the mandate to rule, and it remains a necessary condition for political legitimacy for as long as the mandate obtains. As Tang Junyi sees it:

> [*Tian*'s charge] in its true meaning, is therefore the starting point of something to be done, rather than the terminal point of something already accomplished.[43]

In the *Mencius*, the conditions that facilitate moral and political legitimacy are brought about as a result of the associated humanity (*ren* 仁) exhibited by the ruler. Through the personal cultivation of associated humanity, the ruler's "force of character" (*de* 德) becomes authoritative in its influence on the sociopolitical realm: "forces" then turn in favor of the ruler. This is an achievement, but as a "mandate" it is sufficient only so long as the ruler sustains a root in filial piety and continues to govern through associated humanity.

The account of this dynamic in the *Zhongyong* presents as full an explanation as a Si-Meng Confucian could ever desire, satisfying four important standards of evidence—historical example, botanical analogy, appeal to the *Book of Songs*, and words attributed to Confucius himself:

> Confucius said, "Shun was tremendously filial. His character [*de* 德] rendered him a sage, and his honor rendered him a son of *tian* 天. His wealth encompassed all within the four seas. Temple sacrifices were made to him, preserving his reputation.

Hence, with great character one is sure to attain some status, enjoy some prosperity, succeed in achieving a name for oneself, and secure a long life.

So it is with the generation of things by *tian*. Bounty is awarded by virtue of the "capacity" or "wood-stuff" [*cai* 材] of a thing. Thus, well-planted trees are strengthened and those ready to fall are left to collapse.

The *Book of Songs* say, "Admirable and pleasant the exemplary person, character clearly displayed, treating all people appropriately, *tian* grants its favor. Protection, assistance, and favorable conditions [*ming* 命]—from *tian* are these extended." Thus, those of character are certain to enjoy favorable conditions.[44]

To become an exemplary leader, one must first become a person of character. To remain a person of character, one must remain "firmly planted" in the soil that nourishes that state of character; hence, "Shun was tremendously filial." In response to such character, *tian* extends its favor in the form of conditions favorable to continued political success. Favorable conditions are withdrawn only with the moral decline of the ruler to whom the mandate to rule has been charged. In the Mencian framework, it seems in large part to be *tian* as "social forces," "economic conditions," or "the eyes and ears of the people" that bestows the favorable conditions (*ming* 命) that sponsor the legitimacy of a political figure.

The Conditions for Human Achievement

Tian 天 and *ming* 命 denote much more than "social forces and conditions," but they retain the transactional aspect of the "social" across the range of their extended meanings. Judging by the *Dispositions Arise from Conditions* document, "conditions" denote any phenomena encountered in the course of emerging in formative transaction with the world—a broad notion, indeed. Confucians defer to the causal efficacy of the innumerable formative conditions that shape experience. Confucius himself "stands in awe of conditions" and seeks to "understand conditions."[45] Mencius also relates the following about Confucius:

Confucius said, "There are conditions [*ming* 命]." He advanced by way of ritual propriety and retreated by way of appropriateness. Whether he attained his objectives or not he said, "There are conditions."[46]

The contributions of Tang Junyi assist us in understanding *ming* 命 in such contexts not as terminal or ineluctable, but rather as in the political context: "the starting point of something further to be done."

The Confucian notion of pressing forward while accepting conditions, however, has from early on been mistaken for a "fatalist" doctrine. Mozi perceived it as such: he claimed that the "fatalism" of the Confucians amounted to moral passivity and therefore threatened to "overthrow appropriateness in the world."[47] Mozi's reasoning is easily understood. In a descriptive sense, *ming* 命 does refer to objective conditions.[48] These conditions are often not negotiable, as when Confucius attributes Boniu's terminal illness to *ming*, adding that "there is nothing we can do,"[49] or when Sima Niu, lamenting that he has no brothers, is reminded by Zixia that "in death and in life circumstances [*ming* 命] apply."[50] Circumstances are "objective" in such cases, but fatalism does not necessarily follow from this. It is possible that Mozi was aware of Confucians who exhibited a particularly passive attitude toward conditions, and that he considered these thinkers "fatalistic." It is difficult to know for certain. Tang Junyi believes that Mozi was "attacking an imaginary Confucianism, a product of his own mind."[51]

However one understands the "fatalism" question, it is only indirectly registered in the *Mencius*. This debate gives way to a more subtle discussion of what actually concerned the Si-Meng Confucians: the relationship between "conditions" (*ming* 命) and the formation of a disposition (*xing* 性). This is the theme of *Dispositions Arise from Conditions*. Having highlighted the social dimension of "conditions," we are better prepared to address once again the transactional relationship between these two notions in the Si-Meng school.

As suggested in *Dispositions Arise from Conditions*, just to be disposed is to be shaped in predilection and possessed of some measure of efficacy (*shan* 善) in relation to the world. As such, a disposition is the expression of a limit. Predilections and efficacy take shape in the process of encountering "conditions" as one emerges into the world. This formative transaction is registered through feeling (*xin* 心). The emotional content (*qing* 情) of a disposition—pleasure, anger, grief, and sadness—

indicate emerging habits that define the parameters of one's personal character. "Emotions" attest to the limits of predilection and efficacy in relation to conditions as they stand. They are also expressions of the aspiration to go beyond them.[52]

One's disposition to feel and act is not wholly dictated by conditions, however, as a "fatalist" might contend. Mencius is very clear about this. While everything is shaped by conditions, one does not capitulate to conditions completely. He explains:

> There is nothing that is without conditions [*feiming* 非命]. One goes along with and accommodates only those conditions that are proper to accept; thus, one who comes to understand conditions will not go on standing beneath a wall on the verge of collapse. One who dies after bringing to optimal term the most productive course [*dao* 道] has lived within conditions properly; one who dies in fetters and chains has not.[53]

This statement can be understood in a number of ways. In the political realm, one resists the oppressive conditions of an age by cultivating one's person in solitude if need be. This is to break free from the "fetters and chains" of an oppressive political system. Likewise, in the moral realm, if one fashions one's disposition through education and effort and resists the "desire" (*yu* 欲) for things "external" (*wai* 外) that might otherwise condition one's predilections, one has broken free of the "fetters and chains" that work to hamper genuine, moral development. However the above passage is understood, it states unequivocally that "conditions" (*ming* 命) are *not* wholly determinative of the human experience. Human effort has a role to play.

This is where "aspiration" enters the picture. The dynamic between the conditions of the "age" and the aspiration (*zhi* 志) of the scholar-official is like that between the initial human disposition (*renxing* 人性), also shaped by conditions, and one's effort to get the most out of this inheritance through the extension of feeling and human virtue. Both dynamics reflect the manner in which human aspiration contributes to the advancement of the most productive course (*dao* 道) over and against conditions. Humans, one might say, "conspire" with existing conditions while always "aspiring" to surpass their limits.[54]

The human virtues consist of "getting the most" (*jin* 盡) out of conditions as they present themselves. The term *jin* is closely associated with ritual propriety (*li* 禮), particularly with the burial rites and sacrifices due to one's parents. The death of one's parents is an occasion for "getting the most out of oneself" (*zijin* 自盡) according to Mencius,[55] and Confucius suggests the same.[56] The relationship between the notion of "getting the most out of oneself" and the funeral rites provides insight into the participatory and emergent nature of all human virtues in the Mencian tradition. Since the "substance" of the four human virtues is not given, Mencius, like Confucius, does not provide any definitive, once-and-for-all statement of what constitutes wisdom, associated humanity, appropriateness, or ritual propriety. There is much discussion, however, about rites associated with the death of one's parents. As a subset of practices that fall under the virtue of ritual propriety (*li* 禮), these rites provide insight into the nature of human virtue generally. By looking at the rites of sacrifice, we come to recognize the dynamic by which the human way itself is advanced.

Human Virtue in the Sacrifices

Recall that, for Mencius, spontaneous reactions at the level of feeling (*xin* 心) historically gave rise to the burial rites of parents; henceforth, these genuinely integrated (*cheng* 誠) expressions of human feeling were codified into ritual propriety.[57] Echoing the Mencian notion of ritual propriety, the *Summary of Sacrifices* (*Jitong*) chapter of the *Book of Rites* submits:

> Of all the ways to effect order among people, there is none more imperative than ritual propriety. There are five kinds of ritual practice, and there is none more important than sacrifices. Sacrifice is not something that comes to a person from outside [*wai* 外]. Focused in the person [*zizhong* 自中] it emerges, being born in feeling [*xin* 心]. When feelings are moved, they are given expression in ritual propriety. Hence, only persons of quality are able to "get the most" [*jin* 盡] out of ritual propriety's significance.[58]

In coming to understand the Mencian notion of emergent human virtues and how these relate to "getting the most" out of one's capacities and feelings, there are points to be drawn from this explanation of ritual propriety.

First, the relationship between ritual propriety and social order is not an instrumental relationship whereby ritual is an "external" (*wai* 外) means by which some antecedent discharge of feeling is directed to a desired end. Confucians like Mencius and the author of the *Summary of Sacrifices* do not consider human beings to be driven by a preexisting set of unruly desires in need of sublimation through ritual propriety, as Xunzi later surmises.[59] Ritual propriety is instead a quality conferred upon genuinely expressed feeling, not a device for the sublimation of some errant feeling. Confucius here concurs. When Confucius says that "deference without ritual propriety is lethargy, and caution without ritual propriety is timidity,"[60] ritual propriety denotes the productive form of expressing deference and caution. Deference, in other words, is not a result produced through the instrumental application of "ritual form" upon a human lethargy that is already present; instead, as Confucius elsewhere says, "deference brings one closer to ritual propriety."[61]

Thus, as a human virtue, ritual propriety is an end as much as a means. Rather than being a tool for the purpose of maintaining social order, ritual propriety is both the expression of well-integrated feeling as well as the form in which an optimal level of self-expression is integrated in a productive, meaningful, and qualitatively "human" way. Within the framework of a *qi* 氣 cosmology, there is no sharp distinction between ritual form and its function. Ritual form is a pattern or configuration that enables the optimal expression of qualitative energies (*qi* 氣) by fitting human experiences and actions productively into the patterns and dispositions of the environing world. Ritual propriety is itself a "disposition" that facilitates the discharge of qualitative energies and emotions.

The account given of the generation of ritual form in the *Zuozhuan* locates it within a *qi* 氣 cosmology:

> Ritual form involves three things: the regulative patterning of *tian* 天, the appropriate fit with earth, and the most effective course of behavior for human beings. People genuinely model themselves with respect to the regulative patterning of *tian* and earth. They model what in *tian* is clear, and accord with the dispositions [*xing* 性] of earth. They live by the six *qi* 氣 and

have use of the five phases. *Qi* generates the five flavors, manifests itself in the five colors, and displays itself in the five tones. In excess these qualities confuse and disorder, and people lose their dispositions [*xing*]. Ritual form is generated to furnish [*feng* 奉][62] a disposition.[63]

Ritual forms are an embodiment of patterns generated out of environments in which productive integration is sought. In terms of *qi* cosmology, the functional dimension of ritual form is suggested in the cognate relationship it shares with the body (*ti* 體), which is also an emergent pattern shaped over the course of adjustment to an environment and also filled with configurative energy.[64] As Peter Boodberg observes, "ritual form" and "body" are the only two common terms that share the "vase" phonetic.[65] Both are "container" notions, and as such, both are "shapes" that configure qualitative energies.

For the Confucian, the ideal ritual-based society is one in which people participate in the accreted significance of human experience by contributing their energies to the performance of the rituals that have come to embody, express, and distinguish that experience. Ritual form, in turn, shapes the participants as qualitatively "human" by facilitating the transmission of feelings that have come, over the course of time, to be deemed "human." More is involved than an outward display of behavior. Ritual propriety is a constitutive disposition, both habitual and attitudinal. As a disposition, it is an achievement carved into the world and is maintained only through the focused purposes of those so disposed. Mencius explains how the ancients regarded ritualized behavior and thereby prescribes that it be adopted at the level of a disposition, thus making it constitutive of a person's character (*de* 德):

> Yao and Shun had it as their disposition [*xing* 性]. Tang and Wu reverted back to it. When movements and countenance, all around, become completely focused in ritual propriety; this is the highest concentration of character [*de* 德].[66] Mourning in sorrow for the deceased: not something done for the living. Advancing in virtue without wavering: not done to secure emolument. Invariably standing by one's word: not done to render one's conduct proper. Exemplary persons proceed by this standard [*fa* 法], and simply leave the rest to conditions [*ming* 命].[67]

One's character (*de* 德) indicates the integrity of one's conduct; this is to say that moral and ritualized actions, unmediated by external desires or ends, proceed directly from a disposition that shapes habitual proclivities to behave in such a manner. Exemplary persons aspire to cultivate themselves according to this "standard" of character, regardless of conditions (*ming* 命).

Character is important to the Si-Meng Confucian. The formation of one's character in habitual conduct is the theme of the recently recovered *Five Modes of Conduct* (*Wuxing* 五行) document. The Mencian approach to the internal/external (*nei/wai* 內外) dimensions of cultivating sprouts of virtue into habitudes is subtler than that of the *Five Modes of Conduct*, suggesting that the *Five Modes of Conduct* is a most likely earlier statement of an "internalist" position on these matters.[68] Still, the *Five Modes of Conduct* anticipates the Mencian notion of integrating virtue into one's character through the development of a disposition as opposed to simply "practicing" (*xing* 行) virtuous acts. The text begins:

> Associated humanity taking shape [*xing* 形] on the inside is called the formation of character [*dezhixing* 德之行]; when it does not take shape on the inside it is called simply practice.[69] Appropriateness taking shape on the inside is called the formation of character; when it does not take shape on the inside it is called simply practice. Ritual propriety taking shape on the inside is called the formation of character; when it does not take shape on the inside it is called simply practice. Wisdom taking shape on the inside is called the formation of character; when it does not take shape on the inside it is called simply practice. Sagacity taking shape on the inside is called the formation of character; when it does not take shape on the inside it is called simply practice.[70]

The *Five Modes of Conduct* is concerned with the "internal" formation of habitudes that become constitutive of character.

In the *Mencius*, character (*de* 德) becomes less an "internal" and more a "transactional" notion. Character exhibits its influences in tension with both conditions (*ming* 命) and the characters of others. In the *Mencius*, the term "character" refers primarily to that "force of character" that in the *Analects* is likened to a wind (*feng* 風) that in the absence of coercion transforms the characters of others.[71] Mencius cites this saying of Confucius specifically in describing the influential character of those who wholeheartedly participate in the funeral rites of their parents.[72] The "transforming influence of character" is the prevailing sense of character (*de*) in the *Mencius*.[73]

The "force of character" that Mencius recognizes in those who execute the sacrificial ritual with integrity is one that arises not from "within" the person but rather "in relation" through a form of well-integrated personality associated with filial piety. Family devotion and deference to seniors are identified as the sources of ritual propriety in the *Zhongyong*.[74] When it comes to the burial rites, mourning observances, and seasonal sacrifices to one's parents, these are all rooted in filial piety, which the *Summary of Sacrifices* identifies as the "storehouse" (*chu* 處) of the devotion required to ritually maintain the filial relationship beyond the parent's death.[75]

Just as the "force of character" of a ruler is always in tension with the "mandate" (*ming* 命) and thus, in Tang Junyi's words, "a mutual giving and receiving," the force of character of those who perform sacrifices with integrity can also be understood as in tension with conditions (*ming* 命). Sacrifices boldly deny the finality of mortal death, an irrevocable *ming*. They maintain the filial relationship regardless. Sacrifice is an example of what it means to "get the most" (*jin* 盡) out of experience in spite of the constraints posed by conditions. The performance of the burial, mourning, and sacrificial rites is identified in the *Summary of Sacrifices* as "getting the most out of one's self" (*zijin* 自盡), which is precisely what Mencius considers so important on the occasion of the death of a parent.[76] These three rites allow one to "get the most" out of the parent/child relationship by enabling the most complete expression of one's filial feeling, even as conditions conspire to dissolve their significance.

To maintain and to act upon human feelings when circumstances conspire to undermine them is a great thing. As Mencius says:

> While they live, caring for parents is not to be considered a great thing. Only when that care accompanies them into death is it to be considered a great thing.[77]

In performing the sacrificial rites, the parent, the surviving offspring, and the relationship become sanctified as qualitatively human, over and against what is given by conditions (*ming* 命). As Mencius says, the human is not confined to "die in fetters and chains" by capitulating to each and every condition.[78] This would factor out the tremendous forces of spirit, feeling, and aspiration through which humans engage the world most deeply.[79]

In terms of its religious function, the key to efficacy in ritual is integrity. Ritual must be performed with reverence and genuine feeling. For this reason, it is important that royalty personally participate in ritual observances rather than doing so through emissaries. The *Summary of Sacrifices* explains why this is so:

> It is to give personal expression to their integrity and sincerity [*chengxin* 誠信]. Integrity and sincerity is called "getting the most" [*jin* 盡]. "Getting the most" is called reverence. With reverence and "getting the most," one is able to attend to the spiritual and the holy. Such is the way of sacrifice.[80]

For the Confucian, personal integrity and reverence in the performance of a sacrifice are its most vital elements; in fact, these are deemed even more vital than the presence of the spirits themselves. As the *Analects* say:

> "Sacrifice as though present" is considered to mean "sacrifice to spirits as though spirits are present." But Confucius said: "If I myself do not participate in the sacrifice, it is as though there were no sacrifice."[81]

When it comes to sacrifices, Confucius is mainly interested in the "human" dimension of the experience. While he advocates reverence in sacrifice, the realm of the spirits is among the topics that he "did not discuss."[82] Asked directly by Zilu how to attend to the spirits, Confucius responds, "Not yet able to attend to other people, how can you attend to the spirits?"[83] In one form or another, the priority is always placed on the human dimension as the source of religious meaning.

Mozi considers the Confucian attitude towards sacrifice to be confused: Confucians reverently maintain the sacrifices and yet toward the spirits they are seemingly agnostic. Mozi's own argument for belief in the spirits in his "Clarifying Ghosts" (*Minggui*) chapter is itself a curious mixture. The bulk of his "demonstration" consists of detailed appeals to the written records of various ghostly encounters. Not surprisingly, however, the underlying thrust of his argument is based on his utilitarian principle of benefit (*li* 利). Belief in the existence of retributive spirits, Mozi reasons, will regulate human conduct, and even if such ghosts do not exist, the belief in their presence at the sacrifices will at least serve the purpose of "bringing people together in a pleasant group and generating intimacy among the village community."[84]

As A. C. Graham points out, the Mohists are in a sense less "religious" than those they denounce as skeptics.[85] The Confucian approach to the sacrifices, unlike that of the Mohist, is not instrumental in any bald, utilitarian sense. For the Confucian, sacrifices facilitate the enhancement of one's particular experience by integrating it into an order that both elevates and sanctifies that experience. Like the peppercorn in the pot of soup, when one participates reverently in a sacrifice one is both beneficiary of and contributor to an aesthetic order in which the uniqueness and significance of one's life become more pronounced. Establishing continuity between oneself and one's deceased family members is a uniquely human mode of generating meaning. The religious dividend of sacrifice is that the significance of a human life is enhanced through its sincere performance. Whether this entails the existence of ghosts is beside the point. Confucian spirituality has more to do with the depth and width of one's felt connections and with the formation of a disposition that maximizes this experience.[86]

As a human virtue, ritual propriety (*li* 禮) is something that transforms the human experience; it reconfigures one's very disposition in the world. Humans are made through ritual, but this is accomplished neither through a coercive process like that of "making" cups and bowls from a willow tree, nor through a self-conscious process like that of putting a doctrine into practice. Ritual makes humans by shaping their dispositions. When this is achieved, and ritual propriety is carried through with integrity (*cheng* 誠), there is a real elevation of felt experience. Perhaps all of the Mencian "four sprouts" await this kind of development. Just as the establishment of sacrifices reflect one's "getting the most" out of filial affection, the "fruit" of all human virtues emerge into experience as people find communicable forms through which to articulate, as best they can, the amorphous imperatives of feeling. One wonders if there is any limit to what it means to "become human," thus understood. Mencius, at least, does not appear to place any ceiling on the human capacity.

Aspiration and the Human Way

As suggested above, Mencius allows for discretion in determining which conditions (*ming* 命) are to be regarded as productive and which are to be regarded as unproductive to the advancement of the human way (*rendao* 人道). Since any disposition "arises from conditions," this discretionary prerogative has bearing on the definition of a disposition. Not all conditions deserve equal status in determining what constitutes a "human" disposition. Mencius explains:

> The relationships between mouth and taste, eyes and color, ears and sound, nose and smell, and the four limbs and physical repose: these are a matter of disposition [*xing* 性], and something about them has the quality of conditions [*ming* 命]. Exemplary persons do not consider these as their disposition. The relationships between associated humanity and the parent/child relation, appropriateness and the ruler/subject relation, ritual propriety and the guest/host relation, wisdom and the person of quality, and the sage and the course of *tian* 天: these are a matter of conditions [*ming*], and something about them has the quality of a disposition [*xing*]. Exemplary persons do not consider these as conditions.[87]

Mencius is interested in the definition of a "human" disposition that goes beyond those traits that all Homosapiens share by virtue of biological conditioning. Distinctly "human" traits, here listed as five, correspond with the four Mencian sprouts plus sagacity, a listing also encountered in the recently unearthed *Five Modes of Conduct* document. Experience in the world "conditions" these five modes of conduct, although not in a biological sense; instead, the historical work of sages, family affection, and a Confucian education condition them. Exemplary persons, rather than identify their dispositions with factors that condition animals generally, consider this historical and cultural set of conditions to be formative of their dispositions. In doing so, exemplary persons estimate themselves as distinctly "human."

Mencius, like Confucius, respects the power of conditions generally to limit the possibilities of human achievement. Neither of these thinkers, however, is "fatalist" in the manner that Mozi contends. For Mencius, humans find a way of asserting their aspirations in the face of any and all conditions. Persons who aspire to extend the human way will "take their stands" (*li* 立) within conditions as they present themselves. They will aspire to get the most out of what is available. As a corollary, extending human experience will mean getting the most out of the feelings (*xin* 心) concomitant with their dispositions. To find optimal expression for these feelings in the face of given conditions is to perform a role of enormous spiritual significance to Mencius, one that he identifies with *tian* 天. Mencius says:

> Getting the most out of one's feelings is to realize one's disposition [*xing* 性]. To realize one's disposition, one then realizes *tian*. If one maintains one's feelings and nurtures one's disposition, one thereby does the work of *tian*. Neither premature death nor long life should cause one to be of two minds about this; one should cultivate one's person and await the consequences, and thereby take one's stand [*li* 立] within the given conditions [*ming* 命].[88]

The ability of a person to flourish within conditions as they stand reflects the quality of "integration" (*cheng* 誠) that is initially developed in the *Mencius* and is refined in the *Zhongyong*. The *Zhongyong* begins with the premise that "What *tian* conditions is a disposition" (*tianmingzhiweixing* 天命之謂性),[89] and what *tian* "mandates" in this instance also has the quality of what Tang Junyi describes as "the starting point of something to be done, rather than the terminal point of something already accomplished."[90] Hence the *Zhongyong* states that dispositions are to be furthered along (*jianxing* 建性) and the most productive course for a disposition cultivated (*xiudao* 修道).[91] As in the *Mencius*, this involves the process of "getting the most" (*jin* 盡) out of one's initial disposition—*transforming it*—and thereby participating in the generative function of *tian* 天. The *Zhongyong* describes the process as follows:

> Only those most optimally integrated [*zhicheng* 至誠] into the world are able to get the most out of their dispositions. Once able to get the most out of one's disposition, one is then able to get the most out of the disposition of others. Once able to get the most out of the disposition of others, one is then able to get the most out of the disposition of things and events.

Once being able to get the most of the disposition of things and events, one can assist in the transforming and nourishing processes of heaven and earth [*tiandi* 天地]. Once able to assist in the transforming and nourishing processes of heaven and earth, one becomes the third member in a triad with heaven and earth.[92]

In the *Zhongyong*, those who are able to perform this function are considered the "counterparts" of *tian* 天; elsewhere, they are simply equated with *tian*.[93]

The sage performs this role, and according to Mencius, anyone can become a sage. Sagacity entails nothing more than getting the most out of one's conditions. To do this in the most familiar way is a profound human achievement: "The way of Yao and Shun is simply to be a filial family member [*xiaodi* 孝弟]."[94] For Confucians, the most noble human experiences emerge from and remain rooted in such beginnings. Given this, Yao and Shun provide a "model" (*fa* 法) for human achievement as "the supreme realization of human relationships [*renlun* 人倫]," just as the carpenter's square and compass are the "supreme realization of squares and circles."[95] Modelling the achievements of Yao and Shun does not mean replicating their relationships; rather, it means developing within one's own context one's own human relationships under conditions as they present themselves. To model Yao and Shun is to bring associated humanity to fruition in a novel way in one's own experience.

For those who hold political power, however, this is not enough. Rulers must do more: they must establish socioeconomic conditions that promote the novel expression of human experience collectively. They must bring about order without coercion by facilitating the free intercourse of associated humanity (*ren* 仁), a political model that Mencius identifies with the ancient kings. Mencius addresses rulers when he says:

> Even with the way of Yao and Shun at hand, if one does not bring about order through associated humanity, then one is unable to securely order the world. Today there are those who have feelings of associated humanity and a reputation for it, but the people do not enjoy any benefit from them. They cannot leave a model for future generations since they do not proceed

by the way of the ancient kings. Hence it is said, "Goodness is insufficient for the purpose of bringing about order; a model cannot carry itself into practice."[96]

Rulers wishing to legitimate their rule must not only tend to the cultivation of their own persons; they must also establish the socioeconomic conditions for human flourishing more generally. They must create conditions under which the human experience is allowed to emerge along its aspired way.

Confucius teaches that "it is the human that is able to extend the way [*dao* 道], not the way that is able to extend the human."[97] To be human is to actively participate in extending the way, and there is no destination antecedent to the process of extending it. In the same spirit, Mencius teaches that human virtues do not emerge (*you* 由) from outside (*wai* 外) the human experience itself.[98] Bringing human virtue to fruition (*shi* 實) is a process of nurturing, cultivating, growing, and extending human sensibilities into a world that is always in the making. This process, like any growth process, takes shape within conditions: there are conditions that hamper it and conditions that support it. The most productive course (*dao* 道) is one that makes the most out of these conditions and proceeds most fruitfully given the circumstances.

Mencius, as we have seen, is concerned that the process of becoming human does not stagnate as it makes its way forward. Hence, he disapproves of technical moralities that disengage the human experience from its lived connections at the level of feeling (*xin* 心). Feeling is vital to the nourishment of the evolving human disposition. Recall that the formation of constitutive habit at the level of feeling is what marks the progress of a disposition's growth. Feeling, as the emotional content (*qing* 情) of a disposition, defines the very character of that disposition. Dispositions take shape as feeling extends and becomes reinforced in habit, and as the parameters of a "human" disposition are defined and developed, it is the human way itself that is extended. The human way (*rendao* 人道), one might say, "feels" its way forward in the pursuit of its aspirations.

Recall also that, according to *Dispositions Arise from Conditions*, the feeling (*xin* 心) that is concomitant with an initial, emergent disposition does not have any fixed aspirations (*dingzhi* 定志) prior to the process of transacting with conditions.[99] Once human feeling comes to have its aspirations, however, these become realized through distinctly human forms of expression: poetry, literature, and ritual and musical form. The "art" that this entails is one that is reflected in the Mencian project as well. *Dispositions Arise from Conditions* relates the following:

> Generally, feelings come to have aspirations. Without them nothing is possible. People cannot carry them through in isolation, just as a mouth cannot speak in isolation. An ox born will grow. A goose born will spread its wings. It is disposition that causes this to happen. However, for a human, it is education that brings it about.[100]

> As for the way [*dao* 道], the art of feeling [*xinshu* 心術] is most important. The way has four artistic modes, and the "art of human way-making" [*rendao* 人道] is the only mode that can lay the course. The other three artistic modes only proceed on it.[101]

> In the arts of poetry, writing, and ritual and musical form, their beginnings emerge in and in each case are born of the human experience [*ren* 人]. In poetry, there is something done and it is produced. In writing, there is something done and it is recorded. In ritual and musical form, there is something done and these are established.[102]

In *Dispositions Arise from Conditions*, the process of making the human way (*rendao* 人道) is designated first among the "arts" (*shu* 術): it is the art of "feeling the human way forward." The remaining three arts are only expressions of what humans come to do through the art of feeling, the vanguard of novelty in the human experience.

Feeling, however, forges ahead only by virtue of its aspirations (*zhi* 志), which are not fixed at the start. They do come to be formed, however; for in their absence, no "human" experience is possible. Without aspirations, humans would amount to animals and merely go through their biological motions, as when oxen grow or geese spread their wings. Humans would simply be born, eat, live, and die—all without significance. But humans have more to contribute to the world than the discharge of a biological disposition. Humans, guided by feeling, proceed in the "art" of creating themselves. Even when frustrated, humans will pursue their aspirations in the face of conditions no matter how bleak. This is what Mencius stands for.

Thus, the Mencian way (*dao* 道) demands that humans aspire towards the most that they can possibly achieve. Anything short of this is unacceptable:

> Gongsun Chou said, "The way is lofty and beautiful, but to attempt it is like climbing to *tian* 天 itself; it is something that cannot be reached. Why not replace it with something people can hope to reach so they can be diligent on a daily basis?"
>
> Mencius said, "A great carpenter does not surrender the plumb line to accommodate the inept worker. Yi did not surrender the proper standards for drawing the bow to accommodate the inept archer. Exemplary persons, in drawing the bow, don't just discharge it; they seem to lower themselves respectfully, they find center on the way [*dao* 道] and take their place. Those who are able, follow them."[103]

For Mencius, maintaining the way requires positive human effort and the ability to measure up to standards that challenge the ineptitude of an age. Without such high ideals, human progress stagnates. In the passage that follows directly on that above, Mencius makes the point again:

> When the world is on the way [*dao* 道], that course inspires the person; when the world is off the way, the person aspires for that course. I have never heard of a course inspired by what people just happen to be.[104]

Becoming human is not an idle affair for Mencius, nor is it some irrevocable birthright. While one might be born under human conditions, one must maintain and extend the feelings that distinguish that disposition if one is to remain human. To remain human means keeping pace on the human way, and that way continues to advance. There are some humans whose feelings issue into aspirations for a more equitable, harmonious, and beautiful world, and like master archers or carpenters, they have already set the next standard despite the lag of their contemporaries.

Human aspirations are not realized in isolation, however, just as a mouth cannot communicate in isolation. Mencius relates that the ancient sages, in times of success, realized their aspirations by improving the world together with others. And when social forces and conditions required them to pursue their aspirations in solitude, this was done only to present themselves as inspirations to the age.[105] The Mencian way is one that emerges locally through personal cultivation and individual sagacity, but the goal is communal growth and social transformation. The society that best facilitates these goals is one governed by the free intercourse of associated humanity (ren 仁). In endorsing associated humanity, Mencius is endorsing the unhindered growth of human feeling as it proceeds from its germinal beginnings in the family. What grows from there becomes "human." As Mencius says, "associated humanity is human feeling [renxin 人心],"[106] and "associated humanity coming together in what is 'human' is called the way [dao 道]."[107] Where this way leads is the fruit of our collective, human experiences. Its quality is measured by how well we manage to integrate and transmit feeling in an evolving world in which we are already inextricably disposed.

Afterword

At the outset of this study, reference was made to a grove of trees at the temple dedicated to Mencius at Zuoxian—a grove designed to be an illustration of his vision of becoming human. Recall that at this site there stand saplings beneath magnificent, towering trees. This illustration was used to introduce the botanical metaphor and to distinguish a particularistic, more open-ended reading of becoming human from the more prevalent reading that takes *renxing* 人性 to mean "human nature" in an essentialist or teleological sense. Now having developed an alternative reading of this Mencian metaphor and having reinterpreted the notion of "human disposition" that it supports, we might reflect upon Mencian thought in light of the present.

As I began writing this book, the world changed. I watched September 11th unfold on a grainy television screen in a cramped tobacco shop west of Beijing University. It was around 10:30 at night in China. I was walking home from a restaurant. There had been a dozen or so Beijingers gathered around a television, and they pulled me in off the narrow, muddy street. "What nationality are you?" they shouted. The second tower had just fallen. The Hong Kong channel in Beijing was airing an American news station with Chinese commentary in the foreground. I was ushered to the television.

Mencius says that for each of us there is that which we cannot bear. Who among us could bear the images of that day? Who among us is that disengaged from human feeling? I told my friends in the shop how close my hometown is to New York City. I feared for my family, my friends, and my country. I struggled for the words to express these feelings. Everyone related. The commiseration in that shop was palpable. As Mencius says, such feelings manifest themselves directly in the eyes and in the face. I sensed compassion all around me. That shop was charged with deep human sympathy—an emotional force as electrifying as the thin, granular hum of the old television.

The screen held an aerial view of Manhattan engulfed in a cloud of destruction, half a world away—the word "Live" inset in the upper corner. After some time, I backed away from the screen and stepped out into the night air. I found a concrete block nearby and sat with my head in my hands. After some time, a Chinese man my age came out and placed a consoling hand on my shoulder. He mumbled something that I failed to hear, but his gesture was one of strength, comfort, and support. I looked up and gave him an appreciative nod. He said nothing more; he only tightened his grip on my shoulder as if to brace me. I will never forget that gesture.

Things have become more complicated in the aftermath of that day. We now live in a world of great moral complexity, thrust into what we are told is a new kind of war in which many more innocents have already died. Something was made clear on that day, however. The events of September 11th demonstrated how readily the world community might recognize acts that so flagrantly defy our basic standards of human feeling and conduct. In the immediate aftermath of the attacks, there was a moment in which the leaders of the world—north and south, east and west—came forth, visibly shaken, to voice their outrage, and in so doing to define themselves and their people over and against something that was clearly *not* human. That moment showed us something of the global power of human feeling, and something of the power of the Mencian vision.

This common, baseline response of outrage and compassion, however, is hardly a reason for complacency—it was not for Mencius, and it is not for us. There is an underlying tone of anxiety in the *Mencius* that suggests a fear that destructive perversity will win out despite how humans generally feel about the tragedies of innocents. We share this fear. Just because everyone would jump at the child by the well, Mencius did not consider the human prospect guaranteed in his time. A humane peace in the twenty-first century stands before us as an equally uncertain proposition.

So, how do we understand Mencius today? How do we learn from him? First of all, the central and perhaps most provocative assertion in the present study is that Mencius is not an essentialist about "human nature" in any genetic or teleological sense. While there are surely biological conditions within which humans make their way, these conditions do not provide a sufficient account of the qualitatively human experience. It is argued here that historical and cultural features serve to distinguish the human experience from that of the brute, whereas biological or genetic features alone do not do this. For Mencius, the designation "human" is forfeited when behavior violates the standards of feeling identified as "human" within the intercourse of associated life. One is not simply born human; one must *become* human and remain so in the high-minded community that maintains the distinction. This is an important dimension of Mencian thought.

For Mencius, the germs of goodness reside in family affection, but there is no human "essence" that is reliably good. The privileging of cultural over genetic conditions, and the location of the process of human becoming in particular sets of circumstances, controvert the kind of essentialism associated with such a "nature." As presented here, the human experience is a product of history, education, nurture, economics, culture, personal relationships, and focused aspirations, influences that are "accidental" rather than "essential" in any standard essentialist framework.

Mencius is not an essentialist. Those saplings in the yard of the Mencius Temple do not represent generic instances of a uniform process. Instead, they represent the potential to remake the grove in which they have "taken their stand" (*li* 立). Metaphorically, those young trees are like the young people that Confucius holds in such high esteem, for as the Master asks, "how do we know that they will not surpass our contemporaries?"[1] Mencius, like Confucius, is committed to the future and is an optimist against all odds, but he is not an essentialist about human nature.

Our hope, like his, is that our children will live in a world free from terror and oppression, a world of greater tolerance, understanding, equity, and felt connection. There are strong forces in our world that work against these ideals: terrorism is such a force, but so too are the social, political, economic, and military forces that perpetuate terrorism. Confucians recognize the power of forces in the world, but they do not capitulate to them. For the Confucian, humans have the capacity to improve human life not by virtue of what they essentially are, but rather by virtue of what they might become if they commit themselves to engaging conditions as they are met. In the Confucian world, every obstacle is a challenge and every crisis an opportunity.

I contend that rethinking the notion of "human nature" (*renxing* 人性) in the *Mencius* makes the text all the more provocative today. The process-oriented interpretation submitted here confers upon the notion of *renxing* relevance that any strict, essentialist reading cannot hope to confer. After all, if the "human" experience in the *Mencius* is understood to be fixed and essential, then it is essentially a fourth-century Confucian experience. The *Mencius* then speaks to none of us. One of the merits of Mencian thought, interpreted from a process-oriented perspective, is its capacity for renewal. Understood as a process notion, *renxing* is "transcendent" in a much more relevant sense than is its ahistorical alternative. As open-ended, the Mencian notion of *renxing* "transcends" the limits of any imperfect age. At no point does the notion of what is "human" or "civilized" become locked into an imaginary, static eternity by the ambitions of one group at a single time and in a single place. At no point can the human experience be declared finished. At no point do we exhaust our capacity to feel more deeply the values in our experience. At no point is our aspiration conquered.

As students and as educators bringing the wisdom of the *Mencius* to bear on the problems of this world, this progressive feature makes all the difference. As long as there is change and growth in the human experience, there is a need for greater integration (*cheng* 誠) and more effective (*shan* 善) transmission of our thoughts and feelings. As long as these normative measures are less than perfectly realized, every aspiration for a better world can become the next standard to which humans are challenged to rise. Mencius teaches us this. I feel that we more urgently need this teaching than we do any stale philosophy that declares humans essentially the same and essentially "good" for all time. Such a doctrine is not only inaccurate; it is really quite useless.

A more challenging, process-oriented conception of becoming human is the central contribution of the *Mencius*, and in my estimation, this is what gives the text its value for today. Mencius embodies a determination that is forever human: the determination to ameliorate conditions and to persevere against all odds. When his world shook in terror, Mencius committed himself to the steady restoration of virtues worthy of the term "Human." We would be wise to follow his lead, and after sincere national self-reflection, commit ourselves with similar resolve.

Notes

Introduction

1. Schwartz (1985) p. 175.
2. Eno (1990) p. 121.
3. Ivanhoe (1997) p. 156.
4. Graham (1989) p. 136. This is Graham's early view, which he later adjusted. See Graham (1991) p. 288.
5. James Legge recorded his visit to the Mencius Temple in 1873. See Legge (1994) vol. 2, p. 15.
6. *Mencius* 1A: 6.
7. Legge (1994) vol. 4, pp. 602–03.
8. *Zhuangzi* 47/17/41. I here adopt Richard Rutt's nuanced translation of *ji* 幾 as "process unfolding" as it is used in the *Great Commentary* of the *Book of Changes*. See Rutt (1996) p. 408.
9. *Zhuangzi* 47/18/40. Cf. Graham (2001) p. 184.
10. *Analects* 9.22.
11. Legge (1994) vol. 4, pp. 64–65.
12. *Mencius* 6A: 7.
13. *Analects* 17.9.
14. Legge (1994) vol. 4, pp. 271–73.
15. Legge (1994) vol. 4, p. 116.
16. Legge (1994) vol. 4, pp. 137, 138, 176, 177, 190–91, 201, 359.
17. Legge (1994) vol. 4, pp. 137, 138, 213, 214.
18. Legge (1994) vol. 4, p. 147.

19. Legge (1994) vol. 4, pp. 176, 177, 190, 191, 201, 217, 414.

20. Legge (1994) vol. 4, p. 334.

21. *Mencius* 6A: 8.

22. Pang (1999.2), p. 7. See also Hendricks (2000), pp. 4–5.

23. Li (2002).

24. A second version of the *Dispositions Arise from Conditions* document surfaced on the Hong Kong market in the spring of 1994. Although we are not presently certain of the latter's origin or dating, there is much similarity to the Guodian cache in physicality and content. This has prompted speculation that it comes from the same vicinity in Hubei province. In any case, the presence of two authentic versions of this document, with little variation in content, suggests that *Dispositions Arise from Conditions* was a well-established and widely circulated work in the Warring States period.

25. Pang (1999.2), pp. 8–9.

26. Tu (1999) pp. 4–6.

27. For instance, however customary it became to think of the author of the *Daodejing* (traditionally, Laozi) and the Confucians as timeless adversaries, documents unearthed at Guodian present us with the possibility that the *Daodejing* was in its earliest form *not* an anti-Confucian text. Wherever debate over this question leads, it is a jolt to our tacit understanding of the period. See Hendricks (2000) p. 13.

28. This document has been translated, interpreted, and published in English, and there has been a significant amount of scholarly activity surrounding it since the release of the text in 1998. See Hendricks (2000).

29. Chen, N. (2002) pp. 18, 36 n. 6.

30. Ding (2000) p. 394.

31. Graham (1989) p. 134.

32. For a discussion of the issues of dating and content in the *Zhongyong*, see Tu (1989) pp. 5–21. I am inclined, along with others, to understand sections of the *Zhongyong* as elaborations upon the *Mencius*. See Hall and Ames (2001) pp. 131–37.

33. Different versions of this document have been unearthed both on bamboo strip and on silk, the former at Guodian in 1993 and the latter at Mawangdui in Changxia in 1973. The bamboo manuscript dates from about 300 B.C. while the silk manuscript and an interlaced commentary date from 168 B.C.

34. Pang (1999.1), p. 32.

35. See *Mencius* 6A: 2.
36. Chen, L. (1999) p. 304.
37. Liao (1999) pp. 59–60.
38. Chen, N. (2002) p. 35.
39. *Mencius* 7B: 16 and 6A: 11.

Chapter 1. The Cosmological Background

1. "Configurative energy" is Manfred Porkert's translation. See Porkert (1974) p. 167.

2. Alan K. L. Chan also argues that coming to terms with *qi* 氣 is crucial to reconstructing the world of Mencius. Chan (2002) suggests that "one could interpret the concept of *qi* in different ways or dispute others' conceptions of it, but by the time of Mencius one could certainly not afford to ignore it" (pp. 61–62). The same applies to interpreting the *Mencius*: we might debate over how *qi* functions within the Mencian framework, but we cannot afford to ignore the notion if we wish to understand the text.

3. Legge (1994) vol. 5, pp. 573, 580–81. There are six phases of *qi* 氣 that represent three sets of correlative qualities in the *Zuozhuan*: *yin/yang*, wind/rain, and darkness/light.

4. In *Guanzi* 4.12, we read, "Where there is *qi* 氣 there is life, where there is no *qi*, there is death. What lives does so by virtue of its *qi*." See Rickett (1985) p. 216.

5. As when Mencius speaks of the effects of "calm morning *qi* 氣" and "evening *qi*" on one's moral temperament. See *Mencius* 6A: 8.

6. Sivin (1987) p. 63.

7. *Daodejing* 42.

8. *Zhuangzi* 58/22/12–13. Cf. Graham (2001) p. 160.

9. Farquhar (1994) p. 34.

10. *Zhuangzi* 3/2/4–9. Cf. Graham (2001) pp. 48–49.

11. Fingarette (1972) pp. 1–17.

12. Tu (1989) p. 9.

13. Joseph Needham was influential in the introduction of this terminology. See Needham (1956) pp. 18–26.

14. Vandermeersch (1988) p. 27.

15. Defoort (1997) p. 167.

16. Jullien (1995).

17. Ames (1983) p. 65.

18. Jullien (1995) pp. 16–17.

19. Ibid., pp. 13, 218.

20. *Mencius* 2A: 1.

21. Jullien (1995) p. 17.

22. In *Mencius* 7A: 36, Mencius, upon noting the haughty demeanor of an unfit royal son, notes succinctly: "He puts on airs (*qi* 氣) because of his position" (*juyiqi* 居移氣). Position, broadly construed, conditions the expression of *qi* 氣. The young man's circumstances give him a particular disposition and, hence, haughty affectations (*qi* 氣).

23. *Daodejing* 51.

24. *Zhouyi* 1/1. Cf. Wilhelm/Baynes (1950) p. 370.

25. *Zhouyi* 4/*Wenyan*. Cf. Wilhelm/Baynes (1950) p. 392.

26. Hall and Ames (1987) pp. 237–41.

27. *Daodejing* 10.

28. *Zhouyi* 43/10. Cf. Wilhelm/Baynes (1950) p. 318.

29. *Zhouyi* 44/12. Cf. Wilhelm/Baynes (1950) p. 324.

30. This state must be understood as "formless" relative to the "shape" that is defined in terms of the "quality" (*de* 德) of Zhuangzi's wife. The only thing that does not have "form" in a Daoist cosmology is *dao* 道.

31. *Zhuangzi* 46/18/15–19. Cf. Graham (2001) pp. 123–24.

32. Graham (1989) p. 383.

33. Ibid., p. 387.

34. Graham (1990) p. 9.

35. Ibid., p. 10. Italics added.

36. Legge (1994) vol. 5, pp. 704, 708.

37. *Mencius* 2A: 2.

38. *Mencius* 7B: 21.

39. *Mencius* 7A: 21.

40. Ibid.

41. *Mencius* 7A: 38.

42. *Zhongyong* 1.

43. The manner in which terms carry these dual connotations at once is a consequence of what Roger T. Ames has identified as the "priority of situation over agency" in classical Chinese thought. See Lau and Ames (1998), 20–22. This characteristic carries over into modern Chinese. For instance, the phrase *shangke* 上課 means both "to attend class" and "to conduct class." *Shangke* is vague as to agency; it instead refers to a situation, holding class. There are numerous examples of the primacy of situation over agency in classical Chinese.

44. Liao Mingchun makes a similar argument employing the same insights but draws a different conclusion. He submits that *shuai* 率 in the *Zhongyong* should indeed be understood as to "lead" (*chang* 長). He maintains that Zhen Xuan and Zhu Xi were the first to interpret *shuai* as to "follow" (*shun* 順) based on their understanding of the *Mencius*. For these Neo-Confucians to impute this reading to the *Zhongyong* based on their reading of the *Mencius* was a mistake, according to Liao Mingchun, and the more process-oriented *Dispositions Arise from Conditions* alerts us to this misreading of the *Zhongyong*. I maintain that Mencius and the rest of the Si-Meng authorship are quite similar in their understanding of *xing* and that *any* reading that makes *xing* merely something to "follow" in the Si-Meng school fails to do the school justice. In other words, Mencius has just as much a process-oriented understanding of *xing* as do other texts in the Si-Meng lineage. See Liao Mingchun (1999), pp. 59–60.

45. *Zhuangzi* 4/2/20. Cf. Graham (2001) p. 51.

46. *Zhuangzi* 4/2/21–22. Cf. Graham (2001) p. 51.

47. *Zhunagzi* 22/9/17. Cf. Graham (2001) p. 205.

48. *Zhuangzi* 16/6/26–27. Cf. Graham (2001) p. 86.

49. *Zhuangzi* 46–47/18/22–29. Cf. Graham (2001) pp. 124–25.

50. *Mencius* 7A: 41, 6A: 20.

51. *Zhuangzi* 3/1/43. Cf. Graham (2001) p. 47.

52. I owe the following insight to Hall and Ames. See Hall and Ames (1994) pp. 63–64. On the notion of the "tally" as a sign of "potency" (*de* 德), see also Lewis (1999) p. 30.

53. *Daodejing* 79. My rendering accords with LaFargue's and Waley's translations, both of which render *shan* 善 an active verb in this passage. See LaFargue (1992) p. 20 and Waley (1958) p. 239.

54. Those with missing body parts are most likely criminals having suffered amputation as a punishment.

55. *Zhuangzi* 14/5/51–52. Cf. Graham (2001) p. 80.

56. *Zhuangzi* 2/1/21. Cf. Graham (2001) p. 44.

57. Tang (1988) pp. 8–9.

58. Ibid. p. 10.

59. Ibid. pp. 11–12; *Daodejing* 40.

60. Cf. *Daodejing* 42.

61. *Daodejing* 11.

62. *Zhuangzi* 74/26/31–33.

63. Tang (1988) p. 16; *Daodejing* 42, 39.

64. Tang (1988) p. 10.

65. Whitehead (1978) pp. 21–22.

66. *Mencius* 7A: 4.

67. One of the earliest, explicit discussions of linear causality in China is that of Wang Chong (c. 27–100 A.D.), who provides an emphatic refutation of this notion. See Chan (1963) pp. 292–304. Evidence of such thinking does, however, appear much earlier in Mohist circles. A consideration of linear causality is found discussed in the *Canons*, where the distinction between a necessary and sufficient "cause" (*gu* 故) is clearly spelled out while more mainstream *yin/yang* 陰陽 or *wuxing* 五行 terminology is avoided. See *Mojing* A: 1. Also, the uniquely Mohist tendency to misperceive the Confucian notion of *ming* 命 as inexorably fixed indicates the presence of a deterministic form of causal reasoning. See *Mozi*, 35. Such deterministic notions are unorthodox and perhaps explain why Mohism was in time marginalized as a counterdiscourse.

68. Tang (1988) p. 20.

69. The term "inscape" is borrowed thirdhand from Gerard Manley Hopkins, via the environmental cosmology of Joseph Grange. Grange employs the term to capture the manner in which value emerges in the coming-to-be of an "environmental event or process . . . absolutely unique in its concreteness." See Grange (1997) pp. 16–17.

70. Tang (1988) p. 22.

71. Graham (1991) p. 287.

Chapter 2. The Role of Feeling

1. Confucius uses the term as such and repeatedly makes the point that when *dao* 道 prevails in the land, it is incumbent on the person to participate in its realization. See *Analects* 5.2, 5.21, 8.13, 14.1, 15.7.

2. *Mencius* 4A: 11.

3. *Mencius* 6B: 2.

4. Cf. Shun (1997) p. 32.

5. Zhuangzi criticizes disputation (*bian* 辯), and specifically, the polemic associations of *dao* 道 and *yan* 言:

> By what is *dao* obscured so that we have the distinction between "genuine" and "false"? By what are *yan* obscured so as to have the distinction between "correct" and "incorrect"? Can *dao* be tread, but somehow not here? Can *yan* be present, but somehow impermissable? *Dao* is obscured in such petty attainments. *Yan* is obscured in such flowery rhetoric. Thus we have the distinction of "correct" and "incorrect" among the Confucians and Mohists; and hence, what is "correct" for one of them is "incorrect" for the other and *vice versa*. If one wishes to correct their errors and deny them their corrections, nothing serves better than clarity. [*Zhuangzi* 4/2/24–27; cf. Graham (2001) p. 52]

Zhuangzi explains this "clarity" (*ming* 明) in terms of something he calls the "pivot of *dao*" (*daoshu* 道樞). Only from the pivot is one granted the clarity and flexibility to respond inexhaustibly to the verbal distinctions that fuel debate, distinctions that in fact form a "continuity" (*yi* 一) one to the next. Zhuangzi intends to remove the term *dao* from the arena of disputation (*bian*). There is no invariably right or wrong *dao* in Zhuangzi's view, no absolute "way" that transcends a given context. *Dao* is no longer forced to serve as a fixed philosophical position, as it is in the *Mencius*. Zhuangzi's *dao*, being beyond the kinds of distinctions that condition disputation (*bian*), does not allow itself to be distinguished. It has no corresponding doctrine (*yan*); for "the greatest *dao* is impartial, and the greatest argument doesn't become doctrine." Since *dao* is something that defies all argument, "the *dao* that is shown [through doctrine (*yan*)] is not *dao*" (*Zhuangzi* 5/2/59–61). Cf. Graham (2001) p. 57. Also cf. *Daodejing* 1.

6. *Mencius* 3B: 9.

7. Yangist thought centers on notions of life (*sheng* 生) and disposition (*xing* 性), and as Mencius presents it, jeopardizes political order. These issues are taken up in chapter four. Mohist thought centers on notions of concern (*ai* 愛) and social benefit (*li* 利), and as Mencius presents it, jeopardizes familial order. These issues are taken up in chapter three.

8. *Mencius* 7B: 26.

9. *Mencius* 7A: 26.

10. See *Analects* 9.4 and 14.32. Also, compare *Analects* 4.10 with *Mencius* 4B: 11. *Mencius* 4A: 17 demonstrates Mencius' impatience with inflexible approaches to ritual propriety (*li* 禮). See also *Mencius* 4B: 6 and 6B: 12.

11. *Mencius* 2A: 2.

12. Ibid.

13. It is unfruitful to call *qi* 氣 moral or immoral. Only embedded configurations are subject to normative evaluation. Recall that the notion of a "flood-like *qi*" is a moral energy nourished through a particular habit or disposition. *Qi* focused in a moral disposition (*xing* 性) expresses moral quality. *Qi* might also focus in formations of illness, anxiety, or any other unproductive disposition.

To suggest that *qi* is morally neutral is not to suggest that it is a propertyless substratum. There is no "*qi* itself" that is propertyless. In chapter one, configurative energy was discussed in terms of the inseparability of form and function. Dispositions (*xing* 性) and shapes (*xing* 形) address determinate limits or forms, while *qi*, in this context, represents unlimited qualitative transformation. This distinction between form and quality is derivative, however, not primary.

14. *Mencius* 2A: 6. It is also said that such considerations do not mediate the impulses of true friendship. See *Mencius* 5B: 3.

15. *Analects* 2.4, 6.7, 14.39, 17.22, and 20.1 (twice).

16. Karlgren (1957) pp. 176–77.

17. See Lau and Ames (1998) pp. 44–53; Schwartz (1985) pp. 184–85.

18. *Mencius* 2A: 6.

19. See Dobson (1963) p. 132; Legge (1994) vol. 2, p. 402; Chan (1963) p. 54.

20. *Xin* 心 covers not only human emotion but also a range of cognitive functions. "Feeling" can be considered shorthand for "thoughts and feelings," which on occasion strikes me as a better translation. This is not a tradition that makes a sharp distinction between feeling and thought. I use "feeling" primarily, as I think it best captures the aspect of *xin* that Mencius most often intends to foreground.

21. *Guan* 官 means, according to Bernard Karlgren, "function" or "to function." See Karlgren (1957) p. 62. The other common meaning of this term is "office" or "officeholder," as in the function of a particular office or its "functionary."

22. *Mencius* 6A: 15.

Notes to Chapter 2

23. Hall and Ames (1987) p. 340 n. 28.

24. *Great Learning* 7.

25. *Analects* 2.15.

26. *Analects* 15.31.

27. *Mencius* 2A: 2.

28. *Mencius* 3A: 5.

29. *Xing* 性 is used as a verb here, thus "cultivates as a disposition."

30. *Mencius* 7A: 21. The language here would tolerate the alternative reading, "the physical body is not a doctrine (*yan* 言), but it instructs." I am not wholly convinced that this is Mencius' intented meaning here, but a critique of doctrine (*yan*) is no doubt within scope.

31. *Mencius* 6B: 6. Cf. *Great Learning* 6. 2. "Whatever is genuinely focused at the center is sure to take shape on the outside. Thus, exemplary persons are ever watchful of their uniqueness."

32. *Mencius* 4A: 15.

33. *Mencius* 2A: 2.

34. *Guanzi* 37, 13.4 b.

35. *Mencius* 7A: 30. Both *xing* 性 and *shen* 身 are used as verbs in this passage. Cf. *Mencius* 7B: 33.

36. See LeBlanc (1985) Introduction, and pp. 191–206.

37. Major (1993) pp. 28–32.

38. LeBlanc (1985) p. 118. LeBlanc's translation is only slightly altered here.

39. See Owen (1992) pp. 44–48; Pauline Yu suggests the antiquity of these notions, (1987) Ch. 2.

40. Henderson (1984) p. 26. Cf. Major (1993) p. 44.

41. Confucius' use of poetic imagery is suggestive in this regard. In *Analects* 17.9, Confucius lists "arousal" (*xing* 興) as one of the important merits of the *Book of Songs*. In *Analects* 13.5, the idea that poetic images can be introduced in a diplomatic environment in order to stimulate mutual agreement among disparate parties is suggested.

42. Major (1993) p. 31.

43. Dewey (1981) p. 139.

44. Ibid.

45. *Huainanzi* 3:3b: 11.

46. Cf. Ames and Lau (1998) p. 40.

47. Dewey (1981) p. 561.

48. *Mencius* 7A: 24. Cf. 4B: 18.

49. Karlgren (1957) pp. 190–91.

50. Legge (1994) vol. 5, p. 624.

51. This character consists of two parts, one meaning "skeletal frame" and the other "ritual vessel," both of which suggest a containing shape.

52. Cf. Lau (1970) p. 77. An alternative translation might be: "Where aspiration is reached, configurative energy is next below."

53. *Mencius* 2A: 2.

54. Graham (1989) p. 27.

55. Mark Lewis understands *zhi* 志 to mean, in major Confucian texts, "the thrust of a person's being." There are other applicable meanings of *zhi* in the tradition, however. The term plays an important role in poetry, which "expresses aspiration." See Lewis (1999) p. 162.

56. Cf. *Analects* 9.26. See also Shun (1997) p. 68.

57. *Book of Rites* 20/9a.5–6 and 20/11a.9–11b.1. See Shun (1997) pp. 66–67.

58. *Mencius* 5B: 1.

59. *Mencius* 7A: 33.

60. *Mencius* 4A: 4.

61. *Mencius* 4B: 28.

62. *Mencius* 2A: 7. Cf. *Zhongyong* 14.

63. The connection between aspiration, self-appraisal, and one's core relationships is also evidenced in the *Zuozhuan*. Zhongni, commenting on the disgrace of King Ling, submits, "This is ancient: that having aspiration, mastering oneself, and returning (*fu* 復) to ritual propriety and associated humanity is to be true as a person and good." See Legge (1961) vol. 5, pp. 638, 641.

64. *Mencius* 4B: 28.

65. *Analects* 4.3.

66. *Mencius* 5B: 7, 6A: 11. Cf. 2A: 7.

67. The two notions are also related in the *Analects*. See *Analects* 2.24 and 17.23.

68. *Mencius* 7A: 21.

69. *Mencius* 2A: 2.

70. Recall that when Confucius reached forty he was "no longer of two minds" (*Analects* 2.4). Mencius adds here that Gaozi, by holding to a doctrine (*yan* 言), achieved such a condition at an even earlier age; hence, the state of unagitated feeling (*budongxin* 不動心) is attainable by holding to a doctrine. Below we consider further why Mencius felt this to be inadequate.

71. There are various interpretations of *yue* 約 in this passage. For a survey of various glosses, see Shun (1997) pp. 73–74. Zhaoji understands *yue* as what is important or essential. Zhuxi, noting that *yue* is applied in two contrasted contexts in this passage, suggests that *yue* does not refer to a specific thing that one holds to. Interpreting *yue* as "a sense of what is important" seems to allow the requisite flexibility.

72. I appeal to *Mencius* 4B: 28 in glossing *suo* 縮 in this passage as "well integrated and attuned." The targets of "self-reflection" (*zifan* 自反) in 4B: 28 are humanity (*ren* 仁), ritual propriety (*li* 禮), and doing one's utmost (*zhong* 忠). These are relational notions, referencing one's degree of integration with others and one's attunement to their needs. In referring *suo* ultimately to appropriateness (*yi* 義), I appeal to the close connection between courage (*yong* 勇) and appropriateness (*yi*) in the *Analects*. See *Analects* 2.24 and 17.23. There are other glosses of *suo* in this passage, among them to be "straight," to have "poise," and to be "bound tight." See Shun (1997) p. 73, 244 n. 29.

73. In the *Zhongyong*, courage (*yong* 勇) is said to be close to shame. In regulating a person's conduct, shame also defies any sharp distinction between internal motivation and external conditioning. See *Zhongyong* 20.

74. Lau surmises that there is a break in this section. See Lau (1970) p. 77.

75. *Mencius* 2A: 2.

76. Ibid.

77. Ibid.

78. Cf. Rainey (1998) p. 101; Shun (1997) p. 163.

79. *Mencius* 6A: 4–5.

80. Shun (1997) pp. 94–112.

81. Ibid., p. 111.

82. This kind of episode locates Mencius within a tradition diverse enough to include his contemporary Zhuangzi. While Mencius and Zhuangzi differ in many respects, they are equally resistant to any move to decontexualize in philosophical discourse. Consider Zhuangzi and Huishi strolling across the Hao River Bridge:

> Zhuangzi said, "The minnows swim out and about as they please—this is the way they enjoy themselves."
>
> Huishi replied, "You are not a fish—how do you know what they enjoy?"
>
> Zhunagzi said, "You are not me—how do you know that I don't know what is enjoyable for the fish?"
>
> Huishi said, "I am not you, so I certainly don't know what you know; but by the same token it follows: since you are certainly not the fish, you don't know what is enjoyment for the fish either."
>
> Zhuangzi said, "Let's go back to your basic question. When you asked, 'How do you know what the fish enjoy?' you already knew that I know what the fish enjoy, or you wouldn't have asked me. I know it from here—above the river Hao." [*Zhuangzi* 45/17/87–91; cf. Graham (2001) p. 123]

Huishi hopes to determine the veracity of Zhuangzi's claim by fashioning a standard that transcends two contexts. Zhuangzi resists such a move and directs the conversation back to the context that first occasioned it.

In Mencius' engagement with Gaozi the pattern is similar. There is also a difference, however. Mencius does not reject pan-contextual standards altogether; he only limits their scope. Consider the passage:

> Gaozi said: "That man there is old, and I treat him as elder. He owes nothing of his elderliness to me, just as in treating him as white because he is white I only do so because of his Whiteness that is external to me. That is why I call (appropriateness) external."
>
> Mencius said: "The case of appropriateness is different than that of Whiteness. 'Treating as white' is the same whether one is treating a horse as white or a man as white. But I wonder if you would think that 'deference to age' is the same whether one is treating a horse as old or a man as elder?"

Mencius does not deny that the category "Whiteness" applies across contexts. The exact status of "Whiteness" as a pan-contextual standard, however, concerns him neither here nor elsewhere. His primary interest is ethical, and he is insisting that such externalized (*wai* 外) standards have little relevance to developing a disposition sensitive to what is morally appropriate (*yi* 義).

83. I concur with Kim-chong chong's assessment that Gaozi introduces the "internal/external" distinction while Mencius reduces it to absurdity. See Chong (2002), pp. 103–04, *passim*.

84. Lau (1970) p. 257.

85. *Mencius* 6A: 5.
86. *Mencius* 6A: 4.
87. Lau (1970) p. 253.
88. *Mencius* 6A: 13.
89. Cf. *Mencius* 7A: 24.
90. *Mencius* 6B: 18.

91. This is not to say that doctrine (*yan* 言) makes no contribution whatsoever to the moral development of the person (*shen* 身); it may, and Mencius allows this. The point however is that doctrine (*yan*) so used is appurtenant only to the person (*shen*). It may not be employed as a standard by which to measure the moral development of others. Consider *Mencius* 7B: 32:

> Mencius said: "A doctrine (*yan*) close at hand, pointing the way for extension, is a productive (*shan* 善) doctrine. A course that maintains a sense of what is important (*yue* 約), giving it broad application, is a productive course (*dao* 道). The doctrines (*yan*) of exemplary persons (*junzi* 君子) may never fall below the sash of their robes, yet the most productive course (*dao*) is contained therein. Exemplary persons tend to the cultivation of their persons (*shen*), and this brings order to the world. The problem with people is that they depart their own gardens to weed the gardens of others. They make demands upon others while allowing themselves to be frivolous.

The point is not that doctrine (*yan*) is useless in the moral development of the person (*shen*). The point is that unless one appropriates doctrine (*yan*) at the level of genuine feeling (*xin* 心) it is not contributing to the growth of the person (*shen*). It is the person (*shen*) that brings order to the world, not the doctrine (*yan*).

Doctrine, however, can contribute. Even Shun, in separating himself from the birds and beasts, is reported to have responded powerfully to the productive (*shan* 善) words (*yan* 言) and behaviors (*xing* 行) that he saw and heard. Mencius likens his response to "water breaching the dams of the Yangzi or the Yellow River." See *Mencius* 7A: 16. In this context, the momentum of Shun's response at an emotional level was vital to his development, and the word or doctrine (*yan*) that initiated it was only secondary.

92. *Mencius* 2A: 2.
93. For example, *Xunzi* 22.1a.
94. We find this also in the *Guanzi* and *Mozi*. See *Guanzi* 2/16.2–3; *Mozi* 43/88–90. See also Shun (1997) pp. 99–100.

95. See Ames and Lau (1998) pp. 72–73.

96. Legge (1967) vol. 2, p. 96.

97. Hence, one must guard against committing the genetic fallacy in interpreting *xing* 性. The same theme is found in the *Dispositions Arise from Conditions* document from Guodian, which will be examined in chapters four and five.

98. *Mencius* 7B: 35. This passage does not employ the term "inner" (*nei* 內). "Within" is derived from the particle *yan* 焉. Lau derives "within oneself" from *yan*, but it is unclear what completes the preposition. See Lau (1970) pp. 201–02. I would complete the preposition with "within the process of development," since that seems to be in keeping with the theme of the *Mencius*.

99. *Mencius* 6A: 8, 7A: 1, 7B: 35.

100. *Mencius* 4B: 28.

101. Legge (1994) vol. 4, pp. 374, 439, 553.

102. *Mencius* 6A: 7.

103. Mencius does not use the term "coherence" (*li* 理) regularly. However, he does liken the sagacity of Confucius to the "coherence" of an orchestra piece in *Mencius* 5B: 1.

104. Cf. *Mencius* 6A: 6, where this portion is repeated.

105. *Mencius* 7A: 3.

106. *Analects* 2.4.

107. *Mencius* 2A: 7.

108. *Mencius* 7A: 4.

109. *Analects* 4.4.

110. *Zhongyong* 25.

111. These two terms, "fitting" (*yi* 宜), and "appropriate" (*yi* 義), are cognates and closely related. The latter is defined in terms of the former in *Zhongyong*, 20.

112. Why, then, is integration (*cheng* 誠) not discussed more often in the *Mencius*, and why is the notion of feeling (*xin* 心) entirely absent from the *Zhongyong*? Most occasions of *cheng* in the *Mencius* are of typical vernacular usage, translatable as "genuine" (*Mencius* 1A: 7), "indeed" (*Mencius* 3A: 2), "sincere" (*Mencius* 3A: 5), and "authentic" (*Mencius* 2A: 1). There are instances in which the term is important, however, and these will be treated in chapters to come. Of the two philosophically significant occurrences of *cheng* in the *Mencius*, one overlaps with the *Zhongyong*, a fact that does not tell us much

about the relation between the two texts. The overlapping passages are *Mencius* 4A: 12 and portions of *Zhongyong* 20. One might take this overlap as an indication that, as Tu Wei-ming maintains, much of the *Zhongyong* is in fact premised on Mencian assumptions. See Tu (1989) pp. 72–73. On the other hand, one may, as Kwong-loi Shun does in his treatment of the *Mencius*, purposely "(defer) discussing the notion of *cheng* (in the *Mencius*) . . . because there is insufficient textual basis for reconstructing Mencius' views on *cheng* and *because* of (this parallel) with the *Zhongyong*" [Shun (1997) p. 235 n. 1; italics mine]. It is difficult to determine with any precision the relation between these two texts on the basis of *cheng*. Hall and Ames (2001) raise the possibility that a significant portion of the *Zhongyong* is a gloss on *Mencius* 4A: 12 (pp. 131–37). While the connection between these texts is obscure, the two are certainly bridged by the broader philosophical assumptions that they share within the framework of the Si-Meng lineage and each exhibit an evolving vocabulary within that lineage.

113. *Mencius* 2A: 2.

114. Ibid.

Chapter 3. Family and Moral Development

1. *Mencius* 2A: 2.

2. See *Zhongyong* 25, passim.

3. What is meant here by "technical" might be understood by recourse to the Greek notion of *techne*, a skill based on general principles that are capable of being taught. *Techne* understands its subject matter as a universal and can give a rational account of its activities. The horse trainer, for instance, understands horses and thereby knows the "good" of Horses and is "technically" proficient at handling one. Plato suggests in the *Gorgias* that medicine involves *techne* whereas something like cooking does not (*Gorgias* 501a). The *techne* of medicine knows and treats its subject matter (the human body) as a pancontextual universal. The "good" for medicine is thereby of a different order than that achieved in an instance of good cooking, which Plato considers "pleasant" rather than "good" when well done. The kind of order implicit in such things as cooking in the Chinese tradition is discussed below in terms of harmony (和 *he*). The mainstream Chinese tradition, both Daoist and Confucian, can be understood as appealing to harmony as a normative measure over a more technically oriented "good."

4. *Daodejing* 18, 19. The *Zhujianlaozi* (Bamboo Strip *Laozi*) unearthed at Guodian is free of these overt Confucian terms in its version of chapter 19.

This calls into question the degree of anti-Confucian sentiment in the *Zhujianlaozi*. Robert Henricks (2000) discusses the implications of the Guodian substitutions in his study of the strips (pp. 12–15). Henricks notes that the Guodian collection is largely made up of Confucian materials, so perhaps the text was cleansed for a Confucian readership. His own conclusion is that *Zhujianlaozi* chapter 19 is indeed "anti-Confucian" in tone but not yet "anti-Mencian" in content.

5. *Zhuangzi* 22/9/17. Cf. Graham (2001) p. 205.

6. *Analects* 2.3.

7. *Book of Rites* Book 26.

8. Chapter five argues that Mencius is a strong advocate for this form of government.

9. The case of the Confucian Xunzi is more complex. Clearly, distrust in the "spontaneous" tendencies of people would incline one more toward the "technical" side of the fault line. Xunzi distrusts human tendencies; accordingly, he transforms ritual into a more instrumental notion. Ritual for Mencius and Confucius, however, is not instrumental: it is not a means to an end. This will be argued in chapter four. It should be remembered that the technical-leaning Xunzi was the teacher of Hanfeizi, the most proficient and influential exponent of Legalism in the classical period.

10. *Mencius* 4B: 26.

11. There are various interpretations of the "five punishments," but the common set are tattooing, cutting off the nose, amputation of the feet, castration, and death. A. C. Graham has an interesting discussion of the term *fa* 法 in the Legalist tradition. See Graham (1989) pp. 273–78.

12. Even as Mozi speaks of the sages as exemplars of what is right (*yi* 義), it is always with reference to their embodiment of the "standard" (*fa* 法) of Heaven (*tian* 天), which Mozi calls "the clearest (*ming* 明) standard in the world." See *Mozi* 26.

13. See *Mencius* 2A: 1, where King Wen is a "model" (*fa* 法). In *Mencius* 3A: 3, the ruler who has robust "human relationships" (*renlun* 人倫) will be a "model" (*fa*) and tutor to an upcoming king. In *Mencius* 4A: 1, rulers are admonished to leave a "model" (*fa*) for posterity by cultivating their personal characters. In *Mencius* 4A: 2, Yao and Shun are "models" (*fa*), as they are in *Mencius* 7B: 33. There is only one remaining occurrence of *fa* in the *Mencius*, and it pertains to "law." In *Mencius* 6B: 15, Mencius suggests that a state without "legal families" (*fajia* 法家), or perhaps "legal counselors," is sure to fall. *Fajia* are grouped with stimulating scholar-officials (*shi* 士) and outside military adversaries as impetuses to toughen the ruler's countenance and challenge his resolve.

14. *Mencius* 7B: 37 defines the "way' (*dao* 道) of Yao and Shun as a "norm" (*jing* 經), and asserts that once the norm is established, it will arouse (*xing* 興) common people (*min* 民).

15. See note 3 above.

16. For more on Mozi's standards of evidence, see Graham (1989) pp. 36–41.

17. *Mozi* 46.

18. Mozi's utilitarianism is weakly formulated. It does not elaborate on its own criteria for "benefit" (*li* 利). As A. C. Graham (1989) observes, "this is a utilitarianism that never raises the question, 'Useful for what?'" (p. 40). There is no equation of benefit with either pleasure or happiness. As Chad Hansen (1992) notes, Mozi "takes it for granted that we obviously know what benefiting people is." (p. 117). Mozi cites as support for this standard (*fa* 法) the impartiality of "Heaven" (*tian* 天) itself. He claims that *tian* benefits "each without distinction" (*jian* 兼), so in following the standard of benefit, one accords with the way of *tian*. The argument he makes that *tian* concerns itself with the benefit of humankind amounts to an argument by design and is circular. In *Mozi* 27, he claims that *tian* set forth the sun and moon, the seasons, the grains, and so on, to ensure the comfort and prosperity of the human race. The evidence for this, it would seem, is the comfort and prosperity of the human race.

19. *Mozi* 17–19 and 20–22, respectively.

20. *Mozi* 6 and 8–10, respectively.

21. *Mozi* 23–25 and 32–34, respectively.

22. *Mozi* 29–31.

23. *Mozi* 35–37.

24. *Mozi* 39.

25. Confucians consider family affection and deference to superior character to give rise (*sheng* 生) to ritual propriety (*li* 禮). See *Zhongyong* 20.

26. *Mozi* 39.

27. *Mozi* 26.

28. This is one of the few theory/practice distinctions one finds in classical China, and it is perhaps the earliest. Mozi is here criticizing anyone who, under such a scenario, would affirm impartial concern in practice but would deny it in theory.

29. The idea that one's behavior towards the families of others conditions the well-being of one's own dawns on Mencius, too, as recorded in *Mencius* 7B: 7:

Mencius said, "It has recently occurred to me how serious it is to kill the intimates of another person. If you kill a person's father, that person will kill your father; if you kill a person's son, that person will kill your son. While this is not to kill them yourself, it is only a step removed."

30. *Mozi* 47.

31. *Mencius* 7B: 30. Cf. 7B: 26.

32. *Mencius* 1A: 1. See also *Mencius* 6B: 4. Here too *ren* 仁 and *yi* 義 are presented as an alternative to *li* 利.

33. *Analects* 4.16. Cf. *Analects* 14.12.

34. One might ask if Mencius is fair to Mozi in doing so. It does appear that in Mozi's argument for "impartial concern" there is an appeal to self-interest underlying this otherwise philanthropic doctrine. On the other hand, to reduce Mozi's broader interest in social welfare to motivations of self-interest, in my estimation, leaves Mozi shortchanged. The issue really hinges on Mencius' insistence that moral motivation arise not from "technical" calculations but rather from the "spontaneous" inclinations of a genuine disposition. This idea is further developed below.

35. *Mencius* 7A: 25.

36. Graham (1989) p. 41.

37. *Analects* 20.2 and *Mencius* 7A: 13.

38. *Mencius* 6B: 4. Cf. Shun (1997) pp. 166–69.

39. See Hall and Ames (2001) pp. 75–76; Ames and Rosemont (1998) pp. 57–58.

40. Graham (1989) p. 426. See also pp. 398–99, 423–27.

41. Legge (1994) vol. 3, pp. 217–18.

42. Graham (1989) p. 424.

43. *Mencius* 7B: 25. This is what Graham calls a "loose" definition. See Graham (1989) pp. 146–47.

44. Cf. *Analects* 3.25, where music is discussed in terms of beauty (*mei* 美) and goodness *shan* 善.

45. *Mencius* 2A: 8. Cf. *Analects* 12.16.

46. *Analects* 13.23. Cf. 1.12.

47. David L. Hall is perhaps the person and thinker on Chinese philosophy who is most sensitive to particularity in the aesthetic order. He writes,

"The aesthetic perspective is one which concentrates, no matter how extensive the context, upon the harmony of insistently particular details" [Hall (1982) p. 25].

48. In the *Book of Songs*, the harmonious soup is that which is "carefully prepared and balanced (*ping* 平)." See Legge (1994) v. 4, p. 634. The *Book of Documents* also describes soup as *he* 和. See Legge (1994) v. 3, p. 260.

49. Legge (1994), vol. 5, p. 684.

50. *Analects* 16.1.

51. For an epistemology of value relating to harmony that might augment discussions here, see Neville (1981) pp. 94–97, passim.

52. *Guoyu* 16.

53. *Analects* 8.16.

54. Legge (1994) vol. 4, p. 138. Cf. the song "Cherry Tree" (ibid., pp. 252–53). It is sung in praise of the relationship among brothers and pays homage to the harmony of family itself, which is similar to that of music:

> Dishes may be abundant. And wine consumed to the limit.
> But when brothers are in attendance.
> This is harmony, joy, and happiness.
>
> Happy union of wife and children: it is the melody of lutes.
> But when brothers are joined.
> The harmony and joy are profound.
>
> It is fitting (*yi* 宜) to have a home and a family.
> It is a joy to have a wife and children.
> As soon as one considers it, it is just as soon the case.

55. *Mencius* 5B: 1.

56. *Analects* 7.32.

57. *Analects* 1.12.

58. Confucius says that exemplary persons are not mere vessels, meaning that they are not merely taking on the form of a ritual but actually expressing themselves through it. See *Analects* 2:12 and 5.4. Cf. *Analects* 3.4.

59. *Analects* 17.11.

60. The "delineating," "supporting," and "ennobling" functions of *li* 禮 are inspired by A. S. Cua. See Cua (1989) pp. 209–35. In chapter five I treat in more detail the manner in which these functions work in a Mencian context.

61. Dewey (1985) p. 239.

62. *Mencius* 6A: 7.

63. Note that Mencius never uses the derogatory term "partiality" (*bie* 別) to indicate what he stands for. "Identity" (*fen* 分) is a Confucian term employed in the *Xunzi* and the *Book of Rites* to refer to the kinds of social distinctions that Confucians prize and that Mozi intended to criticize. Prior to Mencius, *bie* is employed by Confucians as a positive term describing what it is that they stand for. This is evident in the newly recovered "Six Positions" (*Liuwei*) document from the Guodian collection. By the time that Mencius wrote, the Mohists appear to have succeeded in rendering *bie* irredeemably negative.

64. Chad Hansen claims that the Confucian resistance to addressing standards (*fa* 法) reveals that they fail to understand normative theory when faced with it. He further asserts that the Confucian critique of the doctrine of impartial concern elides consideration of the standard of benefit that underwrites it. Hansen (1992) writes:

> The Confucian tendency to focus on [the doctrine of impartial concern] instead of [the standard of benefit] reflects a characteristic Confucian confusion. Confucians systematically confuse moral psychology with normative ethics. . . .
>
> By focusing on [the doctrine of impartial concern] Confucian critics of Mozi shift the spotlight from normative ethics to descriptive sociology, where they feel on stronger grounds. They word the dispute in descriptive terms: "are humans naturally partial or naturally universal?" Confucians can certainly point to the natural family partiality of our emotions. They assume that in doing so they are refuting Mozi. In fact, this is simply to miss the point of normative theory. (p. 129)

As for the Confucian failure to focus on the Mohist standard of benefit, Mencius, at least, spotlights that in the very first exchange of his text and elsewhere. According to my reading, Mencius knows what he is doing in refuting the doctrine of impartial concern and he does not miss the point of normative theory in doing so. An argument can certainly be made that Mencius misrepresents the Mohist standard of benefit by identifying the term, as Confucius does, with self-interest. There is a normative dimension to Confucianism itself, however; Hansen does not, to my knowledge, closely consider the notion of harmony (*he* 和) in his work.

65. Accordingly, the translation of *ben* 本 will here oscillate between "fundamental," "root," and "ground" in order to accommodate its seamless range

of meaning. "Fundamental" in this context should not be confused with "inalienable," for what is *ben* can certainly be lost (*shi* 失).

66. Cf. *Mencius* 4A: 5, 4A: 12, and 4A: 19 with *Great Learning* 1.

67. The characteristic that Hall and Ames identify as "aesthetic" order is here most in evidence. See Hall and Ames (1987) pp. 131–38.

68. *Analects* 1.2.

69. Legge (1994) vol. 3, p. 195.

70. *Analects* 2.21.

71. *Mencius* 7A: 15.

72. *Book of Filial Piety* 1/1/4–6.

73. *Mencius* 4B: 13.

74. *Mencius* 3A: 5.

75. This is not Mozi's position, as I understand it.

76. *Mencius* 5A: 1 and 6B: 3. Cf. 4A: 28.

77. *Mencius* 4A: 11.

78. *Mencius* 6B: 2.

79. See Karlgren (1957) p. 113. It is important to maintain the growth metaphor in translating *shi* 實. *Shi* can also be understood more generically as "providing substance" to something. Its botanical associations, however, are well established. In a manner similar to the *Zuozhuan* and the *Book of Documents*, Mencius uses *shi* elsewhere to refer to the "fruit" of a plum tree (*Mencius* 3B: 10). Human virtue, like fruit, is something grown. The family is the soil in which human virtue grows.

80. *Mencius* 4A: 27. Cf. 7A: 15.

81. *Analects* 1.2.

82. *Mencius* 6A: 19.

83. Shun's family life, as it turns out, was far from ideal. Shun was a common man who "rose from the fields" (*Mencius* 6B: 15). He rose to imperial power on Yao's recommendation and, more importantly, by the propensity of *tian* 天 and the people (*Mencius* 5B: 3). Shun's family objected, and he subsequently hid from them his royal marriage. Shun's father, who was blind, plotted against his son's life. Sending him out to repair a barn, the father removed the ladder and set the building on fire. Shun survived, only to have his brother make an attempt on his life. Shun was sent out to dredge a well, and his brother blocked the well over him (*Mencius* 5A: 2). Despite these outrageous attempts on his life, Shun harbored no ill will against his brother

(*Mencius* 5A: 3) nor against his parents (*Mencius* 5A: 4). Shun's narrative certainly makes his filial piety all the more remarkable. To modern ears, it is rather fantastic. This does not detract, however, from the ideal that Mencius locates in Shun. For a more detailed account of Shun's life, see Lau (1970) pp. 225–27, *passim*.

84. *Mencius* 4B: 32 and 6B: 2.

85. *Mencius* 4B: 14.

86. *Mencius* 6B: 2.

87. *Mencius* 4A: 18. Mencius' claim that the ancients did not engage in the instruction (*jiao* 教) of family members is not consistently borne out in the literature. The *Great Learning* suggests that if one is unable to instruct one's own family (*jia* 家), then one is unable to instruct others. (*Great Learning* 15.1) Mencius removes instruction from the home, and in doing so he is not precluding filial piety from the content of instruction. When King Xuan of Qi proposes shortening the period of mourning for one's parents, Mencius suggests that he be instructed (*jiao*) in filial and fraternal responsibility (*Mencius* 7A: 39). The Mencian ideal, however, would be to have such sensibilities nourished by the unlearned feeling of family affection (*qin* 親). King Xuan has perhaps lost the "unlearned" root of his moral sensibilities; hence, he now requires such instruction. *Mencius* 7A: 40 provides a positive account of instruction (*jiao*); however, it does not include the elements of filial piety. Mencius says:

> The exemplary person instructs in five ways. The first is by having a transforming influence like a timely rain. The second is by bringing about the culmination of efficacious virtue. The third is by helping to extend abilities. The fourth is by responding to questions. The fifth is by offering private assistance in refining gracefulness. These are the five ways in which the exemplary person offers instruction.

These five modes of instruction are apparently, according to Mencius, most effectively administered outside of the home.

88. *Analects* 1.4, 1.6, 1.7, 1.8, 5.26.

89. *Analects* 1.8.

90. *Analects* 4.18. Along these lines, we find a fuller treatment of remonstrance and filial restraint in the "Patterns of Family" (*Neize*) chapter of the *Book of Rites* 12.15. However, in the *Book of Filial Piety*, remonstrance in the form of "contention" (*zheng* 爭) with respect to the behavior of one's father is endorsed. See *Book of Filial Piety* 4/15/3–7.

91. *Mencius* 4B: 30.

92. Cf. *Daodejing* 76.

93. *Analects* 13.18.

94. This is endorsed with the aim of facilitating a more self-generative social order that remains rooted in the family and is thereby governed by shame. But what of the poor fellow who loses his sheep? The point is often made that Confucian thought does not supplement family-based order with a sufficiently clear notion of commonwealth. I tend to agree. Chinese culture has traditionally been plagued by the consequences of this imbalance. Anyone familiar with China knows that "personal connections" (*guanxi* 關係) trump any nominal standard or regulation. With China's ascension into the World Trade Organization, economic and legal restructuring is under way, and it is no surprise that these new, binding standards are everywhere in tension with "homegrown" corruption, nepotism, and graft. It is a deeply set problem. I believe that Confucianism is dynamic enough to generate a stronger notion of commonwealth, that it is designed to, and that it should. Mencius would caution that a genuine disposition toward the common good is not something that can be established by logical argument or enforced by rule of law; rather, it must evolve and grow from genuine feeling. This is the Mencian ideal, with which I am also sympathetic.

95. *Mencius* 3A: 3.

96. *Mencius* 1A: 3.

97. *Mencius* 7A: 14.

98. *Mencius* 6B: 16.

99. *Mencius* 4B. 7.

100. Hall and Ames explore the notion of instruction (*jiao* 教) in the *Zhongyong* in a manner that elucidates an interesting dimension of this notion that also applies to the *Mencius*. Like in the *Zhongyong*, the Mencian notion of moral education, with a stress on extension, nourishment (*yang* 養), and the individualized nature of moral upbringing, captures the important etymological components of the English word "education". The word has two principal roots: *educare* and *educere*. *Educare* means "to cultivate, to rear, to bring up," while *educere* means "to evoke, to lead forth, to draw out." Mencius' notion of moral education is an *educare* in that it involves cultivation through relationships that provide nourishment for growth. Family ties furnish a stable, sustainable environment for moral development and continue to rear the moral individual as long as their integrity is maintained. The Mencian notion is also an *educere* in that the individual genuinely emerges into a moral world that he or she can advance by "extending" the sensibilities reared by his or her funda-

mental relationships. Both the formal and creative components of "education" are satisfied in the Mencian notion of moral learning. Cf. Hall and Ames (2001) pp. 50–51, 66–67.

101. *Mencius* 4A: 19.

102. *Mencius* 1A: 7.

103. In discussing the King Xuan episode, Kwong-loi Shun notes that there is some uncertainty over whether Mencius is encouraging the king to extend his actions or extend his concern (*ai* 愛). Such ambiguity speaks to the fact that dispositions (*xing* 性) entail both feelings (*xin* 心) and the concomitant proclivity to act on those feelings. See Shun (1997) pp. 143–44.

104. *Mencius* 7B: 1. Mozi, of course, advocates doing the same in his doctrine of impartial concern. The crucial difference is that Mencius endorses doing so not by accepting a doctrine, but rather by developing the disposition to do so.

105. The Mencian attitude towards "bearable" suffering in the nonhuman world is one that can be further reconstructed. He suggests that one can and ought to regulate the extension of one's sensibilities towards animals. Allowing that once a living animal is seen, one cannot bear to see it killed, and once its painful cries are heard, one cannot bear to eat its meat, Mencius recommends that "the exemplary person stay away from the kitchen" (*Mencius* 1A: 7). Mencius apparently feels that there is a proper measure of empathy that ought to be maintained toward animals, and overexposure to their suffering would complicate that measure. In suggesting the proper parameters of one's graded sensibilities, Mencius locates one's proper feeling toward the nonhuman world:

> Exemplary persons grudge and show concern [*ai* 愛] for living things, but they do not enter into associated humanity with them. They enter into associated humanity with the general population [*min* 民], but they do not feel family affection [*qin* 親] for them. They feel family affection for their family members, but only associated humanity for other people [*ren* 人]. They show associated humanity for other people, but are only sparing and concerned [*ai*] with living creatures. (*Mencius* 7A: 45)

One might here challenge Mencius and still remain a Mencian. For instance, it is the prerogative of groups like People for the Ethical Treatment of Animals (PETA) to bring the "unbearable" kitchens and slaughterhouses into our living rooms with the aim of arousing our sensibilities and, hence, changing our dispositions toward eating meat. If the aspirations of PETA are realized, the day will come when it is considered "inhumane" to treat animals as factory food. In chapter five, the relation between aspiration (*zhi* 志), feeling (*xin* 心), and the evolving "human way" (*rendao* 人道) is discussed at greater length.

106. Cf. *Mencius* 3B: 3. "Boring holes and scaling walls" represents all forms of dishonest, illicit, or duplicitous behavior.

107. *Mencius* 7B: 31.

108. Karlgren (1957) p. 86.

109. *Mencius* 3A: 5.

110. In this instance, we begin to see the development of *cheng* 誠 from its more vernacular meaning of "genuine" to its more philosophical meaning of "integration."

111. Watson (1963) p. 13. It is commonly held that the Mohist movement arose from the lower echelons of society, from those without access to the remnant high culture of the Zhou, which the Confucians sought to revitalize. See Graham (1989) p. 34.

112. Cf. *Daodejing* 25.

113. *Book of Filial Piety* 2/9/28.

114. *Mencius* 6A: 6.

115. *Mencius* 4B: 19.

116. *Mencius* 5B: 7.

117. *Mencius* 1B: 16.

118. *Mencius* 5A: 4. The reference in the *Book of Songs* is to King Wu. See Legge (1994) vol. 4, p. 459.

119. *Mencius* 7A: 24.

120. *Mozi* 27.

Chapter 4. The Human Disposition

1. *Analects* 1.2.

2. *Book of Filial Piety* 2/9/28.

3. *Book of Filial Piety* 1/1/4–5.

4. *Zhongyong* 17 and 19.

5. Lewis (1999) p. 358.

6. The sociologist Ambrose King makes this argument. See King (1985) p. 58. See also Hall and Ames (1995) pp. 276–77.

7. *Mencius* 4A: 28.

8. Li (2002) p. 131; *Liuwei* 6:1.

9. Irene Bloom and Roger T. Ames have established the two clearest positions on the issue.

Bloom (1994) argues that *renxing* 人性 for Mencius means "human nature" in a genetic or "fundamentally biological" sense. It is one, however, "intelligible in both normative and descriptive terms" (p. 44). According to her reading, this is a position Mencius establishes in relation to three counterpositions advocated in the text, the most important of which is advocated by Gaozi in *Mencius* 6A: 3. Bloom calls this a "narrow biologism" that maintains that *xing* can be wholly reduced to biological life and physical appetites. According to Bloom's reading, Mencius maintains in *Mencius* 6A: 7 that "the faculty of the moral mind" (*xin* 心) is just as "biological" as other physical drives and dispositions. Accordingly, Mencius affirms the presence of the moral "faculties" in terms referred to as "the capacities sent down from Heaven' or what in modern terms we would recognize as genetic." Mencius' assertion that "the sage and we are the same in kind" further reflects, for Bloom, the genetic status of these faculties and affirms the fundamental identity of human beings. See Bloom (1997) p. 27. Thus, this heaven-endowed, genetic identity is what Mencius means by "human nature."

Ames argues that "human nature" is not an adequate translation of *renxing* since the term is not intended as a description of what human beings "genetically" or "biologically" share. According to Ames, "genetic" readings reflect an "interpretive prejudice" that privileges an "ahistorical given" over what human beings themselves achieve. See Ames (1991) p. 143. Noting that the differences between the human being and the animal are considered "infinitesimal" (*xi* 希) in *Mencius* 4B: 19, Ames identifies these differences as cultural rather than biological. Appealing to the fact that *xing* 性 in the *Mencius* is also used verbally (see *Mencius* 7A: 21, 7A: 30, 7B: 33, and Ames (1991) pp. 159–60), Ames maintains that the human virtues for Mencius are not "givens," but are instead, as *Mencius* 7A: 21 states, are "what the exemplary person cultivates as *xing*," or, literally, what they "*xing*." Being culturally achieved rather than biologically given, the human virtues identified with *renxing* are neither genetic nor inalienable. They can be forfeited or "lost" (*shi* 失) by morally inattentive people. Thus, for Ames, "when (Mencius) says 'there is no human being who is not good (*shan* 善),' he is also saying that 'anyone who is not good is not really human.'" See Ames (1991) p. 162.

The interpretation forwarded here is more in line with Ames's cultural reading, as will be demonstrated presently.

10. *Mencius* 7A: 15.

11. *Mencius* 6A: 7.

12. Tang (1988) p. 22.

13. The phrase "The human and *tian* 天 are joined in continuity" (*tianrenheyi* 天人合一) is conceived not as the coordination of two separate and independent spheres, but rather in terms of the continuity (*yi* 一) of interdependent processes mutually emergent.

14. The episode is found in *Mencius* 3A: 4.

15. For more on Shenneng movement, see Graham (1989) pp. 66–74.

16. The *Six Positions* document from Guodian also identifies basic human relationships with the instruction (*jiao* 教) of the first king (*xianwang* 先王). The document is unusual in that it treats the distinction (*bie* 別) between male and female as prerequisite to the establishment of affection (*qin* 親) between father and son. The patriarchal character of Confucian thinking in this period is nowhere more in evidence than in the *Six Positions*.

17. Legge (1994) vol. 3, p. 44.

18. *Mencius* 3A: 4.

19. *Analects* 8.19.

20. *Mencius* 3B: 9.

21. *Mencius* 4B: 19.

22. The question is more complex in the *Book of Filial Piety*, where filial piety is described as arising out of respect for the physical inheritance of one's skin and hair from one's parents. It is difficult to say whether such a notion is indicative of the kind of thinking that, Irene Bloom might say, "in modern terms we would recognize as genetic." See *Book of Filial Piety* 1/1/4–6 and n. 9 above.

23. *Mencius* 6A: 7.

24. *Mencius* 4A: 1.

25. *Mencius* 2A: 1.

26. *Analects* 17.2.

27. "Close by" (*xia* 狎) and also, by extension "intimate with" (*xiajin* 狎近).

28. "Intimately connected to" (*mier* 密邇) and also, by extension, "near to" (*erjin* 邇近).

29. Legge (1994), vol. 3, pp. 203–04.

30. *Mencius* 5A: 7.

31. *Mencius* 7B: 31.

32. *Mencius* 3B: 6.

33. *Analects* 5.13 suggests that beyond his observation of the relation between disposition and proximity, Confucius did not discuss the topic.

34. *Mozi*, 25; Watson (1963) pp. 75–76.

35. Kwong-loi Shun shares this inference. See Shun (1997) p. 29.

36. *Mencius* 7A: 5.

37. In *Mencius* 6A: 4, Gaozi suggests that disposition reduces to these functions.

38. *Mencius* 6A: 3.

39. Shun (1997) pp. 93–94.

40. To some degree, however, the human disposition as Mencius understands it does rely on "biological" conditions. Birds, dogs, or plankton cannot adopt a human disposition, and one would presume that there are some "biological" factors that explain why not. Be that as it may, it is Mencius' intention to elevate cultural conditions over biological conditions in his presentation of *renxing* 人性. To be "biologically" human is a necessary but not sufficient condition for having a *renxing*.

41. *Analects* 18.6.

42. *Mencius* 6A: 6.

43. Li (2002) p. 105; *Xingzimingchu* 1.

44. Li (2002) p. 105; *Xingzimingchu* 2.

45. Li (2002) pp. 105–06; *Xingzimingchu* 5–6.

46. *Liang* 良 means "good" and, in its extended sense, "fertile." It is also associated with "grain" (*liang* 糧). See Karlgren (1957), p. 194. *Liang* here means "good" in the sense of "good land." Maintaining the botanical metaphor here is important. To translate *liang* simply as "good" is to lose the sense of being "good for" or "productive," which is also the sense in which Mencius uses the term *shan* 善.

47. *Gu* 梏 has the extended sense of "binding" as in "binding one's hair in a knot." See Karlgren (1957) pp. 91–92. Presumably it is the unencumbered flow of configurative energy that is being "constricted" by unproductive, daily habits.

48. *Mencius* 6A: 8.

49. *Cai* 才 is also associated with the notion of "planting" (*zai* 栽). See Karlgren (1957) pp. 247–48. *Zhongyong* 17 employs the notion of botanical "capacity" in a philosophical context.

50. Shun (1997) pp. 216–17.//
51. *Mencius* 6A: 1.
52. *Mencius* 6A: 2.
53. A. C. Graham (2001) demonstrates that the Yangists and Mohists have points in common in terms of their terminology and technique of debate:

> For example, the later Mohist dialectical chapters, the Yangist chapter *Shenwei* ("Be Aware of What You are For") in the *Lüshichunqiu*, and the second and third dialogues of "Robber Chi" all share a technical use of the falling tone *wei* 為, "for the sake of," to pose the question of what one is for, one's end in life, the final criterion by which all actions are to be judged. (pp. 221–22).

Hence, Graham translates the Mencian condemnation of Yang Zhu in these terms: "What Yang was *for* was self" (*weiwo* 為我). See *Mencius* 7A: 26 and Graham (2001) p. 223. The Mohist interest in benefit (*li* 利) is clear enough throughout the *Mozi*. In Graham's reconstruction of the Yangist teachings, he proposes that Yangism "starts from the same calculations of benefit and harm as does Mohism." See Graham (1989) p. 56.

54. *Mencius* 4B: 26.
55. Cf. *Mencius* 1B: 8.
56. *Mencius* 2A: 6.
57. *Mencius* 4A: 28. "If one is not engaged in family affection, one cannot be considered human."
58. *Mencius* 3A: 5.
59. *Book of Filial Piety* 2/9/26–29.
60. *Mencius* 4A: 27. Cf. 7A: 15.
61. *Mencius* 7B: 25. What is good (*shan* 善) in a person becomes aesthetically best when it is "given fullness so as to be brought to fruition" (*chongshi* 充實). *Shi* in this instance is the resultative compliment of *chong*.
62. *Mencius* 6A: 7.
63. *Mencius* 2A: 2.
64. *Book of Filial Piety* 2/9/28.
65. In the spirit of Mencius, we "extend" the significance of certain episodes in order to suggest this point. What if, in *Mencius* 1A: 7, King Xuan felt that he could not bear the sacrificial slaughter of *any* animal? And what if the exemplary person *did* go into the kitchen? What if Mencius himself, so

quick to call others animals, could experience the equivalent impact of a Warring States March on Birmingham and the wearing of placards that read, "I am a Man"? The point suggested has the merit of being true. Standards of morality and feeling are transformed and redefined with human experience. And there is always further to go.

66. *Analects* 1.2.

67. *Mencius* 6A: 11.

68. *Mencius* 7B: 16.

69. *Mencius* 2A: 6.

70. *Mencius* 4A: 27.

71. *Mencius* 2A: 2.

72. Cf. Hall and Ames (2001) p. 24.

73. *Mencius* 6A: 7.

74. *Analects* 4.15.

75. *Mencius* 6A: 7.

76. In scholarship more inclined to understand *renxing* 人性 in genetic terms, it is presented as "significant" that Mencius "repeatedly" uses the phrase "each and every human" in attributing "the natural tendencies he then specifies" [Bloom (1997) p. 24]. There are seven instances in which Mencius uses the term "human" without qualification in connection with "each and every" (*jie* 皆), and they are not always important where they do occur. There are the significant uses connected with the four sprouts, which "each and every human" has (*Mencius* 2A: 6). And there is the equally important discussion concerning that which "each and every human" is unable to bear (*ren* 忍); the claim, however, is that each and every person has limits, not that there is a uniform threshold (*Mencius* 6A: 6). There is the claim that "each and every human" can become a sage (*Mencius* 6B: 2). And there is also the claim that "each and every human" has, as part of his or her parental feeling (*xin* 心), the wish to see offspring happily married and not involved in shameful or illicit conduct (*Mencius* 3B: 3). In the "Fish or Bear's Paw" passage, discussed below, there is the claim that "each and every human" has a sense of dignity and self-worth that prevents him or her from surviving at any cost. We learn, however, that this dignity can be lost and it is only maintained in persons of quality (*Mencius* 6A: 10). The remaining claims, that "each and every human" believes that Chenzhong would refuse the state of Qi if offered under inappropriate circumstances and that "each and every human" would hold his or her nose while passing by Xishi covered in filth, would appear to be less significant as "natural tendencies" (*Mencius* 7A: 34 and 4B: 25). The list of substantive traits shared

77. *Mencius* 6A: 10.

78. Zhaomeng is the title of chief minister of Jin, a title held by four ministers in the house of Zhao. In the *Zuozhuan*, Zhaomeng is presented as capable of "observing the aspirations" (*guanzhi* 觀志) of senior officers by having them chant a song of their own choosing. Zhaomeng then evaluates their characters accordingly. See Lewis (1999) pp. 162, 424.

79. *Mencius* 6A: 17.

80. See *Mencius* 3B: 9, for his own explanation of his polemic purpose. Here, as elsewhere, his program is associated with safeguarding the original work of the sages.

81. *Mencius* 7B: 36.

82. Hall and Ames (1987) p. 273.

83. On the use of names as "claims" in character, see Lewis (1999) p. 33.

84. *Analects* 15.20.

85. Here we note that surname (*xing* 姓) is cognate with disposition (*xing* 性); both are initial starting points, but insufficient for the purpose of distinguishing one human from another.

86. *Mencius* 2A: 2.

87. *Mencius* 6A: 6.

88. *Mencius* 7A: 38.

89. *Cong* 從 is yet another illustration of the priority of situation over agency characteristic of Chinese language (see Ch. 1 n. 43). The term suggests both "to" and "from," meaning both "to follow" and "to come from." In this instance, understanding *cong* as "to pursue" retains the notion of "to follow" while leaving room for the emergent dimension.

90. *Mencius* 6A: 15.

91. Mencius is not suggesting that one neglect the body and senses; he comments instead on the failure of some to apply the same concern that they have for their physical preservation to the preservation of their feeling (*xin* 心) (*Mencius* 6A: 12). He makes clear, however, that these two sorts of components (*ti* 體) have different values (*gui* 貴), and that the greater component ought not to be neglected for the sake of cultivating the lesser component. He

uses botanical imagery to make his point, noting that some trees are more valuable than others. (*Mencius* 6A: 13). Cf. *Mencius* 6A: 11 and 6A: 13.

92. The terms "bringing something to fullness" (*chong* 充) and "getting the most out of something" (*jin* 盡) have a verb/compliment relationship in the *Mencius*. In *Mencius* 5B: 4, the content of appropriateness (*yi* 義) as a sort (*lei* 類) is discussed. The suggestion is made that taking anything that is not one's own might count as theft. "Fully expressing [*chong*] the sort to such an extreme," Mencius says, "is getting the most [*jin*] out of appropriateness."

93. I suspect that *jin* 盡 does not involve an inherent *telos* in any classical Chinese context. The term does have a different connotation in the *Zhuangzi*, however, and this is important to point out.

In chapter one it was argued that Zhuangzi does not endorse the Mencian project of developing one's disposition (*xing* 性). Recall that Zhuangzi, in the "Inner Chapters," focuses instead on the "shape" (*xing* 形) of things and feels that the "character" (*de* 德) of each shape is sufficient. Hence, for him, dispositions (or shapes) are not to be improved upon by a program of education, as the *Zhongyong* prescribes (See *Zhongyong* 1). As a corollary to this, shape is not to be improved upon through ritualized practices.

This difference in attitude between the Confucian school and Zhuangzi comes to bear on the translation owed *jin* in the *Mencius* and the *Zhuangzi*. For Zhuangzi, to *jin* something is not to "get the most" out of it, but simply to "exhaust" it or allow it to go into "extinction." For Zhuangzi, "The moment we obtain a shape we await its 'exhaustion' [*jin*]" (*Zhuangzi* 4/2/18; cf. Graham (2000) p. 51). For Zhuangzi, special effort and concern is not required to improve upon one's shape; for as he sees it, a shape will run its own course and in the process be exhausted (*jin*). A teleological end does not dictate this process of "exhaustion" any more than "getting the most" out of something involves a predetermined end in a Confucian context. Shape for Zhuangzi is an expression of the transformation of things—the shaping and reshaping of things as they transform one into the next. Since there is no "essence" or "species" posited that transcends shape, there is nothing that furnishes any particular shape a *telos* over the course of its being exhausted.

94. *Book of Rites* 18.9. See Legge (1967) vol. 2, p. 89.

95. *Book of Documents* 6.4.11. See Legge (1994) vol. 3, p. 219.

Chapter 5. Advancing the Human Way

1. *Mencius* 2A: 4 and 4A: 8 quote the *Book of Songs* regarding the "calamity" that *tian* 天 is capable of reaping. *Mencius* 1B: 10 also makes refer-

ence to the calamity that might issue from *tian*, although here too the words are not Mencius' own. In *Mencius* 2B: 1, Mencius speaks of the "seasons" of *tian*, the meteorological counterpart of the geographical features of the earth. In Mencius 1A: 6, *tian* also refers to the sky.

2. Eno (1990) p. 101.
3. *Mencius* 5A: 5. Cf. *Analects* 17.19.
4. *Mozi* 48. Cf. Schwartz (1985) p. 139.
5. *Mozi* 26–28.
6. *Mencius* 5A: 5.
7. *Mencius* 5A: 6.

8. *Shou* 受 means both to "bestow" and to "accept." In keeping with the primacy of situation over agency, these notions are resolved in the event of "allowing" something to occur by both permitting it and sponsoring it. For more on the "priority of situation over agency," see Ames and Lau (1998) pp. 20–22. See also Ch. 1 n. 43.

9. *Mencius* 5A: 5. See also Legge (1994) vol. 3, p. 292.
10. Li (2002) p. 86; *Qiongdayishi* 1.
11. *Mencius* 7A: 9.
12. *Mencius* 1B: 16.
13. Li (2002) p. 86; *Qiongdayishi* 2.
14. Pang (1999.1), p. 27.
15. *Mencius* 7A: 33.

16. "Parent" (*fumu* 父母) of the "people" (*min* 民) is a notion that occurs in *Mencius* 1A: 4, 1B: 7, and 3A: 3. "Parent to the People" is also the title of a newly released document from the Shanghai Museum, which at the time of writing I have not yet read.

17. *Mencius* 4A: 7.
18. *Mencius* 4A: 5.

19. *Mencius* 4A: 2. As associated humanity (*ren* 仁) is understood as a noncoercive form of governing, its opposite, *buren* 不仁, can be understood as any coercive form.

20. *Mencius* 2A: 4, 4A: 1, 4A: 3, 4A: 8, 4A: 9, 6A: 18, and 7B: 13.
21. *Mencius* 2A: 7 and 4A: 16.
22. See *Mencius* 2A: 5 for quoted references.
23. *Mencius* 1A: 7 and 3A: 3.

24. *Mencius* 6A: 7.

25. *Mencius* 7A: 23.

26. *Mencius* 1A: 7.

27. *Mencius* 3A: 3.

28. *Mencius* 7A: 22, 4A: 13, and 1A: 7.

29. This is a strongly glossed translation of *tian* 天, proposed only to underscore that "prevalent social, economic, and political forces" lie within the term's range of meaning in this context.

30. *Mencius* 4A: 7.

31. This despite his optimistic assertion in the passage above that once the way of King Wen is established, order will emerge in five to seven years.

32. *Mencius* 1B: 14.

33. *Mencius* 2A: 1.

34. Ibid.

35. *Mencius* 2B: 13.

36. Legge (1994) vol. 2, p. 37.

37. *Mencius* 2B: 13.

38. *Mencius* 7B: 15.

39. *Mencius* 4B: 22.

40. *Mencius* 7B: 38.

41. Li (2002) p. 139; *Zundeyi* 5.

42. Tang (1962) vol. 1, p. 195.

43. Ibid., p. 201.

44. *Zhongyong* 17.

45. *Analects* 16.8 and 20.3.

46. *Mencius* 5A: 8.

47. *Mozi* 35.

48. The analytic distinction between the "descriptive" and "prescriptive" dimensions of *tian* 天 and *ming* 命 has been introduced and profitably examined by Robert Eno and Kwong-loi Shun. See Eno (1990) pp. 102–06 and Shun (1997) pp. 17–21. I prefer to proceed without this distinction and to allow these dimensions to dissolve as much as possible back into the more synthetic understanding evident in the tradition itself.

49. *Analects* 6.10. The phrase "there is nothing we can do" is found in the recently unearthed Dingzhou text. See Ames and Rosemont (1998) p. 240 n. 93.

50. *Analects* 12.5. Hall and Ames point out that in fact Sima Niu did have a brother, a man who threatened the life of Confucius. Apparently Sima Niu no longer considered this individual his brother. Thus, "far from justifying fatalism," Hall and Ames argue that this episode "demonstrates the fluidity of *ming* 命 and the inseparability of fact and value in the description of one's causal context." See Hall and Ames (1987) pp. 214–15.

51. Tang (1962) vol. 2, p. 29.

52. Martha Nussbaum has recently argued that emotions are not undergone passively, but rather indicate the conferral of value upon objects not completely within one's control yet deemed important to one's own flourishing. The account of emotional content in *Dispositions Arise from Conditions* might resonate with this view. See Nussbaum (2001) pp. 19–33, passim. My suggestions here are tentative. The nature of "emotion" in early Chinese thought is something that still needs to be brought into greater focus. This may be possible with the help of newly found documents.

53. *Mencius* 7A: 2.

54. The words "conspire" and "aspire" share the common Latin root *spirare*, "to breathe." To conspire is to "breathe with" and to aspire is to "breathe on." There is something of the transactional nature of human becoming captured in the etymology of these terms, as breathing is a function that resists any strict reduction to internal or external.

55. *Mencius* 3A: 2.

56. *Analects* 19.17.

57. *Mencius* 3A: 5. See pg. 68 above.

58. *Book of Rites* 26/1/25–26. As for placing the *Jitong* chronologically, it is difficult to say whether the text predates Mencius. Legge notes that "the concluding paragraph shows that [the *Jitong*] was written while the state of Lu was still had an existence; and if the whole book proceeded from the same hand, it must have been composed some time after the death of Confucius and before the extinction of Lu," which took place in 248 B.C. [Legge (1967) vol. 1, p. 37]. Mencius lived from 372–289 B.C.

59. *Xunzi* 19.1a and 23.1 a–b.

60. *Analects* 8.2.

61. *Analects* 1.13.

62. *Feng* 奉 is another term that illustrates the primacy of situation over agency. It means both to "receive respectfully with both hands" and to "offer or serve respectfully." See Ch. 1 n. 43.

63. Legge (1994) vol. 5, pp. 704, 708.

64. *Mencius* 2A: 2.

65. Boodberg (1953) p. 326–27. See also Hall and Ames (1987) pp. 87–89.

66. The phrase *shengde* 盛德, which occurs as well in *Mencius* 5A: 4, can be rendered "abundance of character." As a transitive verb, however, the character *sheng*, pronounced *cheng*, means to "fill" or "put into a container." The grammar of *Mencius* 7B: 33 would tolerate the adjective more readily than the transitive verb; however, given the "container" dimension of ritual form and the mention of "focus" (*zhong* 中), I render *shengde* here as "concentration of character."

67. *Mencius* 7B: 33.

68. Pang Pu suggests that, after the death of Confucius, Confucians divided into two camps: the "externalists" (*wai* 外) and "internalists" (*nei* 內). He suggests that, in responding to the question of how humans have the capacity for associated humanity (*ren* 仁), the "internalists" begin with feeling (*xin* 心), whereas the "externalists" begin with *tian* 天. In the former category, he includes Mencius and Zisi, and in the latter category, Xunzi and the author of the *Great Learning*. See Pang (1999.1) pp. 23–24. While I do think there was an important *nei/wai* debate in this period, Mencius is not nearly as "internalist" as the *Five Modes of Conduct* document. I think Mencius is moving beyond the dichotomy altogether. One can only speculate in attributing a position to Zisi.

69. Roger T. Ames suggests that the phonetic play between "taking shape" (*xing* 形) and what is in its first instance rendered "formation" and in its second, "practice" (*xing* 行), entails the "formation of character" (*dexing* 德行) in the first instance (unpublished translation). The notion of "character" in *Mencius* 7B: 33 and the similar use of *xing* 行 in *Mencius* 4B: 19 as the emergent "course" of virtue in juxtaposition to the idea of its mere "practice" would suggest that this is so.

70. Li (2002) p. 78; *Wuxingpian* 1.

71. *Analects* 12.19.

72. *Mencius* 3A: 2.

73. Most of the thirty-seven occurrences of "character" (*de* 德) in the *Mencius* can be understood within the framework of "transforming influence."

The question of how much "character" is required to become an effective king is one such instance (*Mencius* 1A: 7). What D. C. Lau translates as the "transforming influence of morality" (*de* 德) is deemed vital to the king who seeks to effect associated humanity (*ren* 仁) among the populace (*Mencius* 2A: 3). In effecting order in the world, such influence of character is said to "overflow and fill the four seas" (*Mencius* 4A: 6). Friends are to be sought based on their character (*Mencius* 5B: 3), and there is a correlation between the prevailing character (*de*) of a state and the "quality" (*xian* 賢) of those in positions of influence (*Mencius* 5A: 6 and 4A: 7). The transforming influence of character is to be "prized" and "respected" (*Mencius* 2A: 4, 2B: 2, and 7A: 9); it is considered more important that the influence of rank and age in governing people (*Mencius* 2B: 2).

74. *Zhongyong* 20.
75. *Book of Rites* 26/2/1 to 26/3/5.
76. *Book of Rites* 26/4/7.
77. *Mencius* 4B: 13.
78. *Mencius* 7A: 2.

79. Burton Watson, commenting on Mozi's condemnation of the ancient burial practice of "ascending the roof" to call back the deceased, describes the Confucian purpose in retaining this ritual as being, according to the *Book of Rites*, "not because such rituals were believed to have any efficacy, but because they were regarded as fitting expressions of love for the deceased." See Watson (1963) p. 125.

I do not endorse this characterization of Confucian ritual or of the *Book of Rites*. While I have my doubts that "ascending the roof" ever produced a spirit, one cannot so easily divorce "expression" and "efficacy" in a Chinese world when expression is understood in terms of a disposition. Dispositions have efficacy and propensity; they may not raise the dead, but they certainly alter the world of the living.

As for the *Book of Rites*, it is not so easy to make generalizations about its teachings on ritual. Certain texts, such as the *Jitong*, are Mencian in spirit and describe ritual as emerging directly from feeling (*xin* 心). Other texts, however, have a Xunzian spirit and describe ritual as established by the ancient kings for more functional purposes. The *Questions about the Three Years* (*Sannianwen*) for instance, is a portion of Xunzi's *Discourse on Ritual* nearly verbatim. See *Book of Rites* vol. 2, bk. 35; cf. *Xunzi* 19.9a–19.9c.

80. *Book of Rites* 26/5/15.
81. *Analects* 3.12.
82. *Analects* 7.21.

83. *Analects* 11.12.

84. *Mozi* 31.

85. Graham (1989) p. 48.

86. The Confucian focus on integrity (*cheng* 誠), while prioritizing the human dimension, does not negate the beliefs of popular religion. In the classical tradition, there is a well-established relationship between *cheng* and the spiritual (*shen* 神). In the *Book of Documents* it is said that spirits will only accept the sacrifices of those who are *cheng*, and that only *cheng* can influence the spirits (see Legge vol. 3, pp. 66, 209–10). Likewise, the *Zhongyong* identifies *cheng* with efficacy in the realm of the spiritual (see *Zhongyong* 24 and 16). Integrity in the *Mencius* is considered to have the power to "move" (*dong* 動) other people (see *Mencius* 4A: 12).

87. *Mencius* 7B: 24.

88. *Mencius* 7A: 1.

89. *Zhongyong* 1.

90. Tang (1962) vol. 1, p. 201.

91. *Zhongyong* 1.

92. *Zhongyong* 22.

93. *Zhongyong* 31 and 32.

94. *Mencius* 6B: 2.

95. *Mencius* 4A: 2.

96. *Mencius* 4A: 1.

97. *Analects* 15.29.

98. *Mencius* 6A: 6.

99. Li (2002) p. 105; *Xingzimingchu* 1.

100. Li (2002) p. 105; *Xingzimingchu* 3.

101. The feature of "situation over agency" is very pronounced in this passage, where *dao* 道 is used as a verb in two senses. "Laying the course" is *dao*, but *dao* is also "proceeding on the course" that is laid by the art of feeling, that is, the art of human way-making (*rendao* 人道). For a discussion of "situation over agency," see Ch. 1 n. 43 above.

102. Li (2002) p. 106; *Xingzimingchu* 8.

103. *Mencius* 7A: 41. Cf. 6A: 20.

104. *Mencius* 7A: 42.

105. *Mencius* 7A: 9.

106. *Mencius* 6A: 11.
107. *Mencius* 7B: 16.

Afterword

1. *Analects* 9:23.

References

Ames, Roger T. 1983. *The Art of Rulership: A Study in Ancient Chinese Political Thought.* Honolulu: University of Hawaii Press.

———. 1991. "The Mencian Conception of Renxing: Does it Mean 'Human Nature'?" *Chinese Texts and Philosophical Contexts: Essays Dedicated to Angus C. Graham,* ed. Henry Rosemont, Jr., 143–175. La Salle: Open Court Press.

Ames, Roger T., and David L. Hall. 1987. *Thinking through Confucius.* Albany: State University of New York Press.

———. 1995. *Anticipating China: Thinking through the Narratives of Chinese and Western Culture.* Albany: State University of New York Press.

———. 2001. *Focusing the Familiar: A Translation and Philosophical Interpretation of the Zhongyong.* Honolulu: University of Hawaii Press.

Ames, Roger T., and Henry Rosemont, Jr. 1998. *The Analects of Confucius: A Philosophical Translation.* Albany: State University of New York Press.

Bloom, Irene. 1994. "Mencian Arguments on Human Nature." *Philosophy East and West* 44 (1): 19–53.

———. 1997. "Human Nature and Biological Nature in Mencius." *Philosophy East and West* 47 (1): 21–32.

———. 2002. "Biology and Culture in the Mencian View of Human Nature." *Mencius: Contexts and Interpretations,* ed. Alan K. L. Chan, 91–102. Honolulu: University of Hawaii Press.

Boodberg, Peter. 1953. "The Semasiology of Some Primary Confucian Concepts." *Philosophy East and West* 2: 317–32.

Chan, Alan K. L. 2002. "A Matter of Taste: *Qi* (Vital Energy) and the Tending of the Heart (*Xin*) in Mencius 2A: 2." *Mencius: Contexts and Interpretations,* ed. Alan K. L. Chan, 42–71. Honolulu: University of Hawaii Press.

Chan, Wing-Tsit. 1963. *A Sourcebook in Chinese Philosophy.* Princeton: Princeton University Press.

Chen, Lai. 1999. "Initial Study of the *Xingzimingchu* in the Jingmen Chu Strips." *Guodian Chujian Yanjiu*, ed. Jiang Guanghui, 293–314. Liaoling Province Education Publishing Company, Series in Chinese Philosophy, Vol. 20.

Chen, Ning. 2002. "The Ideological Background of the Mencian Discussion of Human Nature: A Reexamination." *Mencius: Contexts and Interpretations*, ed. Alan K. L. Chan, 17–41. Honolulu: University of Hawaii Press.

Chong, Kim-Chong. 2002. "Mencius and Gaozi on *Nei* and *Wai*." *Mencius: Contexts and Interpretations*, ed. Alan K. L. Chan, 103–125. Honolulu: University of Hawaii Press.

Cua, Antonio. 1989. "The Concept of *Li* in Confucian Moral Theory." *Understanding the Chinese Mind*, ed. Robert E. Allinson, 209–35. Oxford: Oxford University Press.

Defoort, Carine. 1997. "Causation in Chinese Philosophy." *A Compainion to World Philosophies*, ed. Eliot Deutsch and Ronald Bontekoe, 165–73. London: Blackwell Press.

Dewey, John. 1981. *The Philosophy of John Dewey*. Ed. John J. McDermott. Chicago: University of Chicago Press.

———. 1985. *John Dewey: The Later Works 1925–1953*, Vol. 5. Ed. Jo Ann Boydston. Carbondale: Southern Illinois University Press.

Ding, Sixin. 2000. *Research on the Thought of the Bamboo Strips of the Chu Tomb at Guodian (Guodian Chumu Chujian Sixiang Yanjiu)*. Beijing: Dongfang Publishing Company.

Dobson, W. A. C. H. 1963. *Mencius*. Toronto: University of Toronto Press.

Eno, Robert. 1990. *The Confucian Creation of Heaven: Philosophy and the Defense of Ritual Mastery*. Albany: State University of New York Press.

Farquhar, Judith. 1994. *Knowing Practice: The Clinical Encounter of Chinese Medicine*. Boulder: Westview.

Fingarette, Herbert. 1972. *Confucius: The Secular as Sacred*. New York: Harper and Row.

Graham, Angus C. 1989. *Disputers of the Tao*. La Salle: Open Court.

———. 1990. "Background of the Mencian Theory of Human Nature." *Studies in Chinese Philosophy and Philosophical Literature*, 7–59. Albany: State University of New York Press.

———. 1991. "Reflections and Replies." *Chinese Texts and Philosophical Contexts: Essays Dedicated to Angus C. Graham*, ed. Henry Rosemont, Jr., 267–322. La Salle: Open Court Press.

———. 2001. *Chuang-Tzu: The Inner Chapters.* Indianapolis: Hackett Press.

Grange, Joseph. 1997. *Nature: An Environmental Cosmology.* Albany: State University of New York Press.

Hall, David L. 1982. *The Uncertain Phoenix: Adventures Toward a Post-Cultural Sensibility.* Albany: State University of New York Press.

Hansen, Chad. 1992. *A Daoist Theory of Chinese Thought.* Hong Kong: Oxford University Press.

Henderson, John B. 1984. *The Development and Decline of Chinese Cosmology.* New York: Columbia University Press.

Henricks, Robert G. 2000. *Lao Tzu's Tao Te Ching: A Translation of the Startling New Documents Found at Guodian.* New York: Columbia University Press.

Ivanhoe, P. J. 1997. "Human Beings and Nature in Traditional Chinese Thought." *A Compainion to World Philosophies*, ed. Eliot Deutsch and Ronald Bontekoe, 155–64. London: Blackwell Press.

Jullien, François. 1995. *The Propensity of Things: Toward a History of Efficacy in China.* New York: Zone Books.

Karlgren, Bernhard. 1957. *Grammata Serica Recensa.* Goteborg: Elanders Boktryckeri Aktiebolac.

King, Ambrose. 1985. "The Individual and Group in Confucianism: A Relational Perspective." *Individualism and Holism: Studies in Confucian and Taoist Values*, ed. Donald Munro, 57–70. Ann Arbor: University of Michigan Press.

LaFargue, Michael. 1992. *The Tao of the Tao Te Ching: A Translation and Commentary.* Albany: State University of New York Press.

Lau, D. C. 1970. *Mencius.* New York: Penguin Books.

———. 1984. *Mencius.* Hong Kong: The Chinese University of Hong Kong Press.

Lau, D. C., and Roger T. Ames. 1998. *Yuandao: Tracing Dao to its Source.* Albany: State University of New York Press.

LeBlanc, Charles. 1985. *Huai-nan Tzu: Philosophical Synthesis in Early Han Thought.* Hong Kong: Hong Kong University Press.

Legge, James. 1967. *Li Chi: Book of Rites*, 2 vols. New York: University Books.

———. 1994. *The Chinese Classics*, 5 vols. Hong Kong: University of Hong Kong Press.

Lewis, Mark E. 1999. *Writing and Authority in Early China.* Albany: State University of New York Press.

Li, Ling. 2002. *A Textual Study of the Guodian Chu Strips (Guodian Chujian Jiaodu Ji)*. Beijing: Beijing University Press.

Liao, Mingchun. 1999. "Jingmen Guodian Chu Strips and Pre-Qin Confucianism." *Guodian Chujian Yanjiu*, ed. Jiang Guanghui, 36–74. Liaoling Province Education Publishing Company, Series in Chinese Philosophy, Vol. 20.

Major, John S. 1993. *Heaven and Earth in Early Han Thought: Chapters Three, Four and Five of the Huainanzi*. Albany: State University of New York Press.

Needham, Joseph. 1956. *Science and Civilisation in China*, Vol. 2. Cambridge: Cambridge University Press.

Neville, Robert C. 1981. *Reconstruction of Thinking*. Albany: State University of New York Press.

Nussbaum, Martha Craven. 2001. *Upheavels of Thought*. Cambridge: Cambridge University Press.

Owen, Stephen. 1992. *Readings in Chinese Literary Thought*. Cambridge: Harvard University Press.

Pang, Pu. 1999 (1). "Between Confucius and Mencius: Confucian discourse on *Xin* and *Xing* in the Chu strips." *Guodian Chujian Yanjiu*, ed. Jiang Guanghui, 22–35. Liaoling Province Education Publishing Company, Series in Chinese Philosophy, Vol. 20.

———. 1999 (2). "New Knowledge from an Ancient Tomb." *Guodian Chujian Yanjiu*, ed. Jiang Guanghui, 7–12. Liaoling Province Education Publishing Company, Series in Chinese Philosophy, Vol. 20.

Porkert, Manfred. 1974. *The Theoretical Foundations of Chinese Medicine: Systems of Correspondence*. Cambridge: MIT East Asian Science Series, Vol. 3.

Rainey, Lee. 1998. "Mencius and His Vast, Overflowing *Qi*." *Monumenta Serica* 46 (1998): 103–16.

Richards, I. A. 1932. *Mencius on the Mind*. New York: Harcourt, Brace and Co.

Rickett, Allyn W. 1985. *Guanzi: Political, Economic, and Philosophical Essays from Early China: A Study and Translation*. Princeton: Princeton University Press.

Rutt, Richard. 1996. *The Book of Changes: A Bronze Age Document*. New York: Curzon Press.

Schwartz, Benjamin I. 1985. *The World of Thought in Ancient China*. Cambridge: Harvard University Press.

Shun, Kwong-loi. 1997. *Mencius and Early Chinese Thought.* Stanford: Stanford University Press.

Sivin, Nathan. 1987. *Traditional Medicine in Contemporary China.* Ann Arbor: University of Michigan Press.

Tang, Junyi [T'ang Chün-I]. 1962. "The T'ien Ming (Heavenly Ordinance) in Pre-Ch'in China." *Philosophy East and West* 11 (4) 195–218 and 12 (1) 29–49.

———. 1988. "Exposition on the Unique Kind of Basic Spirit in Chinese Culture." *Zhongguowenhuagenjujingshenzhiyijieshi.* Taipei: Student Book Store.

Tu, Wei-ming. 1989. *Centrality and Commonality: An Essay in Confucian Religiousness.* Albany: State University of New York Press.

———. 1999. "Guodian Chu Strips and the Repositioning of Pre-Qin Confucian and Daoist Thoughts." *Guodian Chujian Yanjiu,* ed. Jiang Guanghui, 1–6. Liaoling Province Education Publishing Company, Series in Chinese Philosophy, Vol. 20.

Vandermeersch, Léon. 1988. "Tradition chinoise et religion." *Catholicisme et Sociétés asiatiques.* Paris: L'Harmattan.

Waley, Arthur. 1958. *The Way and its Power: A Study of the Tao Te Ching and its Place in Chinese Thought.* New York: Grove Press.

Watson, Burton. 1963. *Mo Tzu: Basic Writings.* New York: Columbia University Press.

Whitehead, Alfred N. 1978. *Process and Reality: Corrected Edition*, ed. D. R. Griffin and D. W. Sherburne. New York: Free Press.

Wilhelm, Richard, and Cary F. Baynes. 1990. *The I-Ching or Book of Changes.* Princeton: Princeton University Press.

Yu, Pauline. 1987. *The Reading of Imagery in the Chinese Poetic Tradition.* Princeton: Princeton University Press.

Zhang, Liwen. 1999. "*Shi* and *Yu* in *Qiongdayishi.*" *Guodian Chujian Yanjiu,* ed. Jiang Guanghui, 217–20. Liaoling Province Education Publishing Company, Series in Chinese Philosophy, Vol. 20.

Index

aesthetic
　dimension of *shan*, 56
　mindedness, 68–69, 70
　order, 58, 150–151n47, 153n67
Ames, Roger T., 27, 137n52,
　　153n67, 168n69
　on education 155–156n100
　on fatalism, 167n50
　on focus/field, 7
　on *renxing*, 158n9
　on situation over agency, 137n43
　on *Zhongyong*, 147n112
appropriateness (義)
　and associated humanity, 34–35
　defined, xxvi, 146n111
　and integration, 45–46
　as internal/external, 38–41
　as pleasurable, 92–95
　as social, 44–45
archery
　and aspiration, 33–34
　and virtue, 33–35
arousal (興), 30
　and norms, 50
　and poetry, 141n41
aspiration (志)
　and archery, 33–34
　defined, xxvi–xxvii
　and the human way, 124–127
　and limits, 113

　as psychophysical, 32–33
　and the scholar-official, 102–104
associated humanity (仁)
　and appropriateness, 54–55
　defined, xxv–xxvi
　and the human way, 90–91
　as political model, 104–106,
　　123–124, 127
　and self-reflection, 34–36, 44–45

benefit (利)
　as Mohist standard, 50–53
　for Confucians, 54–55
bian 辯
　see disputation
bie 別
　see partiality
Bloom, Irene, 159n22, 162n76
　on *renxing*, 158n9
body
　and configurative energy, 28–29,
　　33, 116
　priority of, 163–164n91
　and ritual form, 116
Boodberg, Peter, 116
Book of Changes
　and causality, 4
　cosmology of, 6–8, 20, 43
　prognosticative function, 19

179

Book of Documents
  on getting the most, 99
  on harmony and soup, 56, 151n48
  on human relationships, 75
  on moral terms, 55
  on social order, 60
  Taijia episode in, 77–78
  on *tian* 天, 102
Book of Filial Piety, 159n22
  on family feeling, 61, 73, 88–89
  on governance, 69, 90
Book of Rites, 41, 114, 169n79
  on striking a bell properly, 98–99
Book of Songs, 26, 43, 70, 105
  on harmony, 56–58, 151n48, 151n54
  on plants and trees, xv–xvi
  on seeds, xiv–xv
botanical model/metaphor
  and adjustment, 19
  and capacity, 84–85
  in classical China, xi–xv
  and flexibility, 65, 86, 90
  and growth, 39–41, 63, 67, 153n79
  and internal/external, 37–41
  and site-specificity, xv–xvi, 61–62, 88
  and sorts, xv–xvi
  vs. production model, 85–86
burial of parents
  discussed, 114–120
  origin of, 68

causality
  in classical China, 3–6, 138n67
Chan, Alan K.L.
  on configurative energy, 135n2
Chan, Wing-tsit, 26
Chanxiang episode, 75–76

character (德)
  defined, xxv
  in *Five Modes of Conduct*, 117
  force of, 110–111, 117–118
  in *Mencius*, 168–169n73
  and *tianming*, 109–111
  See also qualities
Chen Lai
  on *xing*, xix
cheng 誠
  see integration/integrity
child at the well, 25, 26, 91, 96
  translated, 87–88
Chinese language
  and moral terms, 55
  See also situation over agency
Chong, Kim-chong
  on internal/external debate, 144n83
coherence (理)
  defined, 42–43
  and human satisfaction, 58, 92–93, 94
  Mencius' use of, 146n103
conditions (命)
  Confucius on, 111–112
  defined, xxiv
  and disposition, 121–123
  and human achievement, 111–114
  and political legitimacy, 109–111
Confucius, xv, 44, 45
  on achieving a name, 97
  on associated humanity, 63
  on being human, 80
  on benefit, 54
  on conditions, 111–112
  on disposition, 77, 78, 160n33
  on form and function, 58, 151n58
  on the future, 131
  on harmony, 57

Index

on the human way, 124, 138n1
on learning and thinking, 28
on poetry, 141n41
on productive contribution, 58
and religiousness, 119
on ritual, 115
on seedlings, xiv
on the single thread, 94
on sociopolitical order, 60
on the true son, 65
configurative energy (氣)
 and aspiration, 32–33
 and the body, 28–29, 33, 116
 in classical China, 1–4
 and disposition, 11–12, 136n22
 and resonance, 29–31
 and moral nourishment, 39–40
 and moral pertinence, 140n13
 and ritual, 115–116
 See also flood-like *qi*
courage, 143n72, 143n73
 three kinds of, 35–36
Cua, Antonio S.
 on ritual, 151n60

dao 道
 and the human way, 124–127
 as most productive course, 23–24
 as teaching, 23–24
Daodejing, 2, 7, 14
 on causal propensity, 6
 on Confucian morality, 48
 Guodian, xvii–xviii, 134n27, 147–148n4
 on function, 18
 on impartiality, 16
 on the one and the many, 19
de 德
 see character, qualities
Defoort, Carine
 on causality, 4

desire (欲), 42, 46
Dewey, John
 on emotion, 32
 on human satisfaction, 58
 on reflex-arc concept, 31–32
Ding, Sixin
 on *Dispositions Arise from Conditions*, xviii
Discourse on Music
 on desire and disposition, 42–43
disposition (性), xxiv
 and causality, 5–6
 getting the most of, 122–123
 and process, 20–21
 and proximity, 77–78
 and shape, 11, 13, 14–17
 and spontaneity, 10–14
 See also human disposition
Dispositions Arise from Conditions
 on aspiration, 124–125
 on conditions, 111–112
 on disposition, 81–83
 on emotion, 82–83
 origin and importance of, xvi–xx, 134n24
 theme of, 10
disputation (辯)
 Mencius' attitude towards, 24, 53, 163n80
 Zhuangzi's attitude towards, 139n5
Dobson, W.A.C.H. 26
doctrine (言)
 discussed, 23–26
 Mencius on, 37, 40, 46, 49, 70
 moral pertinence of, 145n91
Duan, Yucai, 27

education
 Mencius on, 65–66, 154n87
 Hall and Ames on, 155–156n100

emotion (情)
  in *Dispositions Arise from Conditions*, 81–82
  Mencius on, 83–84
Eno, Robert, 166n48
  on *tian*, xii, 101–102
extension
  and moral growth, 67–68, 156n103
  towards animals, 156–157n105, 161–162n65

fa 法
  various meanings of, 48–50, 70
  in *Mencius*, 148n13
Failure and Success According to the Times
  on *tian*, 102–104
family
  and human disposition, 73–77
  as location for humans, xvi
  and moral instruction, 64–66
  as root of social order, 59–64
Farquhar, Judith
  on configurative energy, 3
fatalism
  and Mencius, 112–113
  Hall and Ames on, 167n50
  Tang Junyi on, 112
feeling (心)
  defined, xxiv–xxv, 26–32, 140n20
  the human way forward, 69, 124–125
  and ritual, 116
Fingarette, Herbert
  on causality, 4
Five Modes of Conduct, xviii–xiv, 121
  and inner virtue, 117
  origin of text, 134n33
flood-like *qi*, 12, 46, 92
  and moral nourishment, 37–40
  See also configurative energy
four sprouts, 84, 86, 92, 120
  and the family, 87–90
function
  in Chinese cosmology, 2–3, 18, 74–75
  of feeling, 26–28

ganying 感應
  see resonance
Gaozi
  on disposition, 79–80, 85
  on doctrine, 25
  and internal/external debate, 38–39
  Mencius compared to, 37
getting the most
  of disposition, 122–123
  meaning of, 97–99
  and sacrifice, 114–115, 118–119
  in *Zhuangzi*, 164n93
good (善)
  in the family, 64–65
  human disposition as, 79, 80–85
  meaning of term, 55–59
  in technical thinking, 147n3
Graham, A.C.
  on benefit, 54
  on Mohism, 120, 149n18, 161n53
  on moral terms, 55
  on spontaneity, 10–11
  on *xing*, xii, 21
  on Yangism, 161n53
Grange, Joseph
  on inscape, 138n69
Great Learning, 141n31, 154n87
  on feeling, 27
  on root of order, 59
Guanzi
  on the body, 29

Index

Guodian, 74, 102–104, 109
　importance of, xvii–xx

habit
　and custom, 78–79
　and disposition, 12
Hall, David L., 27, 137n52, 147n112
　on aesthetic order, 150–151n47
　on education, 155–156n100
　on fatalism, 167n50
　on focus/field, 7
Hansen, Chad
　on Mohist utilitarianism, 149n18
　on normative theory, 152n64
harmony (和), 2, 69
　as human satisfaction, 92–94
　as normative measure, 56–59, 98
he 和
　see harmony
Henderson, John
　on resonance, 30
Hendricks, Robert, 148n4
Honoring Virtue and Appropriateness
　on social conditions, 109
Huainanzi, 42
　on causality and resonance, 29–31
human disposition (人性), 73–99
　as cultural vs. biological, 74–80, 158n9, 160n40
　default understanding of, xii
　as discretionary, 121–122
　and family, 73–74
　getting the most of, 122–123
　as good, 79, 80–85
　See also disposition
human relationships (人倫), 65, 69, 94
　and human disposition, 75–76

impartial concern
　Mohist notion of, 51–53
integration/integrity (誠)
　defined, xxv
　and getting the most, 122–123
　and growth, 94
　and spirituality, 119–120, 170n86
　as standard of appropriateness, 45–46
　in *Zhongyong*, 45–46, 146–147n112
internal/external, 37–39, 42–46, 94
Ivanhoe, P.J.
　on *xing*, xii

jianai 兼愛
　see impartial concern
jin 盡
　see getting the most
Jullien, Francois
　on propensity, 4–5

Karlgren, Bernard, 140n21
King, Ambrose, 157n6
King Xuan episode, 67–68

LaFargue, Michael, 137n53
Lau, D.C.
　on internal/external debate, 38–39
Le Blanc, Charles
　on resonance, 29–30
Legalism, 5
　compared with Confucianism, 48–50
　five punishments of, 148n11
Legge, James, 26, 108
　on *Summary of Sacrifices*, 167n58
　visit to Mencius Temple, 133n5
Lewis, Mark Edward
　on aspiration, 142n55

li 利
  see benefit
li 理
  see coherence
li 禮
  see ritual
Li, Xueqin
  on *Dispositions Arise from Conditions*, xviii
Liao, Mingchun
  on *xing*, xix
  on *shuai*, 137n44
limit
  and aspiration, 112–113
  and shape, 6–7

Major, John
  on resonance, 29–30
Mencius Temple, xii–xiii, 129, 133n5
ming 命
  see conditions
Mohism, 24, 69, 96, 161n53
  popularity of, 59, 157n111
  on standards, 49–50, 148n12
  as technical, 85–86
  on theory/practice, 69–70, 129m28
  See also Mozi
Mozi
  on fatalism, 112–113, 138n67
  on habit and custom, 78–79
  on religiousness, 119–120
  on *tian*, 102
  teachings of, 50–53, 149n18
  See also Mohism

names (名)
  and reputation, 96–97, 163n83
Needham, Joseph, 30
Neville, Robert C.
  on harmony, 151n51

Ning, Chen
  on Guodian, xviii
  on *xing*, xix
Nussbaum, Martha
  on emotion, 167n52

Owen, Steven, 141n39
ox mountain, xvi, 85
  translated, 83–84

Pang, Pu
  on Guodian, xvii, xviii
  on internal/external debate, 168n68
  on *tian*, 104
  on *xing*, xix–xx
parents of the people (民之父母)
  as political idea, 104–106
  as a document, 165n16
partiality (別)
  Mohist critique of, 51
  use of term, 152n63
Porkert, Manfred
  on configurative energy, 135n1
propensity (勢)
  and aspiration, 33
  and causality, 4–6
  and *ganying*, 30
  and *tian*, 102

qi 氣
  see configurative energy
qing 情
  see emotion
qualities (德)
  in *Book of Changes*, 7
  in *Zhuangzi*, 15–16

Records of the Historian, xviii
religiousness, 119–120, 169n79
remonstrance
  and the family, 64–65, 154n90

ren 仁
　　see associated humanity
renlun 人倫
　　see human relationships
renxing 人性
　　see human disposition
resonance
　　discussed, 29–32
　　and internal/external, 41–42
ritual (禮)
　　as disposition, 116
　　as non-instrumental, 115
　　as transformative, 120
　　as illustrated in burial rites, 114–120
Rutt, Richard
　　on ji, 133n8

Sayings of the States
　　on harmony, 57
scholar-officials (士)
　　and aspiration, 33–34, 113
　　and associated humanity, 106
　　role of, 103–104
Schwartz, Benjamin
on xing, xii
self-reflection (自反), 132
　　and appropriateness, 34–36, 44
　　and courage, 36
Shanghai Museum, xvii, 165n16
shape (形)
　　and causality, 3–6
　　and disposition, 11, 13, 14–17
　　and spontaneity, 6–8
　　in Zhuangzi, 14–17
shi 勢
　　see propensity
shi 士
　　see scholar-official
Shun, 29
　　and family devotion, 62
　　and human relationships, 69
　　life of, 153–154n83
　　as a model, 29, 63–64, 149n14
Shun, Kwong-loi, 160n35, 166n48
　　on cheng, 147n112
　　on four sprouts, 84
　　on internal/external debate, 38
　　on King Xuan episode, 156n103
　　on renxing, 80
si 思
　　see thoughtfulness
Si-Meng lineage, 104
　　defined, xviii–xix
　　on disposition, 82–83
　　social dimension of, 109
situation over agency
　　examples of, 163n89, 165n8, 168n62, 170n101
　　explained, 137n43
Sivin, Nathan
　　on yinyang, 2
Six Positions, 159n16
　　on being human, 74
soup
　　and harmony, 56–58
spontaneity
　　and cosmology, 9–13
　　and ethics, 10
　　and family affection, 60–61
　　vs. technical approach, 48–5)
Spring and Autumn Annals of Master Lü, 11
striking a bell properly, 98–99
Summary of Sacrifices
　　dating of, 167n58
　　on reverence, 118–119
　　on ritual, 114–115

Taijia episode, 77–78
Tang, Junyi, 118, 122
　　on Chinese cosmology, 17–21
　　on fatalism, 112

on *tianming*, 109–110, 112
on *xing*, 74
thoughtfulness (思)
  as function of feeling, 26–28
  as counterpart to learning, 28
tian 天, 94, 164–165n1
  and the age, 102–104, 106–109
  defined, xxiii, 101–109
  doing the work of, 105, 122–123
  and economics, 105–106
tianming 天命
  and political legitimacy, 109–111
Tu, Wei-ming, 4
  on Guodian, xvii
  on *Zhongyong*, 147n112
two roots or one, 61–62, 88

value (貴)
  of persons, 95–99
Vandermeersch, Léon
  on causality, 4

Watson, Burton
  on aesthetic-mindedness, 68
  on ritual efficacy, 169n79
Waley, Arthur, 137n53
Whitehead, Alfred North
  on one and many, 19

xin 心 feeling
  see 性
xing disposition
  see 形
xing shape
  see shape
Xunzi, 41
  on ritual, 115, 148n9

yan 言
  see doctrine
Yangism, 24, 85–86, 96, 106, 161n53
yi 義
  see appropriateness
yinyang 陰陽, 2
yong 勇
  see courage
yu 欲
  see desire
Yu, Pauline, 141n39

zifan 自反
  see self-reflection
Zhongyong, xviii, 14, 45–46, 73
  dating the text, 134n32
  on disposition, 122–123
  on ritual, 118
  on *tianming*, 110–111
Zhuangzi, 14–17, 20, 41
  on configurative energy, 2–3
  on Confucian practice, 48
  on death, 8–9
  on decontextualization, 143–144n82
  on exhaustion, 164n93
  on function, 18
  on seeds, xiv
Zuozhuan
  on aspiration, 32, 142n63
  on configurative energy, 1, 135n3
  on disposition, 11–12, 21
  on harmony and soup, 56–57
  on names, 97
  on ritual, 115–116